NEW MEANS
OF FINANCING
INTERNATIONAL
NEEDS

ELEANOR B. STEINBERG AND JOSEPH A. YAGER
with Gerard M. Brannon

NEW MEANS
OF FINANCING
INTERNATIONAL
NEEDS

THE BROOKINGS INSTITUTION
Washington, D.C.

Copyright © 1978 by
THE BROOKINGS INSTITUTION
1775 Massachusetts Avenue, N.W., Washington, D.C. 20036

Library of Congress Cataloging in Publication Data:
Steinberg, Eleanor B
  New means of financing international needs.
  Includes bibliographical references and index.
  1. Underdeveloped areas—Finance. 2. International
agencies—Finance. 3. International finance. I. Yager,
Joseph A., 1916– joint author. II. Brannon, Gerard
Marion, 1922– joint author. III. Brookings
Institution, Washington, D.C. IV. Title.
HG4517.S84 332.1'5 77-21275
ISBN 0-8157-8116-4
ISBN 0-8157-8115-6 pbk.

THE BROOKINGS INSTITUTION is an independent organization devoted to nonpartisan research, education, and publication in economics, government, foreign policy, and the social sciences generally. Its principal purposes are to aid in the development of sound public policies and to promote public understanding of issues of national importance.

The Institution was founded on December 8, 1927, to merge the activities of the Institute for Government Research, founded in 1916, the Institute of Economics, founded in 1922, and the Robert Brookings Graduate School of Economics and Government, founded in 1924.

The Board of Trustees is responsible for the general administration of the Institution, while the immediate direction of the policies, program, and staff is vested in the President, assisted by an advisory committee of the officers and staff. The by-laws of the Institution state: "It is the function of the Trustees to make possible the conduct of scientific research, and publication, under the most favorable conditions, and to safeguard the independence of the research staff in the pursuit of their studies and in the publication of the results of such studies. It is not a part of their function to determine, control, or influence the conduct of particular investigations or the conclusions reached."

The President bears final responsibility for the decision to publish a manuscript as a Brookings book. In reaching his judgment on the competence, accuracy, and objectivity of each study, the President is advised by the director of the appropriate research program and weighs the views of a panel of expert outside readers who report to him in confidence on the quality of the work. Publication of a work signifies that it is deemed a competent treatment worthy of public consideration but does not imply endorsement of conclusions or recommendations.

The Institution maintains its position of neutrality on issues of public policy in order to safeguard the intellectual freedom of the staff. Hence interpretations or conclusions in Brookings publications should be understood to be solely those of the authors and should not be attributed to the Institution, to its trustees, officers, or other staff members, or to the organizations that support its research.

Foreword

THE MEANS of raising money for international purposes have remained essentially unchanged since the establishment of the United Nations and its principal associated agencies almost a third of a century ago. The international community still depends largely on two sources of finance: voluntary contributions by national governments and funds borrowed in capital markets by the World Bank and other international financial institutions.

The authors of this study argue that voluntary contributions and borrowing cannot be counted on to meet growing international financial requirements. They believe that new financing methods will be needed to cope with the world's environmental problems and to help the developing countries raise the living standards of their people.

After examining a wide range of possibilities, the authors select three for intensive analysis: taxes on trade and on certain other international transactions, charges on polluters of the marine environment, and revenues from the exploitation of nonliving ocean resources. The various problems of establishing and managing these new sources of revenue are explored in some depth.

The authors conclude that a new, more powerful, international revenue system can be created within the present international political order—that is, in a world of sovereign nation states. They recognize, however, that governments may not yet be ready to act jointly to raise large amounts of money for international purposes. This study is therefore not so much a plan for immediate action as a means of helping concerned people in all parts of the world think concretely about the steps that may have to be taken if growing international financial needs are to be met.

vii

Eleanor B. Steinberg, a Brookings research associate when this book was written, left the Institution in 1977 to accept a position in the Department of State. Joseph A. Yager, a Brookings senior fellow, directed the project. Gerard M. Brannon, professor of economics and chairman of the department of economics at Georgetown University, was responsible for the analysis of international revenue taxes presented in chapter 3 and for the technical appendix on international taxes. He also made substantive contributions to other parts of the study.

Patrick D. McTaggart-Cowan served as consultant on the project and commented on successive drafts of the study. David Leahigh, Aeran Lee, Florizelle B. Liser, and Steffi Meyer provided research assistance. Dorothy A. Brizill, who was a Rockefeller Younger Scholar at Brookings, also contributed to the project. Jeanane Patterson served as project secretary. The study was edited by Robert L. Faherty and checked for accuracy by Penelope S. Harpold; the index was prepared by Florence Robinson.

The study was conducted under the general supervision of Henry Owen, director of the Brookings Foreign Policy Studies program. The authors are grateful to him for his helpful comments and suggestions and for those of other present and former members of the Brookings staff, including particularly Henry J. Aaron, William R. Cline, Nina W. Cornell, Edward R. Fried, Gerald R. Jantscher, Emil M. Sunley, Jr., and Philip H. Trezise.

The authors also benefited from the generous advice and assistance of many persons in various parts of the world who were consulted during the course of the project. In particular they record their appreciation for the role played by Maurice F. Strong, who proposed that the study be undertaken and provided valuable suggestions and moral support during all phases of work.

The authors are also indebted to Mostafa K. Tolba, Executive Director of the United Nations Environment Programme, and his colleagues, including Yusuf J. Ahmad, Asit K. Biswas, and Philip Ndegwa. Others from whom the authors received valuable assistance include Robert E. Asher, Gordon Becker, Raoul Branco, William C. Clark, Richard Goode, George Hampson, Jean-Pierre Levy, Leonard C. Meeker, Walter Spofford, Robert M. Steinberg, and Jeremy J. Warford.

In March 1977 the Brookings Institution convened an international conference at the Rockefeller Foundation's Conference Center in Bellagio, Italy, to discuss the issues dealt with here. A draft of the study was made available to participants as background for their deliberations, and a number of the ideas developed at the conference have been incorporated in this volume. A summary of the conference proceedings appears in appendix D.

The project was financed by the Rockefeller Foundation and the United Nations Environment Programme. These sponsors were joined by the Ford Foundation in meeting the expenses of the Bellagio conference.

The views presented in this book are those of the authors and should not be ascribed to the persons or organizations whose assistance is acknowledged above, or to the trustees, officers, or other staff members of the Brookings Institution.

BRUCE K. MACLAURY
President

September 1977
Washington, D.C.

Contents

Text Tables

Appendix Tables

Appendix Figures

CHAPTER ONE

Growing International Needs and Limited Financial Means

THIS STUDY proceeds from two propositions. First, the international community is going to require increasing amounts of money in order to deal with major world problems. Second, it is far from certain that enough money can be raised through currently available measures to make it possible to deal adequately with these problems. The present system of transferring resources from rich to poor countries to help them raise the living standards and improve the quality of life of their people is particularly inadequate.

If these propositions are accepted, the desirability of finding new ways of paying for international needs is clear.

Growing Financial Requirements

It is not difficult to demonstrate that more money will be desired for international purposes in future years. Rapid changes in technology, the continuing increase in the world's population, and the growing interdependence of nations are expanding the tasks—and therefore also the financial requirements—of the various UN agencies, such as the World Health Organization (WHO), the World Meteorological Organization (WMO), and the Food and Agriculture Organization (FAO). It is important to ensure that the capabilities of these agencies keep pace with the

1

growing desires for their services. Even larger amounts of money, however, will be needed to deal adequately with several major international problems: meeting the development needs of the poorer nations, dealing with threats to the environment, maintaining peacekeeping forces in trouble spots, and safeguarding civil nuclear-energy facilities.

The net capital flow to developing countries is already large, but much larger amounts of capital will be needed to sustain an annual growth rate of 6 percent (the target set by the UN General Assembly for the Second United Nations Development Decade). In 1973, the oil-importing developing countries received a net external financing of $18 billion from both private and official sources, including international agencies. As a result of measures taken to deal with the huge increase in oil prices in late 1973 and early 1974, the net capital flow to this group of developing nations rose sharply in 1974 to $32 billion and in 1975 to $37 billion.[1] This level, however, falls short of the capital that would be required to support a growth rate of 6 percent in the gross national products of the oil-importing developing countries during the second half of this decade. Even if fairly optimistic assumptions are made about the growth in the export earnings of these countries, their average annual capital requirements for the period 1976–80 have been projected at between $50 billion and $53 billion in constant 1974 dollars.[2]

Estimates such as this are subject to a wide range of error, and they vary with the particular assumptions used. They cannot, however, be dismissed as mere statistical exercises, since they reflect implicitly one of the major forces in contemporary international politics: the drive by the developing nations for a more rapid rate of improvement in their material well-being. Many of the people and the leaders of the poorer countries are frustrated over their slow progress in the struggle against poverty, and they are resentful of the existing world order in which power and wealth are held largely by others.

The demand of the developing countries for a new international economic order cannot be assumed to be a transitory phenomenon that will soon fade away. Beneath all of the rhetoric, the spokesmen of the develop-

1. U.S. Treasury, "Report on Developing Countries External Debt and Debt Relief Provided by the United States" (January 1977; processed), p. 9.

2. Wouter Tims, "The Developing Countries," in Edward R. Fried and Charles L. Schultze, eds., *Higher Oil Prices and the World Economy* (Brookings Institution, 1975), p. 191.

ing nations are, above all else, calling for a massive, assured, and continuing transfer of resources from the rich to the poor nations of the world. It is unlikely that this demand will be rejected out of hand.

The UN General Assembly has, in fact, gone a considerable distance toward endorsing the major elements of the proposed new international economic order. The fact that the resolutions passed by the General Assembly do not have binding legal effect and were not fully supported by some major industrialized nations reduces their practical significance in the near term, but this does not deprive them of their historical importance.[3] In terms of the present study, perhaps the most relevant of the various propositions endorsed by the General Assembly was contained in a major resolution passed at the assembly's Seventh Special Session in September 1975. It reads in part:

> Concessional financial resources to developing countries need to be increased substantially, their terms and conditions ameliorated and their flow made predictable, continuous and increasingly assured so as to facilitate the implementation by developing countries of long-term programmes for economic and social development.[4]

If statements such as this are to be taken seriously—as they probably must be—they clearly suggest a political, as well as an economic, requirement for large flows of capital from the industrialized to the developing nations. The bulk of the capital flowing to the developing countries will no doubt continue to be provided privately and through national aid programs. If the flow is to be increased substantially, however, a greater proportion will, in all probability, have to be handled by international institutions.

Obtaining the capital needed to achieve traditional development goals is, however, only part of the problem. The aspirations of the developing countries include not only higher incomes for their people but also a better quality of life. It is true that investments that raise incomes, if wisely made, can also improve the quality of life. At the same time, environmental problems clearly add substantially to the capital requirements of the developing nations.

3. The key actions of the General Assembly with respect to the new international economic order are: "Declaration on the Establishment of a New International Economic Order," GA Res. 3201 (S-VI), May 1, 1974; "Charter of Economic Rights and Duties of States," GA Res. 2381 (XXIX), December 12, 1974; and "Development and International Economic Co-operation," GA Res. 3362 (S-VII), September 19, 1975.

4. GA Res. 3362 (S-VII), p. 25.

Some of the most pressing problems confronting the countries of the third and fourth worlds are various kinds of environmental degradation which inhibit agricultural and rural development and interfere with the provision of minimum requirements for human survival in towns and cities. Two of the most pervasive problems in the third and fourth worlds are: providing an adequate water supply for human consumption and for agriculture, and preserving soils and ensuring the availability of sufficient arable land for agriculture.

The problems of environmental degradation only recently became matters for serious international concern. Less than five years have passed since the 1972 United Nations Conference on the Human Environment (the Stockholm Conference), and the United Nations Environment Programme (UNEP), which was formed as a result of that conference, is still in the process of carving out a position within the UN system. UNEP itself—as its role is now defined by the United Nations—is not likely to try to mobilize and manage large amounts of money. There can be little doubt, however, that very large financial resources will be required by other international organizations if the world is to cope adequately with major problems such as decreasing pollution of the atmosphere and the ocean, checking the spread of deserts, and improving living conditions of urban and rural settlements.

Some environmental programs, such as monitoring conditions in the ocean and the atmosphere, call for a high degree of international cooperation, and their funding is therefore properly viewed as an international responsibility. Other environmental programs, such as providing facilities for water purification and waste treatment for cities, are by their nature the responsibility of local or national authorities. In many developing countries, however, those authorities lack the financial resources to carry out even urgent environmental programs. There can be little doubt that, if anything is to be done in such situations, the international community will have to assume much of the responsibility for mobilizing the needed funds.[5]

Estimating the total cost of environmental programs that might appropriately be paid for out of international financial resources in future years

---

5. It is also possible that some international funds may be needed to overcome political obstacles to important environmental programs in the developed countries, even though, in terms of ability to pay, such funding could not easily be justified.

is an all-but-impossible task. A few examples will, however, give some indications of the magnitudes involved:

A World Health Organization survey has estimated that meeting specified goals for human water supply in the developing countries by 1980 would require the expenditure of more than $20 billion during the period from 1975 to 1980.[6]

Upgrading 22.5 million existing squatter housing units by providing basic services and amenities would fulfill about one-quarter of the total estimated housing requirements in urban areas in the developing countries over a ten-year period. The cost of such upgrading would total about $6.5 billion. Provision of an equivalent number of new housing units through construction of simple "core" houses with amenities such as running water and electricity would cost about $20 billion.[7]

A long-range program drawn up by UNEP for international cooperation to combat the further spread of deserts would cost approximately $400 million a year.[8] This amount applies only to the cost of salvaging the estimated 5.8 million hectares of arid and semi-arid lands all over the world which each year deteriorate, become less productive, and fall into the category of desert lands. A program to reclaim the vast accumulation of land that has undergone desertification over the years would cost literally billions of dollars.

The first phase (ten years) of a global environmental monitoring program might include establishing ten new stations for monitoring the atmosphere, monitoring and analyzing samples for perhaps a dozen substances at three open ocean stations for one week twice a year, and expanding the existing U.S. satellite system for land-use monitoring into a global monitoring network. The costs for these components of such a program would be about $75 million (including capital and operating costs). It must be

6. World Health Organization, "Community Water Supply and Wastewater Disposal: Mid-Decade Progress Report," WHO Doc. A29/12, March 29, 1976, Annex 6, Annex 7. All cost figures are in 1975 U.S. dollars.

7. Cost figures are derived from estimates in World Bank, *Housing Sector Policy Paper* (Washington, D.C.: World Bank, May 1975), p. 40; *World Bank Annual Report 1970* (Washington, D.C.: World Bank, 1970), and ibid., 1971–76. The number of new and improved urban housing units needed in the developing countries over a ten-year period is derived from "Global Review on Human Settlements," UN Doc. A/CONF.70/A/1, March 8, 1976, p. 171.

8. Cost figures are from Secretariat of the United Nations Conference on Desertification, *Plan of Action to Combat Desertification*, UNEP, August 1977, p. 11.

emphasized, however, that this figure does not represent the costs of developing and operating a comprehensive global monitoring network with computerized facilities for the storage and transmission of the data collected. Also, the initial capital costs of developing the remote satellite system are assumed to have been borne by the U.S. government and are not included. Moreover, many monitoring programs which are being urged by various components of the international scientific community are not even considered here. For example, this does not include the establishment of centers for studying biological, physical, and chemical changes in plant and animal life which may result from environmental changes; nor does it include sophisticated programs for monitoring and predicting changes in climate. The rough cost figure applies only to extremely simple pilot monitoring programs in a few areas.[9]

The international community will also need to mobilize larger amounts of money in future years to deal with security problems. The cost of maintaining peacekeeping forces, such as those on Cyprus and in buffer zones between Arab and Israeli armies, could as easily increase as decrease. As past experience has shown, new crises can bring unexpected new requirements for peacekeeping forces and an urgent need to find the financial means for their support.

An increase in the cost of reducing the risk of diversion of nuclear materials from peaceful civil uses to military or criminal uses is not a contingent possibility, but a virtual certainty. Today, the International Atomic Energy Agency (IAEA) operates a system of safeguards covering approximately 50 nuclear power reactors. By 1980, as many as 200 reactors may have to be safeguarded, and that number may double by 1985.[10] IAEA's budget would of course have to be expanded correspondingly.

9. Cost estimates for atmospheric monitoring stations were supplied by Dr. Donald Pack, consultant to the International Environmental Programs Committee, Environmental Studies Board, Commission on Natural Resources, National Research Council, National Academy of Sciences. Informal estimates for open ocean monitoring were supplied by the National Oceanographic Data Center, National Oceanic and Atmospheric Administration (NOAA). Costs for land-use monitoring by satellite were supplied by Office of Applications, Earth Observation Program, National Aeronautics and Space Administration (NASA).

10. Sigvard Eklund, director general of the International Atomic Energy Agency, "The International Atomic Energy Agency—Its Activities Within the Framework of the United Nations" (address before the Austrian League for the United Nations, March 17, 1976; processed).

Limited Financial Means

Present means of financing international needs clearly have serious limitations. These limitations can be brought out by examining in turn the ways in which the nations of the world now pay for the operations of the UN system (excluding the international financial institutions), meet the financial needs of the developing countries, and deal with threats to the global environment.

Paying for the Operations of the United Nations

Most of the activities of the United Nations, its specialized agencies, and other associated organizations are financed by assessments on member governments and voluntary contributions from those governments.[11]

The first line of table 1-1 shows expenditures for the period 1965 through 1974 by the United Nations through its regular budget. The UN regular budget can be thought of as a general purpose revenue fund. The assessments paid by member nations are used to pay for the overall administration of the UN system, including the costs of the secretariat in New York, expenses associated with the work of the General Assembly and the UN Economic and Social Council (ECOSOC), and the administrative costs of the regional economic commissions. Some of the various UN peacekeeping forces are financed out of the regular budget, while others are paid for partly or entirely by separate contributions from some member states.

Table 1-1 also shows the expenditures of the various specialized and other agencies. In general, these agencies do not receive substantial funds from the UN regular budget (although some receive relatively small amounts for administrative purposes from this source). They are financed primarily by a system of assessments on the individual countries which belong to the various agencies. Finally, there are the agencies whose principal support is derived from voluntary contributions. Examples include the UN Development Programme (UNDP) and UNEP. Voluntary contributions differ from the assessed contributions in that no formula is used

11. The summary of the present means of financing the UN system presented here is drawn principally from the *Yearbook of the United Nations 1972,* vol. 26 (New York: United Nations, Office of Public Information, 1975), especially pp. 691–719.

Table 1-1. Expenditures by the United Nations, Specialized Agencies, and Other UN Programs, 1965–74
Millions of U.S. dollars

Description	1965	1966	1967	1968	1969	1970	1971	1972	1973	1974
UN regular budget	107.1	118.6	130.5	141.2	155.8	168.4	194.1	208.4	233.8	276.9
UN peacekeeping	42.8	34.4	30.4	18.3	14.3	12.7	12.7	14.2	19.0	115.0
Specialized agencies	142.5	160.9	177.4	192.4	221.2	228.1	261.4	285.7	340.5	394.6
FAO	23.6	27.8	29.7	31.7	36.2	38.3	43.3	45.0	50.9	58.6
IMCO	0.9	0.8	0.8	0.8	1.2	1.2	1.6	1.9	2.2	2.9
IAEA	8.8	10.0	9.3	10.0	11.2	12.2	14.0	16.5	19.9	23.4
ICAO	6.4	7.5	7.0	7.6	7.7	8.4	9.7	10.3	12.4	14.2
Joint Financing Programme	3.8	4.2	4.2	3.6	3.9	3.9	4.1	5.1	5.7	7.6
ILO	21.5	23.5	26.5	29.0	31.1	31.3	32.9	32.7	46.6	51.7
ITU	5.6	7.0	6.8	7.2	7.7	8.7	15.0	15.2	17.6	23.6
UNESCO	27.2	28.6	32.9	37.3	41.8	43.7	49.5	56.7	67.5	81.6
UPU	1.1	1.3	1.5	1.5	1.9	1.9	2.3	2.5	3.3	4.7
WHO	42.1	48.2	56.3	61.1	75.0	75.0	84.7	95.4	108.3	119.1
WMO	1.5	2.0	2.4	2.6	3.5	3.5	4.3	4.4	6.1	7.2
Voluntary programs	235.3	293.8	303.6	357.8	431.9	533.3	833.6	896.9	830.6	915.0
IAEA Operational Programme	1.8	2.0	2.2	3.1	2.3	2.6	3.3	3.7	3.8	3.0
UNICEF[a]	31.2	35.4	39.2	45.9	50.7	55.3	75.9	98.4	91.5	72.1

UNDP	119.5	158.5	170.8	195.4	232.9	257.3	317.1	340.1	354.7	369.1
UN Fund for Population Activity	...	...	...	0.1	1.2	6.7	16.2	19.8	37.1	55.3
FAO										
UN/FAO Sahelian Trust Programme	...	...	...	...	...	...	...	...	9.7	10.8
UN/FAO World Food Programme	19.6	38.3	40.9	58.1	84.4	149.2	134.6	171.2	211.7	226.3
UNEP Environment Fund	...	...	...	...	...	...	...	...	4.2	8.2
WHO special programs[b]	1.9	1.9	...	0.1	0.2	0.4	2.4	5.0	9.5	22.2
WMO Voluntary Assistance Programme	...	...	...	0.8	3.4	4.0	4.5	4.5	5.7	3.0
UNESCO special programs[c]	6.0	...	...	...	...	...	...	...	...	12.0
Other programs[d]	55.3	51.7	50.5	54.3	56.8	57.8	279.6	254.2	102.7	133.0
Total	527.7	607.7	641.9	709.7	823.2	942.5	1,301.8	1,405.2	1,423.9	1,701.5

Sources: Data for 1966–74 are from U.S. Department of State, *United States Contributions to International Organizations*, Report to the Congress for Fiscal Year 1975, H. Doc. 95-11, 95 Cong. 1 sess. (1977), pp. 124–26. Data for 1965 are from ibid., Report to the Congress for Fiscal Year 1974, H. Doc. 94-333, 94 Cong. 2 sess. (1976).

a. Voluntary funded programs of UNICEF include its regular program as well as the Nigerian Relief Programme (1970–71) and the program of Humanitarian Assistance for South Asia.

b. WHO special programs include the Malaria Eradication Special Account, the Medical Research Programme, the Community Water Supply Programme, the Drug Monitoring Programme, the Special Cholera Account, and the Smallpox Eradication Programme.

c. UNESCO's current special programs are Aid to African Education and the Nubian Monuments Programme.

d. Other voluntary programs include United Nations Technical and Operational Assistance to the Congo, United Nations Fund for Development Planning and Projections, United Nations Fund for Drug Abuse Control, United Nations Fund for Namibia, United Nations High Commissioner for Refugees Programme, United Nations Relief and Works Agency (for Palestine Refugees), United Nations Relief Operation in East Pakistan/Bangladesh, United Nations Institute for Training and Research, United Nations Research Institute for Social Development, Special Contributions for Vietnam, UNITAR Stevenson Memorial Fellowships, United Nations Programmes for Southern Africans, International Refugee Organization, United Nations Hungarian Refugee Relief Programme, United Nations Korean Reconstruction Agency, and United Nations Volunteers Programme.

for determining the contributions required from each member. Even so, the total level of voluntary contributions for a particular international agency is not left to chance. The amount of the contribution from each country is arrived at by complex multilateral negotiations.

Reliance upon a combination of assessments and voluntary contributions is not uncommon in the UN system. For example, UNDP turns over part of the voluntary contributions that it receives from member governments to specialized agencies, such as the Food and Agriculture Organization, that also raise money through assessments on their members. UNEP receives most of its financial support in the form of voluntary contributions to the Fund of UNEP, but it also receives smaller amounts under the central UN budget which is, of course, financed principally through assessments. Moreover, a number of the specialized agencies run some of the voluntary programs shown in the table. For example, the Food and Agriculture Organization manages the UN/FAO Sahelian Trust Programme and the UN/FAO World Food Programme.

The assessments and voluntary contributions to specific agencies should be regarded as earmarked funds. The preference of member states for earmarking funds for expenditure within the UN system is clear. In 1974 expenditures by the specialized agencies, by various special programs, and for the peacekeeping forces were more than five times the size of the regular UN budget. That year the UNDP alone spent or authorized the expenditure of more funds than were spent through the regular UN budget.

Members of the United Nations proper are assessed previously agreed upon shares of the annual UN budget that is approved by the General Assembly. A percentage scale of assessments is adopted by the General Assembly every three years on the basis of recommendations by its Committee on Contributions, reporting through its Fifth (Administrative and Budgetary) Committee. The scale of assessments is not based on a mechanical formula. In a general way, however, the scale reflects the relative GNPs of members, modified to take account of differences in GNP per capita.[12] A ceiling (in principle, 25 percent) and a floor (0.02 percent) have been set on the assessments of individual members.[13]

12. In the case of countries whose GNP per capita is less than $1,000, part of total GNP is excluded from consideration in determining assessment shares. The fraction of total GNP so excluded is one-half the difference between $1,000 and GNP per capita, divided by $1,000. In the case of a country whose GNP per capita is $800, for example, 90 percent of total GNP would be counted in determining its assessment share.

13. A ceiling has also been established on the per capita contributions of mem-

The United Nations Charter (Article 19) provides that a member that is two years or more in arrears in paying its assessed share of the budget shall lose its vote in the General Assembly. This sanction has never been applied. In the mid-1960s, several governments, including the Soviet Union and France, did fall more than two years behind in their assessments because of their refusal to contribute to the cost of UN peacekeeping operations in the Middle East and in the Congo. After a prolonged controversy, the assembly agreed to shelve the issue.[14]

The refusal of some members to pay for these peacekeeping operations and for certain other expenditures that they regard as either illegal or politically objectionable has caused the United Nations to incur a gradually growing "short-term" deficit. By the end of 1973, the deficit had reached $70.8 million, an amount 30 percent as great as the total obligations incurred by the United Nations in that year.[15]

Except for a few controversial items, the record of payment of assessments by member states is good, but slow. Thus, at the end of 1973, contributions to the regular budgets had reached the following figures: 99.9 percent of the 1970 budget had been paid, 99.6 percent of the 1971 budget, 98.0 percent of the 1972 budget, but only 74.1 percent of the 1973 budget. This illustrates the cash liquidity problem that has plagued the United Nations for many years.[16]

Most of the UN Specialized Agencies have schedules of assessment that are similar to, although not identical with, the schedule used by the central organization. Exceptions to this general rule include the Universal Postal Union and the International Telecommunication Union, which array their members for assessment purposes in classes that reflect relative size or wealth in only a very general way, and the International Civil Aviation Organization, which bases 75 percent of its assessments on ability to pay and 25 percent on relative interest in and importance of civil aviation.

---

bers. No member may be required to make a larger contribution per capita than does the largest contributor (that is, the United States).

14. See *United Nations Financial Situation: Background and Consequences of the Article 19 Controversy over the Financing of U.N. Peacekeeping Operations,* H. Rept. 1564, 89 Cong. 2 sess. (1966), especially pp. 7–19.

15. If amounts to be paid to member states from surplus accounts for contributions to the Middle East and Congo peacekeeping operations are included, the deficit totals $87.5 million. See *Financial Report and Accounts for the Year Ended 31 December 1973 and Report of the Board of Auditors,* vol. I, UN Doc. A/9607, 1974, pp. 8, 55.

16. Ibid., p. 11. See also *Report of the Special Committee on the Financial Situation of the United Nations,* UN Doc. A/8729, 1972.

Like the central organization, the specialized agencies can penalize members that fall behind in paying assessments by suspending their voting rights, but they never have actually done so. Some specialized agencies charge interest on overdue assessments.

Prospects for raising substantially larger amounts of money through assessments on member governments are not good.[17] The assessments system, with its focus on predetermined shares of an agreed upon budget, creates powerful constraints against efforts to expand revenues. The members assessed the largest shares, such as the United States and the Soviet Union, try to hold down the total level of expenditures, and, in most situations, all members, large and small, can be expected to resist increases in their percentage shares. Voluntary contributions give the overall revenue system some flexibility, but such contributions cannot be easily adjusted to meet new or rising requirements.

Meeting the Needs of the Developing Countries

Of the $37 billion in net external financing received by the oil-importing developing countries during 1975, $13 billion, or 35 percent, was from private sources.[18] Grants, loans, and credits from national governments and from the Organization of Petroleum Exporting Countries (OPEC) provided $10 billion (27 percent) and $5 billion (about 14 percent), respectively. The remaining $9 billion, nearly 25 percent of the total, was accounted for by multilateral grants, loans, and credits.[19] Some of the latter funds were provided through various UN Specialized Agencies and voluntary programs whose expenditures were included in table 1-1. The bulk of the multilateral funds, however, came from international financial institutions, including the World Bank Group, the International Monetary Fund, and the regional development banks.

17. On the financial problems of the UN system, see Robert M. Macy, "Getting and Spending: The UN's Money Headaches," *Vista,* vol. 9 (October 1973), pp. 46–51. See also Richard N. Gardner, "The Struggle for Money, Influence and Effectiveness," *Vista,* vol. 8 (September/October 1972), pp. 93–97.

18. The oil-exporting developing countries, as a group, are net capital exporters, so attention has been focused on those developing countries that are net oil importers.

19. Figures on external financing of the oil-importing developing countries are from U.S. Treasury, "Report on Developing Countries External Debt and Debt Relief Provided by the United States" (January 1977; processed), p. 9.

In one way or another, these institutions depend on their member governments for most of the financial resources that they use to meet the needs of the developing countries. Thus, the ability of the International Development Association (IDA), the World Bank's "soft loan" affiliate, to make loans on highly concessional terms depends on the willingness of member governments to make periodic contributions to replenish its funds. The World Bank itself supports its lending operations by borrowing on capital markets. The Bank's articles of agreement, however, limit its outstanding loans to the total of subscribed capital (both paid-in and callable), reserves, and surplus. The level of subscribed capital—by far the most important of these three items—depends directly upon actions by member governments.

On the basis of what is now known about the intentions of donors and the limits of creditworthiness for private capital, the amount of external financing available to the oil-importing developing countries may not differ greatly in the next few years from the amounts provided in 1974–75. One recent study projected that the average amount of capital available to these countries from official and private sources would be about $33 billion a year during the period 1976–80 (in 1974 dollars). An anticipated increase in projected flows of official capital, both unilateral and multilateral, is all but wiped out by an estimated decline in the availability of private capital.[20]

It will be recalled that the average annual flow of capital required to sustain a 6 percent rate of economic growth in the oil-importing developing countries during the second half of the current decade has been estimated to be $50 billion to $53 billion. Those countries may therefore face an average annual shortfall of about $18 billion. This gap could, of course, be narrowed by an increase in development assistance by the wealthier nations, or by a shift in the terms of trade favorable to the developing countries. Whether either or both of these possible developments will occur is, however, highly uncertain. The relevant question in the context of the present study, therefore, is whether the shortfall could be met by the multilateral financial institutions, using the means of mobilizing capital now available to them. The magnitude of the task involved is suggested by the fact that the shortfall is more than two times the net flow of capital from multilateral financial institutions in 1974.

20. Tims, "The Developing Countries," p. 191.

Prospects for obtaining increased contributions from governments to support the development efforts of the world's poorer nations are not bright. Raising the money needed to keep the UN Development Programme afloat and to replenish the lending capacity of the International Development Association has been a constant, and only partly successful, struggle.

Borrowing more money from the capital markets is, on the face of it, a more feasible course, but trying to close the entire gap in this way would require an enormous and unprecedented effort. The World Bank and its affiliates would clearly have to assume the bulk of the responsibility for such an effort. The World Bank Group has, in fact, already embarked on a program of expanded lending. At the meeting of the Board of Governors of the World Bank Group in September 1975, Robert S. McNamara, president of the Bank, announced an increase in lending by the Bank and its affiliates to the level of about $7 billion annually in the period 1975–80 (in 1975 dollars), as compared with an annual average of about $4.5 billion in the preceding five-year period.[21] This is a gross figure and does not take into account interest and repayments of capital on outstanding loans.

An even greater increase in lending, and therefore in borrowing from the capital markets, would not seem to be in the cards. By the early 1980s, the rate of lending that is already projected will force a substantial increase in the capital of the World Bank. Whether this will be possible appears at best uncertain. An effort in 1975 by the president of the Bank to double the Bank's authorized capital (from $27 billion to $54 billion) failed, principally because of opposition by the United States.[22] Instead, as a result of a U.S. initiative, a much smaller increase of $8.4 billion was approved by the executive directors of the Bank in May 1976 with the understanding that the Bank's lending in fiscal year 1977 and succeeding years would not exceed $5.8 billion annually.[23]

In any event, borrowed funds could not by themselves meet the capital requirements of the poorer nations in the developing world. If those nations are to receive the long-term, low-interest loans that they need, the

21. International Bank for Reconstruction and Development, International Finance Corporation, International Development Association, *1975 Annual Meetings of the Boards of Governors: Summary Proceedings* (Washington, D.C.: IBRD, 1975), p. 22.

22. *Washington Post,* October 4, 1976.

23. *World Bank Annual Report 1976* (Washington, D.C.: World Bank, June 1976), pp. 5–6, 86.

World Bank must be able to blend the money that it has borrowed on commercial terms with money contributed to IDA without charge. The difficulty of obtaining increased governmental contributions has already been noted.

Dealing with Environmental Problems

Environmental programs are the most recent major claimant upon the financial resources of the international community. It is therefore not surprising that they are the least specifically provided for. The only clear and separate provision of funds for environmental purposes in the general budget of the United Nations is in the small allocation of funds ($2.8 million in 1975) for the UN Environment Programme (UNEP).[24] Voluntary contributions by governments amounted to $25.7 million pledged in 1975. Also, some of the UN Specialized Agencies engage in activities that are in whole or in part designed to further environmental objectives, and some of the projects financed by the World Bank Group, the UNDP, and the regional development banks have environmental aspects.

It would be very difficult, if not impossible, to estimate even approximately how much international organizations are now spending for environmental purposes. All that is certain is that the amount falls far short of present, not to mention future, requirements. This judgment can easily be verified simply by observing what is not being done to meet major problems such as water supply and waste disposal, the spread of deserts, and pollution of the ocean and the atmosphere.

Prospects for raising more money for environmental programs through present means of finance can only be described as poor. It is not realistic to expect larger contributions to the Fund of UNEP when UNEP is having difficulty getting governments to pay their existing pledges on time.[25] Any large increase in the support provided UNEP in the central UN budget is also unlikely in the light of competing requirements.

An increase in the environmental activities of the UN Specialized

24. The total appropriation for the biennium 1974–75 was $5,235,000, of which $2,457,919 was spent in 1974, leaving a balance for 1975 of $2,838,051. Fund of UNEP, "Financial Report and Accounts for the Year Ended 31 December 1974 and Report of the Board of Auditors." GAOR, 30th Session, Supplement no. 7F (A/10007/Add-6), p. 4.

25. Ibid., pp. 11–12. As of December 31, 1974, unpaid pledges totaled $74.7 million. See also UN Doc. UNEP/GC/83, May 6, 1976, pp. 9–10.

Agencies is conceivable, but it would be at the expense of other activities, unless those agencies would raise more money by increasing assessments on members. The obstacles to such a course of action have already been noted. The international financial institutions could also provide more money for environmental projects and projects with environmental aspects, but to do so might be seen as interfering with the achievement of traditional economic development goals. In any event, the limitations on the ability of those institutions to meet the capital needs of the developing countries would also inhibit a large-scale program of lending for environmental purposes.

Conclusions

The outcome of the above examination of the ability of the international community to meet growing perceptions of financial needs with currently available means of mobilizing funds is generally pessimistic. This conclusion applies equally to areas where large flows of capital are needed on concessional terms and to international programs which are inherently not self-financing.

The fundamental obstacle to expanding present means of raising money for international purposes is, of course, the partial disillusionment of citizens of many industrialized countries with international organizations. This public attitude is reflected in the reluctance of a number of parliaments to appropriate increased funds for international programs. If growing international requirements are to be met, new means of finance will, in all probability, be required.

Plan of Study

The primary objective of this study is to identify and to analyze in depth possible new means of raising money for any agreed upon international purpose. Special attention will, however, be devoted to the problem of financing international environmental programs. This emphasis is justified by the fact that the need to raise large sums of money to deal with environmental problems is only now being recognized. How that need will be met is even less clear than in the case of requirements that have been recognized for years, such as providing development capital for the poorer nations.

The general approach in this study is to examine what might be done if governments decide that new means of financing international needs are required. Political considerations are not ignored in weighing the advantages and disadvantages of various possible sources of funds, but no possibility is excluded simply because its early adoption appears unlikely.

Some of the revenue-raising measures analyzed in this study represent sharp departures from past international practice. At first sight, they may appear to rest on the unstated assumption that a world government with sovereign powers, including powers to raise revenue by taxation and other means, will be created in the foreseeable future. This is definitely not the case. The study assumes that whatever new revenue-raising measures are adopted must function within the framework of the existing international political order.

Most of the various means of finance examined in this study could in principle be used to support virtually any international purpose. In practice, however, the international community may earmark some funds for specific purposes, such as environmental programs. This study will therefore be concerned with both general purpose and earmarked funds.

The sequence of analysis may be described briefly as follows: Chapter 2 examines a wide range of possible sources of finance, rules out some of them for a variety of reasons, and sets aside a few for further, more intensive analysis in chapters 3, 4, and 5. Chapter 3 analyzes several possible international revenue taxes. Chapter 4 explores several possible taxes on international polluters, not so much as means of raising large amounts of money, but as a way of meeting an international need by inducing a change in the behavior of polluters. Chapter 5 examines prospects for obtaining revenue for international purposes by exploiting the nonliving resources of the ocean beyond national jurisdiction. Chapter 6 analyzes the legal and administrative problems that will have to be solved if the new sources of funds discussed in earlier chapters are actually to be generated and used for various international purposes. Chapter 7 reviews some of the problems that would be encountered in creating new means of financing international needs and suggests possible solutions.

CHAPTER TWO

Possible Sources of Finance

THE WAYS in which the international community might conceivably raise money to pay for environmental or other international programs are limited only by human ingenuity. Many theoretically available sources of funds must, however, be ruled out on grounds of impracticality or political unsuitability. Others are too costly or have other disadvantages that outweigh their revenue-raising potential.

The principal task of this chapter is to screen the large number of possible sources of revenue and select a few that are especially promising for detailed analysis in subsequent chapters. Several other revenue sources that cannot be ruled out of consideration, but that do not deserve intensive treatment, are dealt with more briefly in this chapter.

A wide range of possible means of raising money will be considered, including:

—contributions by participating governments, calculated in different ways;

—a variety of taxes levied directly on firms and individuals;

—taxes on polluters;

—revenue from the exploitation of ocean resources;

—loans from various sources; and

—a number of other measures that cannot easily be classified.

A few of the sources of funds to be considered are by their nature particularly suited to the financing of environmental programs. Most of them, however, could be used equally well for any other agreed upon international purpose.

18

Possible Shadow Taxes

One possible alternative to the present system would be to determine the payments required of each member of the United Nations (or of a component organization) on the basis of the estimated yield from certain hypothetical taxes on firms and individuals residing or doing business in the territory of that member. The emphasis would then be less on budgetary shares, and more on the proper definition of the tax base and on the setting of tax rates that would produce a desired amount of revenue. Assessments calculated in this way can be thought of as "shadow" taxes, since no levies would actually be imposed by the United Nations on firms or individuals. Member governments would be free to raise the funds needed to pay their assessments in any way that they wished.

In principle, shadow taxes could be similar to any of the numerous and varied taxes actually used by national governments. In practice, shadow taxes would probably have to be fairly simple in concept, so their hypothetical yield in each country could be easily estimated from readily available statistics. Also, shadow taxes would have to produce a distribution of burdens among states that would be regarded as fair (that is, politically tolerable). If shadow taxes were used to raise money for a specific purpose, a certain appropriateness or relevance to the purpose to be served would probably help gain acceptance for the taxes as a means of calculating official payments.

A relatively simple shadow tax would use the gross domestic product (GDP) of each contributing nation as the tax base. (This would be equivalent to an income tax on all firms and individuals at a uniform rate and with no exemptions or deductions.) A GDP tax could be calculated fairly easily, using data that most countries compile for other purposes. In 1973, a simple GDP tax at a rate of only 0.1 percent would have yielded an annual revenue of more than $5 billion,[1] which is more than twenty times the central UN budget in fiscal year 1973. Such a shadow tax would produce a distribution of burdens that would not differ markedly from the present percentage scale of assessments. Some of the developing countries would, however, find themselves paying a larger share than they do under the

1. See the estimates of the global product in 1973 and 1974 in U.S. Department of State, Bureau of Intelligence and Research, "The Planetary Product in the Year of the Oil Crunch," Report 166 (October 30, 1975; processed), p. 11.

present system, because a GDP tax would not make an adjustment for their low per capita income levels.

If such an adjustment were made, the GDP tax would be brought so close to the present distribution of burdens that the question would be raised of whether it really amounted to a significant change.[2] The answer would depend on whether, by varying the rate, the UN membership would use the GDP tax as a flexible means of raising revenue, or would merely treat the tax as a schedule of percentage assessments under another name. The latter possibility seems to be the more likely.

Other shadow taxes could, of course, be devised that would depart more sharply from the present system of assessments. But such shadow taxes might be less generally acceptable to the governments concerned. Little would be gained by cataloging and analyzing all of the large number of possibilities. In the context of the present study, however, it is worth asking whether any shadow taxes could be imposed that would be especially well suited to the raising of revenue for environmental purposes.

At first sight, it might appear that a shadow tax on GDP would fit this description, on the ground that GDP could be taken as a rough index of the damage that a nation does to the world environment. This argument, however, will not bear close inspection. Too many factors are involved, including differences in the structures of national economies and differences in the content and effectiveness of national policies of environmental protection.

Other shadow taxes might be devised that would, at least superficially, have a greater relevance to environmental concerns than would a GDP tax. For example, the tax base could be limited to the value of the output of a few industries—such as strip mining, thermal power plants, and copper refining—that are notorious for the damage that they inflict on the environment. But this approach, too, would involve serious conceptual and practical difficulties. For example, it would not seem right to count the output of industrial plants in countries with relatively strict and effective environmental controls to the same extent as the output of similar plants in countries with no controls. If this adjustment in the tax base were

2. There would be little need for adjustment at the upper end of the income scale, since the national product of the United States—the largest contributor—is about 25 percent of the global product, and the ceiling under the present assessment system has, in principle, been set at 25 percent.

actually to be made, it would probably be opposed by the poorer countries that tend to give higher priority to economic growth than to environmental protection, since it would increase the relative burden borne by them.

Even if this and other problems could be solved, it does not follow that a shadow tax on the output of selected polluting industries would be more suited to the raising of funds for international environmental programs than it would for meeting any other international financial needs. It must be remembered that a shadow tax is only a means of determining the levels of official contributions. How governments obtain the money that they contribute is up to them. Thus, in the case under discussion, real taxes might or might not actually be levied on the selected, polluting industries.

It might, of course, be possible to develop a system of inducements that would provide incentives for governments to impose real taxes corresponding to the shadow tax. One possibility would be to reduce the payment required of governments that collected the funds in the desired manner. But this would not be enough to create a special environmental claim to the revenues in question. It might be argued with considerable justification that a tax on the output of polluting industries is only superficially an environmental levy. Since the amount of tax imposed on a firm would not vary with the quantities of pollutants emitted, there would be no incentive for the firm to reduce its emissions.

The only shadow taxes that would be clearly more suited to the financing of international environmental programs than to other uses would be those that caused the governments concerned to impose effluent taxes on designated categories of polluters. The degree of intervention into domestic politics that this approach would involve argues strongly against its adoption, except possibly in areas of clear and strong international concern, such as pollution of the oceans. In those cases, the more direct approach of seeking agreement on the levying of international charges directly on polluters would probably be better than the indirect method of basing official contributions on shadow effluent charges. Such an approach is examined in chapter 4.

Trying to relate the level of official contributions to some index of environmental damage is not the only conceivable means of creating a system of official contributions that would be especially suited to the financing of international environmental programs. Another line of argument asserts the right of the international community to charge for the use of the international commons: the oceans and atmosphere beyond national jurisdiction, and radio and television frequencies or channels.[3] The idea that there is such a thing as the international commons is relatively new and has yet to gain general acceptance. By implication, it runs counter to existing international law which holds that no one owns the high seas and that all may navigate there freely. If it is assumed for purposes of discussion, however, that the concept of the international commons will in time be accepted, it can be made the basis of shadow taxes that would determine the level of official payments on which international environmental programs might plausibly be said to have a special claim.

The first practical problem to be solved in levying a shadow tax on users of the international commons, or any part thereof, is selecting the tax base. Two possibilities appear to exist: taxing the profits derived from use of the commons, and taxing the total income derived from such use. A shadow tax on profits would require the collection and analysis of masses of data that would be very costly and might be beyond the capabilities of international organizations. Estimating the total magnitude of goods and services produced through use of the commons would also not be easy, but such an estimate could probably be achieved without unreasonable effort.

That the latter approach may in fact be technically feasible has been demonstrated by the work of Pacem in Maribus on the Ocean Development Tax (ODT).[4] The base proposed for the ODT is the value or volume of fish, transport services, petroleum, and minerals produced through the use of the oceans, including territorial waters as well as areas beyond national jurisdiction. Because of difficulties in assigning money values to the oceanic fish catch and transport services, these items would be expressed in quantitative terms (metric tons and deadweight ton-miles) that would be adjusted periodically by price indexes. Assuming that the prob-

---

3. No claim to charge for the local use of portions of the electromagnetic spectrum would presumably be made. Charges would, under this concept, be justifiable only if a user in one nation interfered with or preempted use of the same wavelength by users in another nation or nations.

4. A general description of the results of this work is presented by John Eatwell, John Llewellyn, and Roger Tarling in chapter 2 of Elisabeth Mann Borgese and David Krieger, eds., *The Tides of Change: Peace, Pollution, and Potential of the Oceans* (Mason/Charter, 1975), pp. 33–47. Eatwell, Llewellyn, and Tarling give a fuller exposition of their work on the ODT in "Some Economic Implications of the Ocean Development Tax" (Cambridge University, May 1972; processed).

lems of collecting data could be solved, petroleum and mineral output would be expressed in monetary terms. The tax base would therefore not be unitary but segmented.

As is true of all shadow taxes, the economic incidence of the ODT cannot be determined, because national governments would raise their ODT payments in different ways. The distribution of the financial burden of the ODT among nations would, however, clearly be a problem. The authors of the ODT would deal with differences in ability to pay the ODT by varying the tax rate with per capita national income. It would not be as easy to meet the predictable complaints of countries that would be asked to make relatively large payments, because they are more dependent than most countries on fish as a source of protein, or because a large number of ships are registered under their laws in order to avoid stricter regulation elsewhere, or because firms incorporated under their laws are heavily engaged in offshore oil production.

The ODT proposal may suffer from a fundamental conceptual weakness. The underlying rationale for the ODT is that nations should contribute to the development and protection of ocean resources in proportion to their uses of the ocean. In many situations, however, what nation is the "user" is far from self-evident. For example, when a Greek-owned ship registered in Liberia carries a cargo from New York to Rotterdam, to what nation's tax base should the transport service be added? From a legal point of view, Liberia or Greece should be taxed; from an economic point of view, the United States or the Netherlands should be taxed. But which nations should actually contribute, and in what proportions?

Similar difficulties would be encountered in dividing the tax among nations if an effort were made to charge for use of international air space or telecommunication channels. Also, in those parts of the international commons, the need for revenues to develop or protect identifiable natural resources is much less clear or compelling.

A more modest proposal made by the Canadian government several years ago would not encounter the same kind of difficulties as would the ODT or other shadow taxes on users of the international commons.[5] Canada proposed that all coastal states pay over to an interim ocean

5. "Statement by the Representative of Canada to the Enlarged United Nations Committee on the Peaceful Uses of the Seabed and the Ocean Floor Beyond the Limits of National Jurisdiction" (May 24, 1971; processed).

regime "a fixed percentage of all the revenues they derive from the whole of the seabed areas claimed by them beyond the outer limit of their internal waters."[6] This proposal may, however, have been overtaken by events. Deliberations at the Third United Nations Conference on the Law of the Sea have revealed little interest by coastal states in devoting the revenues from their claimed territorial areas and economic zones to any international purpose.

The use of various shadow taxes as a means of calculating assessments for international organizations suffers from the same weakness that plagues other methods of levying assessments on national governments: payment is essentially voluntary, unless effective sanctions can be devised and applied. The only sanctions available at present are denial of rights to vote or, in the cases of a few specialized agencies, denial of the right to participate in various bodies. These sanctions are not severe and they could not be relied on to compel payment by a government that objected strongly either to the financial burden placed on it or to the purposes for which the funds in question were to be spent. The problem of arrearages could, in fact, be expected to increase under an assessment system that was more flexible and more automatic than the present one.

Stronger sanctions than those that now exist can easily be imagined, but it is doubtful that they would be applied, even if they were adopted in principle. The use of military force against a delinquent member is out of the question. Expulsion would appear to be an appropriate response to a long period of financial delinquency, but in any specific case political considerations might well inhibit such a step. Obtaining agreement on economic sanctions would be quite difficult and would be conceivable only if they were carefully tailored to the size of the offense. In that event, however, their impact on delinquent governments might not be enough to induce payment of overdue assessments.

Optimism concerning prospects for finding and applying effective means of enforcing shadow taxes or any other system of assessments on national governments would appear not to be warranted. This fact, plus the limitations on any revenue source that depends upon periodic appropriations, explains the need to look beyond possible improvements in the system of national assessments to other, more novel revenue possibilities.

6. This proposal would, of course, not create a shadow tax, but would provide for a sharing of specified revenues between national governments and an international entity.

Taxes on Firms and Individuals

Although national governments have always financed their operations by levying a variety of taxes on private individuals and organizations, there has never been an international tax. The reason for this is that the power to tax and to compel payment is an attribute of sovereignty, and there is yet to be an international entity with sovereign powers. The fact that under the present international order there cannot, strictly speaking, be international taxes does not, however, preclude arrangements among national governments to use their sovereignties jointly to impose and enforce the collection of taxes on behalf of international organizations. The term "international taxes," as it is used here and in subsequent chapters, refers to levies on firms and individuals imposed and collected under such arrangements among nations. Various forms of such arrangements and the problems that they involve will be considered later in this study.

Like assessments, international taxes depend fundamentally on the acquiescence—and indeed the active support—of national governments. But, because taxes are levied on firms and individuals rather than on governments, taxes have two advantages over assessments. First, the burden that taxes impose on cooperating governments is both less direct and less visible than that imposed by assessments. Legislative approval of taxes would be required in many countries at the time of their imposition, but the annual appropriation process, with all of its political hazards, could subsequently be avoided. Second, governments would be more likely to apply effective legal sanctions against delinquent individual taxpayers than they would be to penalize other governments that were in arrears in their assessments. It is even possible that, once an international tax had been agreed upon, some governments would be willing to permit the United Nations to sue delinquent taxpayers in their courts and even to obtain court orders attaching the assets of such taxpayers.

The vulnerability of any schemes of international taxation to the withdrawal of support by national governments must nevertheless be taken seriously. For that reason, it would be desirable to structure international taxes in such a way that they would be collectible in more than one country. This would reduce dependence on the continued cooperation of each individual government.

For purposes of this study, two kinds of international taxes must be considered: taxes that are imposed solely to raise revenue, and taxes that are intended primarily to change the behavior of taxpayers in directions that are desirable from an environmental standpoint.

Revenue Taxes

Many taxes that national governments employ cannot be expected to be made available to the United Nations or any of its component organizations. In some cases, the infringement of national sovereignty would be too great; in other cases, the administrative problems would be too large for any international organization to handle successfully; and in still other cases, national governments would resist the loss of traditional mainstays of their financial support. For one or more of these reasons, most internal excise taxes (for example, on alcoholic beverages and tobacco), real estate taxes, value-added taxes, income taxes, and charges for the use of public facilities can be ruled out of consideration.

Two possible areas of international taxation appear to deserve serious consideration:
—charges for the use of the international commons (that is, international waters, air space, and telecommunication frequencies), and
—levies on international trade and financial transactions.

CHARGES FOR USE OF THE COMMONS. The international community does not today possess sovereign rights over the international commons. So long as this situation prevails, international charges for use of the commons must be justified on a case-by-case basis. A strong case for imposing a charge can be made if users degrade the commons, and the possibility of such charges is explored in the next section of this chapter. A good case can also be made for taxing the economic rents enjoyed by users of scarce resources outside national jurisdictions. Such rents are, in a sense, windfalls since they represent returns on investment in excess of costs, including a normal return on capital. As such, they would appear to be prime candidates for diversion to international purposes.

The wisdom of charging for the use of an international resource that is not scarce and that is not degraded by use is questionable. To do so would be to make users pay for something that has no economic value. As a consequence, the marginal efficiency of capital in activities involving the use of such a resource would be artificially depressed, and some capital and labor—which are scarce resources—would be diverted into other, less productive activities.

The possibility of obtaining revenue for international purposes by appropriating part of the rent created by exploitation of living and non-living ocean resources is examined later in this chapter. At the present time, there do not appear to be many other scarce resources that produce economic rents for users of the commons.

The high seas and international air space are not yet so crowded as to constitute scarce resources, although this situation may arise someday on heavily traveled sea and air lanes. The right to transit some narrow straits, such as the Strait of Malacca, may become a scarce resource in the not-so-distant future, but the power to tax the resulting economic rents would undoubtedly reside in the coastal states rather than in any international body. Some air lanes over the North Atlantic are already saturated at certain times of the day, but congestion is not yet a serious problem in most other air routes.

Parking spaces, or "slots," for satellites in geosynchronous orbit[7] could one day become a scarce resource. This day has not yet arrived, however.[8] The orbital track along which geosynchronous orbit is possible is a circle with a circumference of 165,000 miles. Moreover, this track is not a narrow line; it is more like a tunnel 100 miles high and several miles wide. The satellite population would therefore have to be quite dense before serious danger of collisions would arise. The more likely problem is radio interference between neighboring communication satellites, but technological advances are making it possible to position satellites using the same radio frequency closer and closer together. Nevertheless, the need to control allocation of the more choice geostationary slots—that is, those well located with respect to land areas that are economically important—may one day arise. Charging "parking fees" for such slots would then be justifiable.

The only significant scarce resources currently associated with the commons, other than the living and nonliving resources in and under the

---

7. A satellite placed in orbit 22,300 miles above the equator, traveling from west to east, will remain approximately above the same spot on the earth below. Such a satellite is said to be in synchronous or geosynchronous orbit and to occupy a geostationary slot.

8. See Brenda Maddox, *Beyond Babel: New Directions in Communications* (London: André Deutsch, 1972), pp. 80–81.

ocean, appear to be telecommunication channels. In principle, the international community could try to appropriate all or part of the economic rents now enjoyed by private radio and television broadcasters and by firms selling telecommunication services. This might be done either by taxing the profits of the firm in question or by charging fees for the use of assigned channels.

In practice, an effort to tax broadcasters would encounter serious complications. The assignment of frequencies is largely in the hands of national governments, and it would be difficult for an international organization to charge for channels when it did not control their assignment.[9] Moreover, an increasing part of the long-distance use of telecommunication frequencies involves satellites belonging to Intelsat (the International Telecommunications Satellite Consortium), which already charges for the use of its circuits. These charges are set at a level designed to cover depreciation of satellites and operating costs, and to yield a return on the investments that members of Intelsat have made in the space segment of the communications system.[10]

These complications might be overcome through an intensive and probably prolonged international effort. The prospects for success, however, do not appear great enough to accord taxes on telecommunication frequencies very high priority among possible new sources of revenue for environmental or other international purposes. One possibility that might be explored would be to impose a tax on the profits received by shareholders of Intelsat as part of a more general system of taxing the international transmission of profits on international investments.

Even though many uses of the commons—such as shipping in the ocean, and air travel and the stationing of satellites in the atmosphere—do not involve the use of resources that are scarce now or likely to be

9. Ranges of frequencies for various international purposes are allocated at periodic Administrative Radio Conferences convened by the International Telecommunication Union (ITU). These allocations are not binding, however, unless or until they have been incorporated in formal international agreements. Specific frequencies for individual users within the agreed upon ranges are assigned by national governments. These assignments are then registered with the International Frequency Registration Board, an agency of the ITU. See Abram Chayes and others, *Satellite Broadcasting* (London: Oxford University Press, 1973), pp. 17–18.

10. Paul L. Laskin, "Background Paper," in *Communicating by Satellite,* Report of the Twentieth Century Fund Task Force on International Satellite Communications (New York, 1969), p. 34.

scarce in the reasonably near future, the international community may someday decide that some of these uses are proper objects of taxation. Economic theory often has little influence on the decisions of those responsible for drawing up tax plans. In practice, such decisions are more likely to depend on whether the proposed levy is regarded as administratively and politically feasible.

Moreover, if the international community, in anticipation of conflicting demands on the use of resources in the global commons, decided to develop an international body to manage the oceans and/or the atmosphere, charges might be imposed on various uses to finance the operations of the international authority.[11] For example, taxes on international air travel could generate a considerable amount of revenue. Such a tax would be relatively easy to administer and to collect. Various sales taxes and other national and local taxes are levied on air travel tickets and are paid by the consumer when the ticket is purchased. The airlines, which already transmit the revenues from these taxes to appropriate government authorities, could also transmit revenues from any agreed upon international taxes to a designated international authority. Other advantages of a tax on air travel are that the tax burden would be borne largely by relatively affluent individuals, and that the tax base is constantly expanding.

TAXES ON TRADE AND FINANCIAL TRANSACTIONS. Levies on international trade and financial transactions have several attractions. The very fact that trade and finance are vital international economic activities lends credibility to the assertion that it is appropriate to impose an international tax on them. Also, since the value of international trade and financial transactions is very large, quite low tax rates could produce substantial revenue, and opposition to the levies might, as a consequence, be moderated. Of greatest practical importance, however, is the fact that in every international trade and financial transaction at least two nations are involved, so more than one point for collection of an international tax would be available. Nevertheless, these general advantages do not provide answers to two important questions. Should all international trade and all

11. The need for new institutions to manage the ocean and the atmosphere and the kinds of regimes that might be proposed have been discussed by a number of scholars. See, among others, Borgese and Krieger, eds., *The Tides of Change,* pp. 324–57; Elisabeth Mann Borgese and Arvid Pardo, "Ocean Management," in Jan Tinbergen, coordinator, *Reshaping the International Order: A Report to the Club of Rome* (Dutton, 1976); Seyom Brown and others, *Regimes for the Ocean, Outer Space, and Weather* (Brookings Institution, 1977), pp. 241–42.

international financial transactions be taxed? If they should not, what components of each should be singled out for taxation? A study such as the present one cannot provide a definitive answer to these questions. In the end, they must be resolved on political grounds. The consequences of selected alternatives can, however, be usefully analyzed, and this is done in chapter 3.

With respect to international trade, both a general trade tax and special taxes on internationally traded fuels, oil, and mineral raw materials will be considered. These particular commodities were selected for two reasons. First, they are depletable resources, and taxing them could contribute to their conservation by discouraging consumption. Second, they are major components of world trade, and taxing them even at very low rates would yield substantial revenue.[12]

With respect to international financial transactions, a general tax can probably be ruled out. Funds are transferred internationally for many reasons, and treating all transactions alike could not easily be justified. Moreover, administration of a general tax on international financial transactions would be complicated and costly. Widespread evasion of the tax could probably not be prevented.

A tax on certain kinds of financial transactions might, however, be more manageable. In fact, a tax on the international transfer of income from international investments has certain attractions from an administrative point of view. The average size of such transfers is probably fairly large, which would tend to hold down the size of the administrative burden relative to the size of the tax base. Preventing large-scale evasion of a tax on income transfers would be facilitated by the fact that many of the firms subject to the tax would be large multinational corporations that are already required to report extensively on their financial status and activities to several governments. A tax on the transfer of income from international investments will therefore be among the revenue taxes analyzed.

Taxes on Polluters of the Ocean and the Atmosphere

For centuries, the free use of the ocean, the atmosphere, and inland lakes and streams as receptacles for waste products or as vehicles for

12. As an alternative to a tax on trade in energy and minerals, it might be possible for the international community to impose a tax on profits of firms pro-

carrying away waste went virtually unchallenged. In recent decades, however, the realization has grown in many parts of the world that this kind of behavior imposes costs on society by destroying amenities or endangering public health. The view has therefore become increasingly widespread that polluters should pay when they use common resources to dispose of their waste.[13]

Taxes on polluters serve two important purposes. First, by requiring economic entities, such as mines or factories, to cover the full social costs of their activities, these taxes facilitate a more rational use of resources. Second, the fact that the taxes vary with the amount of pollution gives polluters an economic incentive to reduce their pollution to the point at which the marginal cost of further pollution control exceeds the charge per unit of pollution. By adjusting the charge per unit, any given target of pollution abatement can in principle be achieved at the least total cost. The reason for this is that polluters are not identical in their ability to reduce pollution, and user charges automatically allocate a larger share of the abatement target to those in the best position to respond (that is, those with the relatively more elastic supply curves for pollution abatement).

Since polluters would continue to pay for the pollution that it was not in their financial interest to abate, taxes on polluters would also produce revenue. The amount of such revenue, however, would be only a partial measure of the resources that the taxes would make available for the achievement of agreed upon international goals. Although they would not pass through the treasury of any international institution, the expenditures made by polluters to abate pollution as an alternative to paying the tax represent in a very real sense funds mobilized for an international purpose. Taxes on polluters are therefore not only valuable tools in working toward social goals, but they also can properly be viewed as useful components of a future international fiscal system.

A good case can be made for devoting the proceeds of taxes on pol-

---

ducing these commodities. A proposal for this kind of tax is described briefly in Robert Gibrat and Tetsuo Noguchi, "Energy, Ores and Minerals," in Tinbergen, coordinator, *Reshaping the International Order*, p. 258.

13. The rationale for this point of view and the various ways in which it might be applied are spelled out in Organisation for Economic Co-operation and Development, *The Polluter Pays Principle: Definition, Analysis, Implementation* (Paris: OECD, 1975). See also Allen V. Kneese and Charles L. Schultze, *Pollution, Prices, and Public Policy* (Brookings Institution, 1975).

luters to environmental purposes. Since the primary reason for imposing such taxes is the desire to change behavior in environmentally desirable directions, it would seem appropriate to use the revenue from such taxes in support of similar objectives. Each taxpayer/polluter is forced by the tax to assume costs for every unit of pollution. Some of these costs are incurred in order to reduce the amount of effluent, and they are therefore clearly in support of an environmental objective. Other costs take the form of tax payments, and consistency suggests that they also be devoted to environmental purposes.

Examples of the use of taxes on polluters by national and local governments are not difficult to find. No international agency has thus far imposed taxes on polluters, but there would appear to be no reason in principle why such taxes should not be levied on all polluters of the ocean and the atmosphere beyond national jurisdictions. On practical grounds, however, distinctions must be made among categories of polluters of the commons.

Land-based polluters can probably be ruled out of serious consideration at this time, primarily for two reasons. First, taxing land-based polluters would probably involve an infringement of national sovereignty that some coastal states would find unacceptable. Second, monitoring ocean dumping (particularly indirect dumping) would present great practical difficulties. It should be noted, however, that the inherent case for taxing ocean pollution from land-based sources is essentially the same as that for taxing pollution from economic activities that take place on the oceans.

Levying taxes on pollution by ocean shipping would probably encounter fewer difficulties. A large part of the polluting hydrocarbons emitted by tankers and other ships are discharged on the high seas outside national jurisdictions. Moreover, on most voyages oceangoing ships enter the ports of more than one country, thereby creating the possibility of collecting taxes in two or more national jurisdictions. The possible application of taxes on pollution from shipping will be analyzed in chapter 4. Tankers and other merchant ships will be treated separately, in part for technological reasons, and in part because tankers account for a larger share of hydrocarbon pollution of the ocean.

The levying of taxes on pollution caused by firms engaged in the offshore drilling of oil will also be considered. Such drilling is already a significant source of pollution in some areas, such as the Gulf of Mexico and the Persian Gulf, and it could become a much larger source in future years. It is true that much offshore drilling is within the territorial waters of coastal states, and a large part of the remainder is within the special economic zones that are being claimed by more and more such states. Questions of national sovereignty would therefore have to be faced, and administration of these taxes might be more difficult than in the case of shipping. On grounds of both consistency and equity, however, it would be hard to justify applying taxes to oil pollution from ships and not to offshore drilling when both are sources of the same kind of pollution of the ocean.

At first sight, consistency and equity might also appear to argue for considering seriously the levying of taxes on polluting emissions from civil aircraft. After all, planes and ships are competitive forms of transport over many routes and both discharge hydrocarbons into the atmosphere or the ocean or both. These facts, however, have less weight than other practical considerations. The hydrocarbons discharged into the international commons by planes are a small fraction of those emitted by tankers and other ships. Therefore, the pollution abatement that might be achieved by levying taxes on planes would be relatively small.

Revenue from the Exploitation of Ocean Resources

The exploitation of the ocean's living resources involves different legal and economic problems than are encountered in the exploitation of the ocean's nonliving resources. The potential of these two kinds of resources as sources of revenue for environmental or other international purposes must therefore be considered separately.

Living Ocean Resources

Fish are by far the major living resource of the ocean. Sea mammals are much less important, and their commercial exploitation has become increasingly constricted by international efforts to protect endangered species. Sedentary species (mostly shellfish) are sizable sources of income in some areas, but they are found largely within the inland and territorial waters of coastal states, or in the special economic zones that are being claimed by more and more such states.

General acceptance of exclusive economic zones extending 200 nautical miles to sea in fact appears likely in the near future, either through agreement at the Third United Nations Conference on the Law of the Sea or through the unilateral actions of coastal states. As a consequence, a large proportion of commercially valuable fish stocks will come under national jurisdictions, and extracting revenue from them for international purposes will become virtually impossible.

Some fish stocks will, of course, remain partly or wholly outside national jurisdictions. In the former case, coordination of management and revenue policies between national governments and a still-to-be-created international ocean authority would involve enormous difficulties. Moreover, an international claim to an interest in one important category, anadromous fish (such as salmon) that spawn in inland streams and rivers and spend most of their lives in the ocean, would encounter strong opposition. Coastal states have traditionally asserted a primary interest in anadromous species and can be expected to do so in the future.

The fish stocks, including migratory species such as tuna, that are located wholly or largely more than 200 miles from land could in principle produce revenue for international purposes. Levying taxes on the deep-sea fishing industry could in fact increase its efficiency.[14] Because fish on the high seas belong to no one, entry into the fishing industry has been open and free. The result has been overcapitalization and overfishing. The economic rents (that is, the financial return above total costs plus a normal profit) potentially obtainable from fishing have been dissipated in the form of higher than necessary costs caused by excessive depletion of fish stocks.

International taxes on the volume or value of fish caught, or charges for the privilege of fishing, or both would tend over time to squeeze out marginal operators, reduce both overcapitalization and overfishing, and increase the profits (before taxes) of the remaining operators. In effect, the taxes or charges would at once re-create economic rents in the deep-sea fishing industry and would appropriate these rents, in whole or in part, for international purposes.

This result, however, is only what might result if serious practical diffi-

14. This proposition is argued more fully by Richard N. Cooper, "An Economist's View of the Oceans," in National Science Foundation, *Perspectives on Ocean Policy: Conference on Conflict and Order in Ocean Relations* (Washington, D.C.: NSF, 1974), pp. 143–65. Cooper develops the argument in greater detail in "The Oceans as a Source of Revenue" (paper prepared for the Workshop on Specific Proposals and Desirable DC Response to LDC Demands Regarding the New International Economic Order, Massachusetts Institute of Technology, May 17–20, 1976; processed).

culties could be overcome.[15] Obtaining international agreement on any scheme to extract revenues from the fishing industry would be quite diffi- ✓ cult. Nations that have large fishing fleets or that are especially dependent on fish as a source of protein would be certain to feel threatened and discriminated against. The economic case for using taxes or charges to limit entry into the fishing industry would not be accepted easily by those who hold the traditional view that fish on the high seas are a free resource.

Even if agreement could be reached on the principle of imposing some kind of tax or charge on deep-sea fishing, working out the specifics of such an arrangement would be complicated. The economics of fishing for different species differ, and conditions vary in different parts of the ocean. Also, the price of a given variety of fish varies widely from country to country, depending on dietary habits and the prices of alternative sources of protein. A further complication is the fact that some governments subsidize their fishing fleets, and they would undoubtedly fear that an international tax on fishing would force an increase in their subsidy payments. A uniform revenue system would probably not work, and information on which to base a variable system could be obtained only at considerable effort and financial cost.

Enforcement would also be difficult and expensive. Lacking a navy, how could the United Nations collect taxes from fishing boats flying the flags of noncooperating nations? Sanctions might, of course, be applied to such boats if they entered the ports of cooperating nations, but they could not be counted on to expose themselves in that way.

The most that could realistically be expected would be that the parties to some regional conservation agreements might see an advantage in adding taxes or other charges to the measures (such as quotas, limited seasons, and restrictions on gear) now used to prevent overfishing of certain fish stocks. In such an event, however, the resultant revenues would almost certainly be used to support the administration of the agreement in question, and they would not be available for more general international purposes. Indeed, the very existence of regional fishing agreements is yet another complication in the way of establishing any general system of raising revenue from the deep-sea fishing industry.

Before leaving the subject of living ocean resources, something should

15. Some of these difficulties are similar to those involved in creating a satisfactory international system for distributing the benefits of the world's fisheries. See Francis T. Christy, Jr., "Distribution Systems for World Fisheries: Problems and Principles," in NSF, *Perspectives on Ocean Policy*, pp. 179–205.

be said about a little-known resource that could have a large potential as a source of revenue for international purposes. That resource is the krill, a small shrimp-like animal found in enormous quantities in the waters surrounding Antarctica. The krill are at present harvested on only a small scale by Soviet and Japanese fishermen, but it has been estimated that krill could be caught in an amount that would more than double the tonnage of fish taken from the ocean each year without damaging the main breeding stock.[16]

Although the bulk of the krill population may lie within 200 miles of land, it does not follow that it is within the exclusive economic zones of coastal states. A number of states have staked out claims, some of them conflicting, to portions of Antarctica. Those claims, however, were suspended for thirty years under the Antarctic Treaty that came into effect in 1961.[17] A further agreement among all interested powers to relinquish all claims to an economic zone in Antarctic waters would not appear to be out of the question. Creation of a special international economic zone would be another way to remove the krill from even contingent national jurisdictions. In either event, the way would be opened to the extraction of international revenue from enterprises engaged in harvesting krill. How large such revenue might become cannot be estimated in the absence of further information on the economics of exploiting the krill stock off the Antarctic continent.

Nonliving Ocean Resources

The nonliving resources of the ocean are varied and extensive.[18] Some are already being exploited on a significant economic scale, and there

16. "Talking About Antarctica," *The Petroleum Economist* (November 1975), p. 412. Similar estimates are presented—with varying degrees of tentativeness—by Yu. E. Permitin, P. A. Moiseev, and J. A. Gulland in M. W. Holdgate, ed., *Antarctic Ecology,* vol. 1 (Academic Press, 1970), pp. 177, 216, and 220.

17. Article IV, section 2, of the treaty states: "No acts or activities taking place while the present Treaty is in force shall constitute a basis for asserting, supporting or denying a claim to territorial sovereignty in Antarctica or create any rights of sovereignty in Antarctica. No new claim, or enlargement of an existing claim, to territorial sovereignty in Antarctica shall be asserted while the present Treaty is in force." 12 UST 794; 402 UNTS 71.

18. The summary discussion of nonliving ocean resources presented here is based principally on the following sources: "Mineral Resources of the Sea, Report of the Secretary-General," UN Doc. E/4973, April 26, 1971, pp. 5–37; Francis T.

can be little doubt that the contribution of the ocean to the gross global product will grow in future decades.

Enormous quantities of minerals—including gold, magnesium, bromine, potassium, and various salts—are dissolved in the water of the ocean. Some—most notably common salt, or sodium chloride—are already extracted in commercial quantities. The ocean water itself is the principal source of deuterium, a heavy isotope of hydrogen, on which the nuclear fusion process of producing energy may one day be based.

Deposits on the surface of the sea floor are also of current or potential economic importance. Most such deposits that are now being exploited are relatively close to shore: ordinary sand, gravel, shell, heavy mineral sands, and iron sands. Lying under deeper waters and awaiting possible future exploitation are manganese and phosphorous nodules, and in a few areas metalliferous brines containing small percentages of copper, zinc, silver, lead, tin, and gold.

By far the most important resources known to exist beneath the ocean floor are oil and natural gas. More than one-tenth of the world's production of these essential sources of energy now comes from offshore wells, and this percentage is expected to rise sharply in future years. Much smaller, but commercially significant quantities of coal are produced by mines extending under coastal waters. Sulphur is found in domes on the continental shelf in some areas, and the bedrock beneath the ocean probably contains large deposits of tin, iron, nickel, copper, mercury, and potash. Knowledge of sea floor geology is, however, still quite limited.

By no means all of the nonliving resources of the ocean are possible sources of revenue for international purposes. The exploitation of some resources is much too costly. Other resources are now largely under the control of individual nations, or they will probably become subject to such control in the not-too-distant future. Most nonliving resources of the ocean are found close to shore,[19] or they can be extracted more easily from close-in waters than from waters farther out to sea. This fact plus the pre-

Christy, Jr., "Marigenous Minerals: Wealth, Regimes and Factors of Decision," in *Symposium on the International Regime of the Sea-Bed* (Rome: Accademia Nazionale dei Lincei, 1970), pp. 113–31; and summaries of papers presented by V. E. McKelvey and John B. Rigg to the National Ocean Industries Association meeting, March 1974, in *Ocean Industry*, vol. 9 (April 1974), pp. 208–19.

19. "Economic Significance in Terms of Sea-bed Mineral Resources, of the Various Limits Proposed for National Jurisdiction," UN Doc. A/AC.138/87, June 4, 1973, especially pp. 37–39.

viously noted tendency of coastal states to claim exclusive economic zones extending 200 miles from shore sharply reduces the resources from which revenues might conceivably be derived for international purposes.[20]

The only nonliving resources that appear to deserve more intensive examination are hydrocarbons (oil and natural gas) and manganese nodules.[21] The potential of these resources as sources of revenue for environmental or other international purposes is analyzed in chapter 5.

Borrowings from Capital Markets

Loans already are the principal means of financing internationally sponsored development programs. In principle, there would appear to be no reason why loans could not also be used to finance international environmental programs. In fact, some of the projects financed by the World Bank and other international financial institutions have had environmental aspects. Possible arrangements between UNEP and these institutions that might increase such lending are explored in chapter 6.

Another possibility would be for the Fund of UNEP, or a new environmental institution created specially for the purpose, to borrow directly from the money market by issuing its own bonds. In order for such an effort to succeed, the fund or other borrowing institution would have to establish its creditworthiness, which might require some or all of the following actions:

—A commitment to use the proceeds of bond sales only for self-liquidating projects, such as financing construction of waste disposal plants that would be paid for by charges levied on users.

—Guarantee of the bonds by a group of UN members.

—Earmarking of some other UN revenues, such as assessments or taxes, to meet interest and repayment schedules on the bonds.

20. The current state of international law, and possible future developments, concerning jurisdiction over offshore resources are discussed in greater detail in chapter 5.

21. The possibility of harnessing ocean currents or producing energy through exploiting the temperature differences in ocean water at various depths will not be treated here. The economic feasibility of such projects has not yet been proved, and it is impossible to estimate whether, and to what extent, they might become potential sources of revenue for international purposes.

Even with all of these measures, it is possible that the bonds could not be marketed on terms comparable to those obtained by the World Bank. If this proved to be the case, the proceeds of the bond sales could not be re-lent on terms that would be acceptable to many potential borrowers, especially governments of the poorer developing countries. It might then be better to leave the raising of money from the capital markets to the World Bank and to induce the Bank to expand its support of environmental projects. This approach is explored in chapter 6.

Other Possible Sources of Finance

A number of possible sources of finance in addition to those treated above also deserve at least brief consideration. These include charges for technical services, private contributions, compulsory insurance against accidental damage to the environment, various revenue taxes, and the use of Special Drawing Rights (SDRs) and the profits from gold sales.

Charges for Technical Services

As UNEP gains experience, it will be increasingly able to provide technical services for which it could demand and receive compensation, if its costs prove to be competitive with private sources of similar services. Services for which charges might be levied include surveys of environmental problems, planning and technical supervision of environmental projects, and monitoring environmental conditions. Other international agencies active in the environmental field might also be able to charge for their services.

In some cases, the cost of technical services could be included in the sum advanced by the World Bank or a regional development bank to finance a project with environmental aspects. In other cases, the services might be sold directly to a national government, a municipality, or even a private business firm. Monitoring information might be particularly valuable to private enterprises that are trying to prove their compliance with local or national environmental standards.

UNEP and other international organizations would probably encounter some opposition if they attempted to charge for technical services. Some governments that had made substantial contributions to the organization making the charges might argue that they were being asked to pay twice for the same services. Other governments that face serious problems in acquiring the resources needed for economic development might see the charges as only one more burden and an unfair one at that.

As a relatively new organization, UNEP may face something of a dilemma. If UNEP does not soon establish the principle that its services are not always free, it will have a hard time initiating charges in later years. On the other hand, if it moves too aggressively to put part of its operations on a self-sustaining basis, it may lose the international backing that it needs to gain access to really substantial sources of revenue. The solution (which might also be adopted by other international organizations) may be to distinguish between normal services, which are provided without charge, and special services, for which charges are levied on the basis of ability to pay.

Private Contributions

Campaigns to raise money for international programs from private individuals, foundations, and corporations are not a new idea. One well-known example is the annual sale of holiday greeting cards and gift wrapping paper by UNICEF. There is no reason why UNEP should not contemplate a similar effort. Before actually launching a fund-raising campaign, however, several practical problems would have to be faced, including the purposes for which contributions would be used and the cost of the campaign itself.

An alternative to a far-flung campaign on the UNICEF model also deserves consideration. This would be a more carefully targeted effort to obtain large contributions from a relatively small number of wealthy corporations and individuals, who could be convinced of the social need for a larger effort to protect the environment, and who might also hope to benefit from being associated in the public mind with such an effort. The same impulses that lead to large gifts to charities and to the endowment of foundations dedicated to promoting the public interest could also produce substantial contributions for international environmental purposes.

Such contributions would be made much more likely, however, if they could be deducted from the income subject to taxation in the country of origin. It might therefore be necessary to induce countries whose tax laws do not permit such deductions to make appropriate amendments to those laws. Alternatively, some governments might be willing to encourage private gifts to UNEP by offering to match such gifts by increased contributions from public funds.

Compulsory Insurance against Accidental Damage to the Environment

Some damage to the environment is, of course, accidental. Examples are collisions involving oil tankers, temporary breakdowns of waste-processing systems, and blowouts during oil-drilling operations offshore. These and other accidental damages to the environment are probably insurable risks, in that experience provides a basis for estimating the frequency of their occurrence and the extent of their resultant damage.

If industries subject to environmental risks were required to carry adequate insurance, one kind of financial requirement in the field of environmental protection would automatically be provided for.[22] Moreover, a useful incentive to avoid accidental damage to the environment would be provided if insurers would agree to reduce premiums for firms with better-than-average safety records.

The risks insured against should go beyond those involving demonstrable damage to specific persons or governments. Damage to the international commons should also be covered, and UNEP or another international agency should be empowered to submit and collect claims for such damage. Insurance against environmental damage would, of course, mobilize resources and direct them into environmentally desirable uses. Insurance would therefore reduce requirements for environmental financing. Insurance would not, however, be a significant source of revenue for

---

22. A precedent for such a requirement is provided by the International Convention on Civil Liability for Oil Pollution Damage, which establishes the liability of shipowners for pollution damage and requires them to maintain insurance or other financial security against such liability, if they wish to avail themselves of the limitation on total liability provided by the convention. See "Official Documents," *American Journal of International Law,* vol. 64 (April 1970), pp. 481–93. According to the U.S. Department of State, this convention came into force in June 1975 for some participating nations, but as of June 1977 it had not come into force for the United States.

environmental programs, since receipts (premiums) and payments (compensation for damage) would be kept as nearly in balance as possible.

Taxes on Arms Transfers and on National Defense Budgets

From time to time a proposal surfaces that taxes should be levied either on the transfer of arms among countries or on national defense budgets. These proposals are usually made in the context of discouraging the global arms race. Given the enormous sums that are spent for these purposes by many governments, either of these ways of "levying a tax on war" could yield enormous revenues in addition to attempting to promote world peace. There are several problems with both of these levies that appear to make them less viable from an operational standpoint than the other revenue taxes examined in greater detail in this study.

With respect to taxes on trade in arms, a problem arises from the fact that national governments are virtually always the importers in this trade. Governments are frequently involved on the export side as well—either directly, or indirectly as providers of export credits or guarantees to manufacturers of weapons. Thus, taxes on arms transfers would essentially be levied on governments. As noted earlier, one of the principal purposes of this study is to identify ways of raising revenue that differ from government contributions on grounds that voluntary governmental contributions seem unlikely to expand a great deal.

The major problem with a tax related to national defense expenditures is that this amounts to a tax on a particular component of national GNP. Again, as discussed previously, a tax on GNP (or one component of it) is essentially the same thing as a government contribution. Moreover, a tax on national defense expenditures is basically a shadow tax and suffers from one of the chief drawbacks of a shadow tax imposed on any specific activity—namely, there is no way of assuring that the national defense budget would bear the burden of the tax. The national government could pay this tax, if it were levied, out of general revenues paid to the treasury.

Special Drawing Rights

Special Drawing Rights are the "paper gold" issued by the International Monetary Fund (IMF) to its members as reserve assets. The use of SDRs to finance the development of the poorer nations of the world has been under discussion in international financial circles for many years.[23] If agreement on such use is ever reached, it might be argued that SDRs should also be used to finance international environmental programs. Certainly, there should be little question about developmental projects with environmental aspects. A good case could also be made for purely environmental expenditures on the ground that international concern over the environment is in fact inextricably linked with the need to raise living standards in the developing countries.

Early agreement to link the issuance of SDRs and economic aid does not, however, appear likely. Many industrialized countries remain unconvinced of the merits of the concept. Even if agreement on some kind of SDR-aid link is one day reached, however, it does not follow that substantial additional resources would then become available on a sustained basis to finance developmental, environmental, or any other international program of international agencies.

Over the years, the various proposals pertaining to the linkage of SDRs and economic development have undergone considerable change. Some of the proposals of the 1960s envisioned that the SDRs issued for development be channeled through a multilateral institution, usually the International Development Association (IDA). More recent proposals put forth by the developing countries have envisioned the distribution of SDRs directly to governments. If these proposals were accepted, there would be no additional funds for programs administered by international organizations. Instead, a direct resource transfer to the developing countries would take place.

Even if the industrialized countries were willing to agree to the link, however, a number of considerations reduce the attractiveness of SDRs as a means of resource transfer. One possibility is that aid donor countries might use the link as an excuse to reduce their official bilateral and/or multilateral aid contributions. A second factor is that the IMF charges interest on the net use of SDRs, so that the amount of concessional aid available from SDRs depends on the difference between the rate of interest charged by IMF and commercial interest rates.

23. The various forms of the proposal to link SDRs and developmental assistance are described and analyzed in William R. Cline, *International Monetary Reform and the Developing Countries* (Brookings Institution, 1976). The discussion of the linkage of SDRs and aid presented here is based in large part on this study, especially pp. 91–95.

Another problem lies in the distribution of SDR emissions. The initial emissions of SDRs in 1970–71 went to IMF members in proportion to their quotas. This meant that the larger part of the SDRs went to industrialized, rather than developing, nations. Moreover, the developing countries that were better off received more than those with the lowest per capita incomes. Recognizing this problem, the group of developing countries that has been pushing for the SDR-aid link has proposed a different pattern of distribution that would give a somewhat greater share of future SDR emissions to the poorest countries.

Within the present international monetary framework, perhaps the greatest drawback of the link is that the emission of SDRs seems unlikely to result in a substantial mobilization of resources for aid, at least in the near or medium term. SDRs are issued by the IMF to meet requirements of the international monetary system for additional liquidity. If no additional liquidity is needed, which is the case today and may continue to be the case for the next few years, no new SDRs would be issued. The existence of large financial requirements for developmental assistance or environmental programs would make no difference. The leading advocates of the SDR-aid link have accepted this basic principle. The magnitude of SDR emissions over the longer run cannot easily be predicted. The emissions will depend not only on total needs for liquidity but also on the extent to which those needs are met by gold and foreign exchange reserves.

Despite these problems and limitations, it is possible that over the longer run SDRs will become an important means of economic assistance or transfer of resources. It may be that SDRs will ultimately play a greater role in the international monetary system. If creation of international reserves through the accumulation of foreign exchange and gold were phased out and SDRs became the dominant or exclusive reserve asset, then substantial annual SDR emissions would probably be needed. If this happened, and if the industrialized countries moderated their opposition to the link, considerable resources could be made available for economic development.

Gold Sales

More recently, another proposal for using the international monetary system to provide assistance to the developing countries has received greater attention than the SDR-aid link. This proposal has been stimulated by the rise in the market price of gold to a level several times that of its official price. The proposal is that the IMF gradually sell part of its gold holdings and use the resulting profits to help the non-oil-exporting developing countries adjust to the impact of the higher oil prices imposed by the oil-exporting countries in late 1973 and early 1974.

The IMF acted favorably on this proposal at a meeting of its Interim Committee of Twenty in Kingston, Jamaica, in January 1976.[24] The sale of 25 million ounces of gold was authorized, with the profits going into a trust fund to aid poor nations. The managing director of the IMF estimated that gold sales would bring the less developed countries (LDCs) about $500 million in 1976. Profits in future years depend upon the future price of gold. The proceeds from gold sales are not likely to exceed the needs that the special trust fund was set up to meet. Gold sales do not therefore appear to be a promising means of financing environmental or other international programs.

Conclusions

The following principal conclusions emerge from the above examination of a variety of possible means of financing environmental and other international programs:

First, the present system of assessments and official contributions might usefully be replaced or supplemented by "shadow taxes," calculated in any of a number of possible ways. The use of shadow taxes might shift the emphasis away from budgetary shares and toward defining a tax base and setting tax rates so as to yield a desired amount of revenue. Shadow taxes, however, share with the present system of assessments and official contributions the basic characteristic of being essentially voluntary.

Second, international taxes on firms and individuals also would depend on the acquiescence, and indeed the active support, of governments. They would have the advantage over assessments of being less visible, less direct, more automatic, and more enforceable. Prospects of collecting international taxes could be greatly increased by so structuring them as to make them collectible in more than one country.

24. R. J. Levine and C. N. Stabler, "Monetary Officials Reach Final Accord on 'Floating Rates,' Aid to Poor Nations," *Wall Street Journal,* January 9, 1976.

Third, the most promising kinds of international taxes are levies on international trade and financial transactions, and taxes on polluters of the international commons. Within each of these categories, some specific taxes appear on practical grounds to be most promising, and they have been selected for more intensive analysis in subsequent chapters of this study.

Fourth, the possibility of obtaining revenues for international purposes from hydrocarbons and manganese nodules under or on the ocean floor deserves serious consideration and will be explored more fully later in the study.

CHAPTER THREE

International Revenue Taxes

IN CHAPTER 2 several possible international revenue taxes were identified that appeared to deserve more intensive study: a general tax on international trade, a variety of taxes on energy materials, a tax on international trade in mineral raw materials, and a tax on international investment income. The present chapter takes up these taxes in turn, examining in each case the technical features of the tax, its incidence, and the distribution of its burden internationally. The chapter concludes with an assessment of these taxes in terms of certain generally accepted criteria for judging the merits of taxes.

General Tax on International Trade

A major attraction of a general tax on international trade is the enormous tax base. In 1977 total world trade should reach $1,000 billion. An ad valorem tax levied at a rate of only 0.1 percent would then yield $1 billion in revenue.

A disadvantage of a general trade tax is that—to the extent that it increased the prices of internationally traded goods—such a tax would constitute a burden on international trade. It would depress the total volume of international trade in the same way that the tariffs imposed by national governments do. This effect could be minimized by keeping the tax rate low. Nevertheless, before imposing a general trade tax (or a tax on specified internationally traded commodities), the international community would have to decide whether the revenue produced by the tax would yield benefits that outweighed the adverse impact of the tax on international trade.

Technical Features

The legal and administrative arrangements needed to impose and enforce various international taxes are taken up in chapter 6. It should be noted here, however, that an important feature of a trade tax is the possibility of collecting it at either the point of importation or the point of exportation. In the normal case, the tax would probably be collected at the point of importation. If, however, a particular country refused to tax its imports, the trading partners of the country in question could levy the tax on their exports to that country.

The definition of the tax base for an international trade tax raises several questions. The first is whether to include so-called invisible items. In principle, there is no particular reason to decide this question one way or the other. On purely practical grounds, however, it would appear wise to include some invisibles and to exclude others. Thus, insurance and freight charges are easily ascertained at the point of importation, so the tax could be imposed on the c.i.f. (cost, insurance, and freight) value of the goods without difficulty. On the other hand, attempting to tax other invisibles, such as the expenditures of tourists or those of diplomats and military personnel stationed abroad, would require separate and complicated administrative arrangements that would not be worth the trouble and expense, even if they proved to be politically feasible.

Another technical problem is the handling of reexports. It can be argued that it is not fair to tax a material such as steel when it is imported into one country for processing and then to tax it again when it is shipped to another country in the form of finished goods such as knives. In principle, it would seem that an exporter should be given a credit (or a rebate) for a tax paid on imported materials when he can show that his exports include those same materials in identifiable form. On the other hand, verifying claims for credits would involve physical checks that would be quite time consuming and expensive relative to the amount of revenue that would usually be involved.

On grounds of practicality, it would probably be best at first not to give credits for reexports. As the tax collection system matured, however, it might be able to handle more refinements and credits for reexports might then be introduced. There is, in fact, a historical precedent for this approach. Many advanced countries now impose a value-added tax, which can be described as a trade tax with a sophisticated system of credits for the cost of goods purchased and resold. In many of these countries, the immediate predecessor of the value-added tax was a turnover tax, which is a simple trade tax with no credits for the cost of goods purchased and resold.

Even at the outset, double taxation of one category of reexports could easily be avoided. Goods that were reexported without being cleared through customs for internal use need not be taxed until they reached their ultimate destination. Such an exemption would, in principle, apply both to goods held in bond before being reexported in their original form and to goods that were reprocessed in a free-trade zone before being shipped on.

Still another question about the definition of the tax base concerns the treatment of capital goods. If an international trade tax is viewed as analogous to national consumption taxes, capital goods would be excluded from the base. Argument by analogy, however, is not very convincing. More weight might be given to the argument that excluding capital goods would lighten somewhat the burden on developing countries, since such goods bulk larger in their imports than they do in the imports of advanced countries.[1] Administering an exclusion of capital goods would, however, be very difficult. Some imported items, such as steel, could go into either consumers' goods or capital goods, and there would be no easy way of determining what would ultimately happen to particular shipments when they arrived at the point of importation. There are better ways of reducing the tax burden on developing countries that will be taken up later in this study.

Largely on practical grounds, it can be concluded that, at least initially, an international trade tax should be levied on the c.i.f. value of all internationally traded goods passing through customs. But this conclusion leaves open the question of what is international, as opposed to domestic, trade. This is far from a trivial question from the political point of view. A few examples may help to bring out the nature of the problem. Trade between New York and Pennsylvania is clearly domestic, but how about

1. In 1973 roughly three-eighths of the imports of developing countries were in the category "machinery and equipment"; only about one-quarter of the imports of developed countries were in this category.

trade between New York and the Commonwealth of Puerto Rico? Similarly, trade between England and Scotland is (at least as of this writing) domestic, but should not the same be said of trade between Belgium and Luxembourg which also does not go through customs? And if the latter trade is domestic for present purposes, must not all trade between members of the European Community be similarly regarded, even though (except for the special relationship between Belgium and Luxembourg) it still passes through customs?

The fundamental problem is deciding what constitutes a separate country. It would seem that this could be resolved in terms of the degree of political autonomy enjoyed by a given entity, but such an approach would lead to endless controversy. Some simple rule of thumb is needed. At first sight, membership in the United Nations might appear to be the answer, but several clearly autonomous trading areas (Switzerland, Taiwan, North Korea, and South Korea) do not belong to the United Nations, and two UN members (Byelorussia and the Ukraine) cannot be regarded as countries separate from the Soviet Union. A practical solution might be simply to regard all trade that passes through customs as international and make special provisions for exceptional cases like the trade between Belgium and Luxembourg. This approach has the obvious advantage of ensuring that almost all trade subjected to international taxation would be evaluated and recorded.

A final technical problem with respect to an international trade tax is the evaluation of goods moving internationally under state trading agreements. Such agreements, which are particularly important in the trade of the countries with centrally planned economies, can involve either barter or trade at negotiated prices rather than market prices. If, as appears likely, the tax rate were quite low, there would be little danger that the state trading agreements would be deliberately rigged to reduce liability under an international trade tax. What would be more probable would be a chronic overcharging or undercharging of some categories of trade transactions.

For example, trade among the centrally planned economies of Eastern Europe is based on "adjusted historical world market prices," which are often fixed for a long period and which are generally above world market prices.[2] Using these prices would overstate the tax liability of the state

2. For a discussion of the foreign trade prices of East European countries, see Paul Marer, *Soviet and East European Foreign Trade, 1946–1969* (Indiana University Press, 1972), pp. 344–46.

trading organizations concerned. Attempting to correct this distortion commodity by commodity for the numerous transactions involved would be a very large task. A more practical procedure would be to study periodically the relationship between market prices and negotiated prices and to adjust the exchange rate under which tax collections would be remitted to a central receiving office. Thus, if it developed that Soviet imports from Eastern Europe are overpriced relative to world market prices by 10 percent, the international taxes collected on such imports could be converted to, say, U.S. dollars at the rate of 0.99 rubles to a dollar, rather than at the official rate of 0.9.

Incidence of the Tax

Before attempting to determine how the burden of any international tax might be distributed among participating nations, it is first necessary to estimate the incidence of the tax. That is, how much of the tax will be absorbed by producers in exporting countries and how much will be shifted to consumers in importing countries? In the case of a general tax on international trade, it is virtually impossible to answer this question precisely. Too many commodities, produced and marketed under different conditions, are involved. Assembling information on the demand and supply for just the major commodities traded internationally would be difficult enough. But even then it is questionable whether existing techniques of econometric analysis are refined enough to determine the effect on import prices (and, consequently, on consumers) of a tax that would probably be levied at a very low rate—say, 0.1 or 0.2 percent ad valorem. Under these circumstances, only a few speculative and nonquantitative generalizations concerning the incidence of a general tax on international trade are possible.

How much of a tax on a particular internationally traded commodity would be shifted to consumers would depend on the elasticities of demand for that commodity in the countries to which it is exported and on the elasticities of supply in the countries from which it is exported. An individual country could therefore expect to do better on some of its exports than on others; that is, it could shift more of the tax to foreign consumers. Thus, the proportion of the tax reflected in the prices received for its exports would vary from commodity to commodity. The same would be true with respect to the imports of a given country. Cases in which a country paid more than half of the tax on a particular import or export transaction would tend to be balanced by cases in which it paid less than half. The balance would rarely be exact, however, and most countries would pay a larger or a smaller share of total tax revenues than they would if the tax burden were distributed exactly in proportion to each country's share of total world trade.

At first sight, it might not appear to matter much, in terms of the incidence of the tax, whether a country is a net importer or a net exporter. In actual fact, there are grounds for believing that, over the long run, countries that chronically import more than they export would tend to pay a larger tax on a given level of total trade than would countries that usually experience export surpluses. (It is not possible to make a similar generalization about the incidence of this tax in the short run.)

Over the long run, the elasticity of supply for exported commodities is probably quite high, whereas the elasticity of demand for imports appears to be much lower.[3] In this situation, exporters would have a strong incentive to shift most of the tax to consumers in importing countries and they would be able to do so. The high elasticity of supply suggests that if exporters absorbed the tax many of them could not cover their costs over the long run and would be forced out of business.[4] They would therefore try to shift the tax. The fact that demand for imports is relatively inelastic

3. A high elasticity of supply for manufactured goods can be deduced from the fact that over the long run the economies of scale in manufacturing industries are not great. See Frederick T. Moore, "Economies of Scale: Some Statistical Evidence," *Quarterly Journal of Economics,* vol. 73 (May 1959), pp. 232–45. The evidence for nonmanufactured goods is less clear, but one estimate puts the elasticity of supply for all U.S. imports at 8.5 and for all U.S. exports at 11.5. See Stephen M. Magee, "Prices, Incomes, and Foreign Trade," in Peter B. Kenen, ed., *International Trade and Finance* (Cambridge: 1975), p. 204.

Several studies conclude that the demand for imports is neither very elastic nor very inelastic. One source argues that the elasticity of demand tends to be unitary. See Hendrik Houthakker and Stephen M. Magee, "Income and Price Elasticity in World Trade," *Review of Economics and Statistics,* vol. 51 (May 1969), pp. 111–25. Two recent sources conclude that the elasticity of demand for imports in the major industrialized countries lies between one and two. See William R. Cline and others, *Trade Negotiations in the Tokyo Round: A Quantitative Assessment* (Brookings Institution, forthcoming). Also see Robert M. Stern with the assistance of Jonathan H. Francis and Bruce Schumacher, "Price Elasticities in International Trade: A Compilation and Annotated Bibliography of Recent Research" (Ann Arbor, 1975; processed).

4. The pressure on exporters to shift the tax will be increased by the fact that they must compete for resources (that is, labor and capital) with firms in the exporting country that are producing for the domestic market and whose output would not be subject to the tax.

(that is, consumer resistance to a price increase is not strong) means that exporters would not suffer a large decrease in sales. Moreover, whatever loss of volume they did experience would not force the unit costs of production up very much because the economies of scale are not large.

To the extent that the tax was shifted, the prices of domestic, as well as imported, commodities in the importing countries would rise slightly, and the share of the domestic market enjoyed by local producers would increase. In this respect, the consequences of an international trade tax would be similar to those of national customs duties on imports.

Distribution of the Tax Burden

The burden of an international trade tax on a particular country would depend on both the incidence of the tax and the absolute value of the country's imports and exports. In the absence of contrary evidence, countries whose imports and exports roughly balance over a period of years would have a particularly good reason to assume that the incidence of the tax would be relatively unimportant for them. Countries with chronic trade deficits would, however, have reason to presume that they might pay a disproportionate share of the tax, if the incidence of the tax is more on importers than on exporters, as was suggested above. Even some countries with balanced trade might feel that the tax would fall particularly heavily on them. These countries, which might include some of the more advanced developing nations, might argue that, on the one hand, their demand for imported capital goods is so inelastic that they must bear most of the tax on their imports and that, on the other hand, the demand for the light manufactures that they export is so elastic that they must absorb most of the tax on their exports.

Since the tax would normally be levied at the point of importation, the public perception in most countries would, in all likelihood, be that the tax was being paid by consumers of imported goods. Little attention would be paid to the possibility that some of the tax would be absorbed by producers in the exporting countries. International discussion of a general trade tax would probably proceed on the basis of this perception and would assume that the burden of the tax would depend solely on the value of each country's imports.

On this assumption, the burden of the tax relative to GNP would vary widely if it were to be levied at a uniform rate and if there were no exemptions, rebates, or retentions of tax proceeds by collecting countries. This is the case because of the great differences in the ratio between imports and gross national product (GNP) from country to country. For all countries in the world, total imports in 1974 were about 15 percent of the sum of their gross national products. The ratio of imports to GNP in large countries tends, however, to be considerably below the average and in small countries considerably above the average. (See table 3-1 for examples of this phenomenon.)

At first sight, it might appear that the ratio of imports to GNP would be higher in rich countries than in poor countries. The examination of trade and income data for about 120 countries indicates that this is not the case. This data is summarized in table 3-2. At all levels of per capita income, the imports of large countries are a relatively low percentage of GNP and the imports of small countries a relatively high percentage (see the footnotes to table 3-2).

The fact that a 0.1 percent ad valorem tax on imports would amount to considerably more than 0.1 percent of the GNP of Trinidad-Tobago but less than 0.01 percent of the GNP of the United States (to take two extreme examples) would clearly be unacceptable. If a general tax on international trade is ever to be adopted, some means of narrowing the disparity between the burden on small states and that on large states would have to be found.

A promising approach is to permit all but the largest countries to keep

Table 3-1. *Imports as Percent of Gross National Product for Four Large and Five Small Countries, 1974*

Country	Population (millions)	Imports as percent of GNP
China, People's Republic of	811.0	2.0
India	582.0	6.2
Soviet Union	250.0	4.3
United States	210.0	6.5
Hong Kong	4.2	102.0
Norway	4.0	40.0
Mauritania	1.3	59.0
Congo, People's Republic of	1.2	55.0
Trinidad-Tobago	1.1	116.0

Sources: The GNP and population data for 1974 were taken from *World Bank Atlas 1975* (Washington, D.C.: World Bank, 1975), pp. 14–22. Imports were, in general, taken from data as reported in United Nations, *Monthly Bulletin of Statistics*, various issues, especially vol. 30 (July 1976), and vol. 31 (June 1977). In some cases imports were taken from International Monetary Fund, *Direction of Trade* (January and February 1976). Where data were reported on f.o.b. basis, they were raised 10 percent to a c.i.f. basis.

Table 3-2. *Distribution of World Imports and GNP by Level of Per Capita Income, 1974*
Money amounts in U.S. dollars

	GNP (billions)	Imports (billions)	Imports as percent of GNP
Developed market economies			
Over 5,500 GNP per capita	2,036	251	12[a]
4,000–5,500	538	156	29[b]
2,000–4,000	791	173	22[c]
1,000–2,000	276	60	22[d]
Centrally planned economies	1,061	75	7[e]
Oil-exporting countries	158	39	25[f]
Developing countries			
500–1,000 GNP per capita	185	39	21[g]
200–500	88	27	31[h]
Below 200	122	14	11[i]
Total	5,255	834	16

Sources: See table 3-1.
a. Excluding United States (7.6 percent), the average is 23 percent.
b. Includes Belgium-Luxembourg (56 percent), Netherlands (50 percent), Norway (40 percent).
c. Includes Ireland (52 percent), Singapore (178 percent), Japan (15 percent).
d. Includes Hong Kong (103 percent), Argentina (8 percent).
e. Excluding Soviet Union (5 percent) and People's Republic of China (2 percent), the average is 18 percent.
f. Includes Bahrain (18 percent), Oman (54 percent).
g. Includes Malaysia (59 percent), Costa Rica (48 percent), Republic of China (61 percent).
h. Includes Jordan (49 percent), Liberia (58 percent), Mozambique (13 percent).
i. Includes Somalia (47 percent), Burma (5 percent). Excluding India (7 percent), the average is 19 percent.

part of the tax proceeds that they collect and to vary the portion retained inversely with the size of the country. This approach is illustrated in table 3-3. This table first shows the burden distribution that would result from the levying of a straight trade tax at the rate of 1 percent ad valorem. It then shows how a 2 percent tax, with differential retention of part of the proceeds, could raise roughly the same amount of revenue and spread the tax burden much more evenly.

The fraction (f) of the tax proceeds to be retained by any given country was determined by the following formula, in which ln P is the natural logarithm of the country's population:

$$f = \frac{0.435 - 0.089 \ln P}{0.51 - 0.089 \ln P}.$$

The derivation of this formula, which is based on the past relationship between value of trade and population, is explained in appendix A.

Table 3-3. Redistribution of the Burden of an International Trade Tax through the Use of a Differential Tax-Retention Formula, 1974
Money amounts in U.S. dollars

Country	Per capita GNP	GNP (billions)	Population (millions)	Revenue from 1 percent tax with no size adjustment		Revenue from 2 percent tax with country-size adjustment	
				Millions[a]	Percent of GNP	Millions	Percent of GNP
DEVELOPED MARKET ECONOMIES							
Per capita GNP above 5,500							
Sweden	6,720	54.8	8.2	165.0	0.30	76.0	0.14
Switzerland	6,650	43.1	6.5	144.0	0.33	62.0	0.14
United States	6,640	1,407.0	211.9	1,071.0	0.08	2,140.0	0.15
Canada	6,080	136.6	22.5	324.0	0.24	205.0	0.15
Germany, Federal Republic of	5,890	365.2	62.0	703.0	0.19	722.0	0.20
Denmark	5,820	29.4	5.0	104.0	0.35	42.0	0.14
Subtotal	...	2,036.1	...	2,511.0	0.12	3,247.0	0.16
Per capita GNP 4,000–5,500							
Norway	5,280	21.1	4.0	84.1	0.40	32.0	0.15
Belgium-Luxembourg	5,230	53.1	10.2	299.0	0.56	146.0	0.27
France	5,190	272.4	52.5	530.0	0.19	494.0	0.18
Netherlands	4,880	66.1	13.5	326.0	0.50	175.0	0.27
Australia	4,760	63.4	13.3	120.0	0.19	65.0	0.10
Finland	4,130	19.4	4.7	68.5	0.35	27.0	0.14
New Zealand	4,100	12.4	3.0	36.5	0.29	13.0	0.11
Austria	4,050	30.5	7.5	90.2	0.30	40.0	0.14
Subtotal	...	538.4	...	1,554.3	0.29	992.0	0.18
Per capita GNP 2,000–4,000							
Japan	3,880	425.9	109.7	621.0	0.15	980.0	0.23
Israel	3,380	11.2	3.3	41.5	0.37	15.0	0.14
United Kingdom	3,360	188.6	56.2	541.0	0.29	524.0	0.28
Italy	2,770	153.3	55.4	409.0	0.27	393.0	0.26

Ireland	2,370	7.3	3.1	38.1	0.52	14.0	0.19
Singapore	2,120	4.7	2.2	83.8	1.78	28.0	0.60
Subtotal	...	791.0	...	1,734.4	0.22	1,954.0	0.25

DEVELOPING COUNTRIES

Per capita GNP 1,000–2,000

Greece	1,970	17.7	9.0	43.9	0.25	21.0	0.12
Spain	1,960	68.7	35.1	153.0	0.22	117.0	0.17
Argentina	1,900	46.9	24.6	36.4	0.08	24.0	0.05
Hong Kong	1,540	6.6	4.2	67.7	1.03	26.0	0.40
Portugal	1,540	13.9	9.0	46.9	0.34	22.0	0.16
Trinidad-Tobago	1,490	1.6	1.1	18.6	1.16	6.0	0.34
South Africa	1,200	29.2	24.3	79.5	0.27	52.0	0.18
Yugoslavia	1,200	25.4	21.2	75.0	0.30	46.0	0.18
Jamaica	1,140	2.3	2.0	9.4	0.41	3.0	0.14
Uruguay	1,060	3.2	3.0	4.9	0.15	2.0	0.06
Mexico	1,000	58.1	58.0	65.2	0.11	64.0	0.11
Subtotal	...	273.6	...	600.5	0.28	383.0	0.14

Per capita GNP 500–1,000

Brazil	900	93.2	104.0	142.0	0.15	213.3	0.23
Chile	820	8.5	10.4	19.1	0.22	9.4	0.11
Costa Rica	790	1.5	1.9	7.2	0.48	2.4	0.16
China, Republic of	720	11.4	15.7	69.8	0.61	39.0	0.34
Peru	710	10.7	15.0	15.3	0.14	8.4	0.08
Turkey	690	26.8	38.9	37.2	0.14	29.7	0.11
Malaysia	660	7.6	11.6	44.6	0.59	22.6	0.30
Nicaragua	650	1.3	2.0	5.6	0.43	1.9	0.14
Dominican Republic	590	2.7	4.6	6.7	0.25	2.6	0.10
Angola	580	3.4	5.8	6.2	0.18	2.6	0.08
Guatemala	570	3.0	5.3	7.0	0.23	2.9	0.10
Tunisia	550	3.1	5.6	11.2	0.36	4.7	0.15
Colombia	510	11.6	22.8	16.0	0.14	10.2	0.09
Subtotal	...	184.8	...	387.9	0.21	349.7	0.19

(continued)

Table 3-3 (continued)

Country	Per capita GNP	GNP (billions)	Population (millions)	Revenue from 1 percent tax with no size adjustment		Revenue from 2 percent tax with country-size adjustment	
				Millions[a]	Percent of GNP	Millions	Percent of GNP
Per capita GNP 200–500							
			DEVELOPING COUNTRIES (continued)				
Syria	490	3.5	7.2	12.3	0.35	5.5	0.16
Zambia	480	2.3	4.8	7.9	0.34	3.2	0.14
Paraguay	480	1.2	2.5	1.7	0.14	0.6	0.05
Korea, Republic of	470	15.8	33.5	68.5	0.43	51.1	0.32
Papua New Guinea	440	1.2	2.7	4.3	0.36	1.5	0.13
Morocco	430	6.9	16.3	20.9	0.30	11.8	0.17
Ivory Coast	420	2.6	6.1	9.7	0.37	4.1	0.16
Mozambique	420	3.6	8.5	4.6	0.13	2.1	0.06
Jordan	400	1.0	2.6	4.9	0.49	1.7	0.17
El Salvador	390	1.5	3.9	5.6	0.37	2.1	0.14
Ghana	350	3.3	9.6	8.2	0.25	3.9	0.12
Honduras	340	1.0	2.9	3.8	0.38	1.4	0.14
Liberia	330	0.5	1.5	2.9	0.58	0.9	0.18
Senegal	320	1.3	4.2	4.6	0.35	1.8	0.14
Philippines	310	13.0	41.4	34.7	0.27	28.6	0.22
Thailand	300	12.1	41.0	31.4	0.26	25.7	0.21
Egypt	280	10.1	36.4	23.5	0.23	18.2	0.18
Cameroon	260	1.6	6.3	4.7	0.29	2.0	0.13
Bolivia	250	1.4	5.5	3.9	0.28	1.6	0.12
Mauritania	230	0.3	1.3	1.2	0.40	0.4	0.12
Togo	210	0.5	2.2	1.2	0.24	0.4	0.08
Kenya	200	2.6	12.9	9.9	0.38	5.2	0.20
Central African Republic	200	0.4	1.7	0.5	0.15	0.2	0.05
Subtotal	...	87.7	...	270.9	0.30	174.0	0.20

Per capita GNP below 200

Sierra Leone	180	0.5	2.9	2.2	0.44	0.9	0.16
Malagasy	170	1.4	8.6	2.6	0.19	1.2	0.09
Uganda	160	1.8	11.2	2.1	0.17	1.1	0.06
Zaire	150	3.6	24.1	10.5	0.29	6.8	0.19
Sudan	150	2.6	17.5	6.6	0.25	3.8	0.15
Tanzania	140	2.1	14.4	8.1	0.39	4.4	0.21
Haiti	140	0.6	4.5	1.0	0.17	0.4	0.07
India	130	79.0	595.6	52.0	0.07	104.0	0.13
Sri Lanka	130	1.8	13.4	6.9	0.38	3.7	0.20
Pakistan	130	8.8	68.2	17.2	0.20	18.8	0.21
Malawi	130	0.6	5.0	1.9	0.32	0.8	0.13
Guinea	120	0.7	5.4	0.9	0.13	0.4	0.06
Yemen Arab Republic	120	0.7	6.4	1.9	0.27	0.8	0.12
Nepal	110	1.3	12.3	0.8	0.06	0.4	0.03
Niger	100	0.5	4.5	1.0	0.20	0.4	0.08
Afghanistan	100	1.6	17.0	2.4	0.15	1.4	0.09
Bangladesh	100	7.3	76.2	7.7	0.11	9.0	0.12
Ethiopia	90	2.6	27.2	2.8	0.11	1.9	0.07
Chad	90	0.4	4.0	0.9	0.22	0.3	0.09
Burma	90	2.7	30.2	1.4	0.05	1.0	0.04
Somalia	80	0.3	3.1	1.4	0.47	0.5	0.17
Burundi	80	0.3	3.7	0.4	0.13	0.2	0.05
Rwanda	80	0.3	4.1	0.6	0.20	0.2	0.08
Upper Volta	80	0.5	5.8	1.1	0.22	0.5	0.09
Mali	70	0.4	5.5	1.3	0.32	0.5	0.13
Subtotal	...	122.4	...	135.7	0.12	163.4	0.13

(continued)

Table 3-3 (continued)

Country	Per capita GNP	GNP (billions)	Population (millions)	Revenue from 1 percent tax with no size adjustment		Revenue from 2 percent tax with country-size adjustment	
				Millions[a]	Percent of GNP	Millions	Percent of GNP
CENTRALLY PLANNED ECONOMIES							
German Democratic Republic	3,430	58.9	17.2	108.0	0.18	62.1	0.11
Czechoslovakia	3,220	47.3	14.7	83.0	0.18	45.3	0.10
Poland	2,450	82.4	33.7	111.0	0.13	83.0	0.10
Soviet Union	2,300	580.8	252.1	274.0	0.05	548.0	0.09
Hungary	2,140	22.4	10.5	55.8	0.25	27.5	0.12
Bulgaria	1,770	15.4	8.7	47.6	0.31	22.2	0.14
Cuba	640	5.8	9.1	11.1	0.19	5.2	0.09
Albania	530	1.3	2.4	1.0	0.08	0.3	0.03
Congo, People's Republic of	390	0.5	1.2	2.6	0.52	0.8	0.16
China, People's Republic of	300	245.8	825.0	48.3	0.02	96.6	0.04
Benin	120	0.4	3.0	1.6	0.40	0.6	0.14
Yemen	120	0.2	1.6	1.9	0.95	0.6	0.30
Subtotal	...	1,061.2	...	745.0	0.06	892.2	0.08
OIL-EXPORTING COUNTRIES							
United Arab Emirates	13,500	4.6	0.3	17.0	0.40	4.1	0.09
Kuwait	11,600	10.8	0.9	15.2	0.14	4.3	0.04
Qatar	5,830	1.1	0.2	2.7	0.25	0.6	0.06
Libya	3,360	7.5	2.2	27.6	0.37	9.3	0.12
Bahrain	2,250	0.6	0.2	11.2	1.87	2.6	0.42
Saudi Arabia	2,080	16.7	8.0	42.2	0.25	19.2	0.12
Venezuela	1,710	19.8	11.6	37.9	0.20	19.2	0.10

Gabon	1,560	0.8	0.5	3.8	0.48	1.0	0.12
Oman	1,250	0.9	0.8	7.1	0.79	2.0	0.22
Iran	1,060	35.1	33.1	54.3	0.15	40.2	0.11
Iraq	970	10.4	10.8	23.6	0.23	11.7	0.11
Algeria	650	9.8	15.2	40.3	0.41	22.3	0.23
Ecuador	460	3.2	7.0	9.6	0.30	4.2	0.13
Nigeria	240	17.8	73.0	27.7	0.16	31.6	0.18
Indonesia	150	18.6	127.0	38.4	0.21	70.2	0.38
Subtotal	...	157.7	...	358.6	0.22	242.5	0.15
Total, all countries	...	5,252.9	...	8,299.2	0.16	8,397.8	0.16

Sources: See table 3-1. The basis of the adjustment formula reported in the two right-hand columns is discussed in the text and in appendix A.

a. This column, with the decimal shifted one place to the left, is the amount of imports in billions of 1974 dollars.

A 1 percent trade tax would impose a burden equal to about 0.15 percent of the total GNPs of all countries taken together. The retention formula is designed to reduce the burden of a 2 percent trade tax on each country to 0.15 of GNP, if the country's ratio of imports to GNP is "normal" for its size. (See appendix A for a definition of the normal relationship between country size and the ratio of imports to GNP.) Countries whose imports are a relatively high percentage of GNP for their size would, even under the formula, bear heavier burdens, and countries whose imports were low for their size would bear lighter burdens. The formula does not provide for any tax retentions by very large countries, since its numerator becomes zero when population reaches about 150 million.

The formula would take care of one major deficiency of a general trade tax. Additional adjustments on either the revenue or the expenditure side (and probably on both) would be needed to achieve a politically acceptable distribution of the tax burden. If, as would be likely, the tax were viewed as a means of transferring resources from rich to poor countries, a reduction in the relative burden of the latter would be required.

Administering a system of tax retentions would involve no special problems. Participating countries that were entitled to tax retentions could be allowed to choose between two alternatives. They could collect the tax at the basic rate and use the portion retained for any domestic purpose that they wished. Or they could collect the tax at a reduced rate, calculated on the basis of the retention formula, and turn all of the proceeds over to the international agency designated to receive the tax.

If it were decided to apply the tax to the imports of nonparticipating countries,[5] participating countries could tax exports destined for nonparticipating countries at the basic rate and turn all proceeds over to the designated international agency. That agency could then calculate and pay the amounts due nonparticipating countries under the tax-retention formula. Or alternatively, such payments could be withheld to give nonparticipants an incentive to participate in the collection of the tax.

Tax on Internationally Traded Oil

If some component of world trade, rather than total trade, is to be taxed for international purposes, oil must be regarded as a leading possibility.

5. See chapter 7 for a discussion of this issue.

No other single commodity accounts for as large a proportion of world trade. This fact, coupled with the present high price of oil, means that a very low tax rate would produce a substantial amount of revenue. For example, a tax of only 0.1 percent ad valorem would yield more than $100 million in revenues each year. A 1 percent tax would yield $1 billion annually, or as much as a 0.1 percent tax on all international trade.[6]

Technical Features

A tax on internationally traded oil would share some technical features and problems with a general tax on international trade. Thus, like a general trade tax, a tax on oil moving between countries could be collected at either the point of importation or the point of exportation. The problem of reexports would also arise in the case of a tax on internationally traded oil, possibly in a more acute form than in the case of a general tax on all international trade. Taxing oil once when it is imported and again when it is reexported in the form of refined products would clearly work against the interests of a few countries, such as the Netherlands and Trinidad-Tobago, and these countries could be expected to object strongly. It might therefore be necessary to exempt reexports from the tax.

An international oil tax would also have special problems of its own. If the tax were levied on an ad valorem basis, it would be necessary to decide whether to tax the full value of refined products or only the value of the crude oil from which they were made. The latter alternative would be both fairer and more acceptable politically, because taxing the full value of refined products would put refineries in oil-exporting countries at a disadvantage relative to refineries in oil-importing countries.

Another problem to be faced in levying an ad valorem tax is establishing constructive prices for oil that is imported, refined, and marketed by the same company. The export prices proclaimed by oil-exporting countries for various grades of oil would probably make this problem manageable, although by no means easy. In the case of oil that did change owner-

6. This is a conservative estimate. The 1974 level of world trade in oil was about 10 billion barrels. See *Statistical Review of the World Oil Industry in 1974* (London: British Petroleum Co., 1975), p. 10. If the price of oil were $10 a barrel, a 1 percent tax would yield $1 billion. In fact, the price of "marker" crude f.o.b. (free on board) the Persian Gulf was $11.51 a barrel in mid-1976. Delivered prices were higher.

ship when it was imported, rules would have to be established concerning what discounts, if any, were allowable from the basic sale price.

Whether the tax was levied ad valorem or on a specific basis (so much a ton or a barrel), a technical problem would arise with respect to refined products. Technical coefficients would have to be established, specifying how many barrels of crude oil (the commodity being taxed) presumably went into every thousand barrels of a given refined product.

Incidence of the Tax

If—as appears likely—a tax on internationally traded oil were levied at a very low rate, it would be difficult to determine how much of the tax was being absorbed by producers in oil-exporting countries and how much was being passed on to consumers in oil-importing countries. Certain non-quantitative generalizations concerning the possible incidence of an international oil tax in both the long run and the short run can, however, be made.[7]

Over the long run, it seems reasonable to assume that the Organization of Petroleum Exporting Countries (OPEC) will evolve in one of two directions. It may become a tight cartel that regulates the output of its members in such a way as to maximize their profits as a group. Or, one or more of OPEC's members could assume the role of price leader and residual supplier. In the second alternative, most members would produce at capacity and the price leader (or leaders) would curtail output to the level required to obtain the price that would maximize its profits.[8]

In both the tight-cartel case and the price-leader case, the incidence of an international oil tax would depend upon the price elasticity of demand for refined petroleum products.[9] Over the long run, this elasticity is probably greater than one, because the price of oil relative to other sources of energy will influence both the kind of equipment that energy users will buy (for example, coal-burning versus oil-burning electric power plants) and the speed of development of alternatives to oil. If so, the oil producers

7. See appendix A for a fuller discussion of the incidence of an international oil tax.

8. For a formal analysis of this oligopoly case, see Edwin Mansfield, *Microeconomics: Theory and Applications,* 2d ed. (Norton, 1975), pp. 341–42.

9. Demand conditions would control profit-maximizing decisions, because the marginal cost of production of the Middle Eastern oil producers (who are key decision makers in OPEC) appear to be constant over a considerable range of output.

could not shift all of the tax to consumers without losing more through reduced sales than they would gain by adding the tax to the price of each unit of oil sold.

In the short run, the situation is somewhat different. OPEC is clearly not a tight cartel because it has not been able to agree on the allocation of market shares. That function has, in effect, been delegated to the oil companies.[10] Each company ships only the amount of oil that its refining and marketing systems can absorb at the OPEC price. Where it gets its oil is determined by commercial and technical considerations (for example, distance from market, desired mix of refined products, and suitability of various types of oil for particular refineries), modified to some extent by the need to maintain good relations with important suppliers. Market shares of the oil-exporting countries are the combined result of these individual company decisions.

This loose—and, from the point of view of the oil-exporting countries, not very satisfactory—system of adjusting output to price may not last. Saudi Arabia, supported by the United Arab Emirates, may assume the role of price leader and residual supplier. The refusal of Saudi Arabia and the United Arab Emirates to go along with the full price increase announced by the other members of OPEC in December 1976 may have reflected their belief that they would have to absorb so much of the resultant shrinkage of the world market that they would lose more than they would gain. If so, they behaved as profit-maximizing residual suppliers could be expected to behave. Saudi Arabia's subsequent announcement of production increases in an effort to force the other members of OPEC to accept its lower price increase was also consistent with such behavior.

Nevertheless, since the potential price followers are not producing at capacity, as would be the case in a stable price-leader system, the role of the companies in determining market shares persists, and the price of oil does not yet appear to be set by a nice calculation of market demand either by OPEC as a group or by a price leader. OPEC is not currently pursuing a policy of maximizing profits in the short run. If it were, the price of oil would be higher than it is today. It is clear that, if the price of oil were increased, OPEC's members would lose less in sales in the short run than

10. For a fuller explanation of how this system operates see Joseph A. Yager and Eleanor B. Steinberg, "Trends in the International Oil Market," in Edward R. Fried and Charles L. Schultze, eds., *Higher Oil Prices and the World Economy* (Brookings Institution, 1975), especially pp. 267–71.

they would gain through higher unit prices. (That is, the price elasticity of demand is less than one.)

If the reason for OPEC's failure to push the price of oil up to the profit-maximizing level can be determined, it should be possible to speculate more intelligently on the incidence of an international oil tax in the short run. There may well be no single reason for OPEC's restraint, but several explanations are plausible.

First, Saudi Arabia and the United Arab Emirates possess large reserves of oil, and they may seek to maximize their returns over the long run. These countries may, with good reason, believe that over the long run, as substitute sources of energy are developed, the demand for oil will be more elastic than it is in the short run and that higher prices would therefore not be in their economic interest. Second, raising the price of oil would require a cutback in production that could dangerously strain OPEC's unity. Third, Saudi Arabia claimed that its relatively restrained price policy in December 1976 was designed to induce the United States to press forward toward a settlement of the Arab-Israeli dispute. Finally, it is possible that some producer states may not want to dampen the recovery from the deepest global recession since the 1930s.

If any or all of these explanations of OPEC's failure to exploit its market power fully are accepted, it follows that a large part (and possibly all) of an international oil tax would be absorbed by the producers in the short run, as well as in the long run. Oil importers might be billed separately for the tax, but the total charge per barrel, including the tax, would still be determined by OPEC largely on the basis of these considerations. The price with the tax would be about what it would have been without the tax. This means that the producers would absorb a substantial part of the tax.

Distribution of the Tax Burden

If the incidence of an international oil tax actually worked out as described above, the burden of the tax would fall largely on the oil-exporting countries in proportion to their oil exports. In terms of their immediate economic self-interest, those countries could be expected to oppose the adoption of the tax. They could probably mobilize support from the other developing countries with which they are allied on a wide range of international economic issues. It is conceivable, however, that the oil-exporting countries might see political advantage in supporting the tax or, more likely, in levying the tax themselves as a means of raising money to provide assistance to the poorer oil-importing countries. In this way, the oil-exporting countries might hope to counter charges that higher oil prices have added to the economic problems of the developing countries.[11]

Different problems would arise if an international oil tax were shifted largely to consumers in the oil-importing countries, or if that were how the incidence of the tax was generally perceived. Table 3-4 presents estimates of the burden on selected countries of a 1 percent ad valorem tax on imported oil, using 1973 data, on the assumption that the tax is shifted entirely to consumers. As would be expected, the burden as a percentage of GNP is highly erratic for both developed and developing countries.

On the one hand, the burden on the United States, Canada, and Australia is relatively low because of domestic oil production. On the other hand, the burden on some developing countries is relatively high, possibly reflecting a lack of coal or unusual needs on the part of local industry. Developing countries with high burdens include the Philippines, Panama, Kenya, Bulgaria, and Cuba. Cuba's burden is remarkable—almost three times the burden of those developed countries that are heavy importers of oil.

On the assumption of full forward shifting, the oil-exporting countries would escape the tax altogether. This would of course include all members of OPEC, but the Soviet Union and China would also pay virtually no tax.

If an international oil tax were perceived as falling largely on consumers, the uneven distribution of the burden of the tax would pose an obstacle to its adoption. The objections would be almost as serious as those that would be raised if the tax were perceived as falling largely on producers. The fact that the two superpowers would bear either a low burden or almost no burden at all would be particularly troublesome.

---

11. Iran in fact proposed such a tax in 1975, but it received little support from other members of OPEC; *New York Times,* September 24, 1975. In November 1976, the representative of Saudi Arabia introduced a resolution in the Second Committee of the UN General Assembly proposing that all oil-producing countries levy "a value-added tax of one cent per barrel" which would be "deposited in a special account of the United Nations Environmental Programme to help save the biosphere for mankind." UN Doc. A/C.2/31/L.7/Rev. 1, November 1, 1976. This resolution was subsequently withdrawn on condition that the committee and the secretary general take note of it.

Table 3-4. *Distribution of the Burden on Selected Countries of a Tax on Internationally Traded Oil, Assuming Full Shifting to Consumers, 1973*
Money amounts in U.S. dollars

Countries	GNP (billions)	Oil imports (Millions of metric tons)			Revenue from 1 percent tax on imports at $12 a barrel	
		Crude oil	Net refined-petroleum energy products[a]	Total[a]	Millions[b]	Percent of GNP
DEVELOPED MARKET ECONOMIES						
United States	1,304.5	161.0	113.0	274.0	264.0	0.020
Sweden	48.1	10.6	15.8	26.4	26.4	0.055
Canada	120.5	45.2	−9.4	35.8	37.8	0.031
Germany, Federal Republic of	329.7	110.0	23.5	133.5	144.0	0.044
France	236.6	135.0	−12.2	122.8	120.0	0.051
Netherlands	58.2	70.4	−42.4	28.0	30.0	0.052
Australia	57.2	8.4	−2.3	6.1	7.8	0.014
Japan	393.0	249.0	−3.0	246.0	233.0	0.059
Israel	9.7	0.8	−0.6	0.2	0.3	0.032
United Kingdom	171.4	116.0	−6.0	110.0	108.0	0.063
Italy	134.5	126.0	−31.0	95.0	101.0	0.075
Greece	16.7	12.3	−1.8	10.5	10.2	0.061
Spain	59.4	41.4	−7.2	34.2	33.3	0.056
Argentina	39.8	2.4	0.8	3.2	3.7	0.009
Portugal	12.7	4.4	0.8	5.2	5.4	0.043
CENTRALLY PLANNED ECONOMIES						
German Democratic Republic	50.9	16.0	−2.1	13.9	14.0	0.028
Czechoslovakia	41.8	14.2	−0.4	13.8	17.9	0.043
Poland	69.9	11.1	0.2	11.3	11.8	0.017
Soviet Union	506.5	13.2	−31.2	−17.8	3.7	0.001
Hungary	19.3	6.6	0.4	7.0	7.3	0.038
Bulgaria	13.7	9.6	1.5	11.1	9.9	0.072
Cuba	4.9	5.0	2.0	7.0	7.6	0.156
China, People's Republic of	216.8	0	0	0	0	0.000

DEVELOPING COUNTRIES

Per capita GNP 500–1,000					
Brazil	77.0	32.1	−1.0	31.1	30.4	0.039
Chile	7.4	3.5	−0.1	3.4	3.3	0.045
Lebanon	2.8	2.5	−0.4	2.1	2.3	0.081
Peru	9.1	1.6	0.3	1.9	1.9	0.021
Turkey	22.6	9.3	−1.1	8.2	8.1	0.036
Nicaragua	1.1	0.5	0.3	0.8	0.9	0.082
Per capita GNP 200–500					
Colombia	9.9	...	−1.8	...	...	0.002
Zambia	2.0	...	0.5	0.5	0.6	0.028
Paraguay	1.0	0.2	0.2	0.4	0.4	0.041
Morocco	5.1	2.2	0.8	3.0	3.1	0.061
Ivory Coast	2.3	1.3	...	1.3	1.3	0.056
Jordan	0.9	0.7	...	0.7	0.7	0.078
Ghana	2.8	0.9	−0.2	0.7	0.7	0.026
Philippines	11.2	9.3	−0.7	8.6	8.2	0.073
Per capita GNP below 200					
Kenya	2.2	2.7	−1.5	1.2	1.3	0.060
Central African Republic	0.3	0	0.1	0.1	0.5	0.175
Uganda	1.6	0	0.4	0.4	0.4	0.021
Zaire	3.2	0.7	...	0.7	0.9	0.026
India	71.6	13.3	2.2	15.5	14.7	0.021
Pakistan	7.7	3.2	0	3.2	3.1	0.041
Ethiopia	2.3	0.7	−0.1	0.6	0.6	0.026
Chad	0.3	0	0.5	0.5	0.5	0.150

Sources: Basic data for GNP in 1973 from *World Bank Atlas, 1975*, pp. 55–87; for oil imports, *World Energy Supplies 1970–73*, UN Doc. ST/ESA/STAT/SER. J/18, 1975, pp. 27–30.

a. Net imports of refined-petroleum energy products means domestic consumption of such products less domestic production of such products. Thus, imports for inventory accumulation and imports resold as bunker fuel for ships are not included in total imports. (Inventory accumulation has been excluded since it is apt to be erratic in any one year. Bunker fuel was excluded, because the burden of a tax on it is not likely to be on the importing country.) Nonenergy refined petroleum products are not included in columns 3 or 4.

b. The tax on imports assumes a tax rate of 12 cents a barrel and 7 barrels in a metric ton. This initial calculation of the tax was increased by 8.2 percent to reflect the fact that that percentage of total oil imports goes into nonenergy uses. Country breakdowns for nonenergy uses were not available, so it was arbitrarily assumed that nonenergy products would be imported in the same proportions as total petroleum imports.

Tax on Both Domestic and Internationally Traded Oil

An international tax that was levied on both domestic and internationally traded oil would have the obvious advantage of a much larger tax base. Also, as will be treated below, the distribution of the burden of such a tax would be somewhat more satisfactory than that of a tax applied only to internationally traded oil. Taxing domestic as well as internationally traded oil would, however, require a degree of cooperation from national governments that would be hard to obtain.

Technical Features

In one respect, a tax on both domestic and international oil would be simpler to administer than one on international oil alone because all crude oil would be taxed and there would be no need to tax the crude content of some refined products in order to get complete coverage. Therefore, the problem of what to do about reexports either would not arise or would be of only minor importance. There would also be no need to define the crude oil equivalents of refined products.

Assuming cooperative attitudes on the part of national governments, it would not be difficult to assess and collect a tax on domestic oil. The experience of several states in the United States with a severance tax[12] would be directly relevant. Records on oil production are probably good in most countries. Where a government is the owner of oil in the ground, procedures are certain to exist for keeping track of the oil extracted in order to prevent illegal diversion of a public asset and, if oil is produced by a private company, to provide the basis for royalty payments. Where private firms and individuals own some oil deposits, as is the case in the United States, efforts to enforce drilling and operating rules in the interest of conservation have generated production records that would facilitate collection of the tax.

Incidence of the Tax

In the short run—say, the next ten years—oil producers would clearly find it easier to shift a tax on all oil to consumers than to shift a tax applied

12. A tax per barrel on oil extracted (that is, "severed") from the ground.

only to internationally traded oil. The demand for all oil is less elastic than the demand for internationally traded oil alone because a large part of the competition for internationally traded oil comes from domestic oil production in the oil-importing countries. If domestic oil is also taxed, the only competition would be from sources of energy other than oil, such as coal, natural gas, and nuclear power.

In the long run, however, the demand for all oil would be more elastic than it would be in the short run, since over time the production of sources other than oil could respond more fully to an increase in the price of oil. Oil producers would then have to absorb more of the tax. Producers who normally cover no more than their total costs (including a fair rate of return on capital invested) would eventually shift their part of the tax backwards to the owners of the oil resources, thereby reducing the owners' royalty incomes.

Distribution of the Tax Burden

If all of a tax on both domestic and internationally traded oil were shifted forward to consumers—as would be possible in the short run—one might at first sight expect the distribution of the tax burden among various countries to be roughly proportional to their gross national products. In actual fact, variations in the use of oil in comparison with other fuels (and probably also differences in ratios between GNP and total energy consumption) could produce a fairly erratic distribution.

Table 3-5 presents for illustrative purposes estimates of the burden of a 1 percent ad valorem oil tax for more than fifty selected countries on the assumption of full forward shifting. These estimates suggest that the burden of such a tax on most developed countries would amount to between 0.03 and 0.05 percent of GNP. The Soviet Union, Canada, Italy, and Israel are at the upper end of the range. The United States is near the middle. The burden on most developing countries is relatively low. However, the burden on a few developing countries—including Lebanon, Nicaragua, the Philippines, and Cuba—is relatively high, running above 0.05 percent of GNP. In the long run, as the incidence of the tax fell more on oil producers and on the owners of oil deposits, the burden of the tax would be borne disproportionately by the oil-exporting countries.

Table 3-5. *Distribution of the Burden on Selected Countries of a Tax on Hydrocarbon Fuels, Assuming Full Shifting to Consumers, 1973*
Money amounts in U.S. dollars

Country	GNP (billions)	Revenue from 1 percent ad valorem tax on							
		Oil		Natural gas		Coal		Oil, gas, and coal	
		Millions	Percent of GNP	Millions	Percent of GNP	Millions	Percent of GNP	Millions	Percent of GNP
DEVELOPED MARKET ECONOMIES									
United States	1,304.5	550.0	0.042	420.0	0.032	254.0	0.019	1,224.0	0.094
Sweden	48.1	19.3	0.040	...	...	1.1	0.002	20.4	0.042
Canada	120.5	54.5	0.045	34.8	0.029	13.4	0.011	102.7	0.085
Germany, Federal Republic of	329.7	99.4	0.030	23.2	0.007	60.9	0.019	183.5	0.056
France	236.6	80.5	0.034	10.9	0.005	22.1	0.009	113.5	0.048
Australia	57.2	19.7	0.034	2.7	0.005	17.2	0.030	39.6	0.069
Netherlands	58.2	15.1	0.026	24.9	0.043	2.1	0.004	42.1	0.072
Japan	393.0	163.0	0.041	4.0	0.001	40.0	0.010	207.0	0.053
United Kingdom	171.4	69.6	0.041	19.8	0.011	65.2	0.038	154.6	0.090
Israel	9.7	4.7	0.048	...	...	...	...	4.7	0.048
Italy	134.5	64.7	0.048	11.5	0.009	6.0	0.004	82.2	0.061
Greece	16.7	6.6	0.039	...	...	2.5	0.015	9.1	0.054
Spain	59.4	24.1	0.041	0.6	0.001	7.8	0.013	32.5	0.055
Argentina	39.8	17.3	0.043	5.5	0.014	0.6	0.002	23.4	0.059
Hong Kong	6.0	2.2	0.037	...	...	...	...	2.2	0.037
Portugal	12.7	4.2	0.033	...	...	0.2	0.002	4.4	0.035

CENTRALLY PLANNED ECONOMIES

German Democratic Republic	50.9	8.8	0.017	2.2	0.004	42.8	0.084	53.8	0.106
Czechoslovakia	41.8	8.7	0.021	2.3	0.005	38.3	0.092	49.3	0.118
Poland	69.9	7.3	0.010	5.2	0.007	64.2	0.092	76.7	0.110
Soviet Union	506.5	223.0	0.044	160.0	0.032	235.0	0.046	618.0	0.122
Bulgaria	13.7	7.9	0.058	0.2	0.001	9.8	0.071	17.9	0.131
Hungary	19.3	5.8	0.030	3.3	0.017	8.8	0.046	17.9	0.093
Cuba	4.9	4.2	0.087	1.3	0.027	1.5	0.031	7.0	0.146
China	216.8	27.8	0.013	2.0	0.001	199.9	0.093	229.7	0.106

OIL-EXPORTING COUNTRIES

Kuwait	10.6	1.9	0.018	3.5	0.033	…	…	5.4	0.051
Libya	7.6	0.8	0.011	4.8	0.063	…	…	5.6	0.074
Saudi Arabia	12.5	3.0	0.024	2.1	0.017	…	…	5.1	0.041
Iran	27.8	8.6	0.031	7.0	0.025	0.5	0.002	16.1	0.058
Iraq	8.9	2.8	0.031	0.8	0.009	…	…	3.6	0.040
Algeria	8.3	1.5	0.018	0.1	0.001	0.1	0.001	1.7	0.020
Indonesia	16.0	6.1	0.038	0.3	0.002	0.1	0.001	6.5	0.041

DEVELOPING COUNTRIES

Per capita GNP 500–1,000

Lebanon	2.8	1.4	0.050	…	…	…	…	1.4	0.050
Panama	1.4	0.7	0.050	…	…	…	…	0.7	0.050
Brazil	77.0	25.5	0.033	0.8	0.001	2.1	0.003	28.4	0.037
Chile	7.4	3.6	0.049	2.3	0.031	0.8	0.010	6.7	0.090
Peru	9.1	4.0	0.044	0.3	0.003	0.1	0.001	4.4	0.048
Turkey	22.6	8.1	0.036	…	…	3.3	0.015	11.4	0.050
Nicaragua	1.1	0.8	0.073	…	…	…	…	0.8	0.073

(continued)

Table 3-5 (*continued*)

Country	GNP (billions)	Revenue from 1 percent ad valorem tax on: Oil, Millions	Oil, Percent of GNP	Natural gas, Millions	Natural gas, Percent of GNP	Coal, Millions	Coal, Percent of GNP	Oil, gas, and coal, Millions	Oil, gas, and coal, Percent of GNP
				DEVELOPING COUNTRIES (continued)					
Per capita GNP 200–500									
Colombia	9.9	4.2	0.042	1.2	0.012	1.5	0.015	6.9	0.070
Zambia	2.0	0.4	0.020	...	...	0.5	0.025	0.9	0.045
Paraguay	1.0	0.2	0.020	...	...	...	...	0.2	0.020
Ivory Coast	2.3	0.8	0.036	...	...	...	...	0.8	0.036
Jordan	0.9	0.4	0.044	...	...	...	...	0.4	0.044
Morocco	5.1	1.6	0.031	...	...	0.3	0.006	1.9	0.037
Ghana	2.8	0.6	0.021	...	...	...	...	0.6	0.021
Philippines	11.2	6.0	0.053	...	...	...	...	6.0	0.053
Per capita GNP below 200									
Kenya	2.2	1.0	0.045	...	...	...	...	1.0	0.045
Central African Republic	0.3	...	...	...	...	...	...	...	...
Uganda	1.6	0.3	0.019	...	...	...	...	0.3	0.019
Zaire	3.2	0.6	0.019	...	...	0.2	0.006	0.8	0.025
Haiti	0.6	0.1	0.016	...	...	...	...	0.1	0.016
India	71.6	13.8	0.019	0.4	0.001	39.1	0.005	53.3	0.074
Pakistan	7.7	2.5	0.032	2.9	0.038	0.4	0.005	5.8	0.075
Ethiopia	2.3	0.5	0.022	...	...	...	...	0.5	0.022
Chad	0.3	...	...	...	...	...	...	...	...
Burma	2.4	0.8	0.033	...	...	0.1	0.004	0.9	0.037

Sources: Basic data for GNP in 1973 from *World Bank Atlas 1975*, pp. 27–30. Data on consumption of oil, gas, and coal used in calculating tax yields were drawn from *World Energy Supplies 1970–73*, UN Doc. ST/ESA/STAT/SER. J/18, 1975. Coal was priced at $50 a metric ton. Natural gas and oil were assigned prices reflecting their heat content relative to that of coal. One metric ton of coal was assumed to have the same heat content as 0.68 metric tons (4.76 barrels) of oil, or 0.75 thousand cubic meters (27,000 cubic feet) of natural gas.

Tax on All Hydrocarbons

Because of the political problems that either of the taxes on oil discussed above would probably encounter, it is worthwhile to examine a tax on all hydrocarbon fuels, both internationally traded and domestic. (There would be little point in looking at a tax on only those hydrocarbons that are traded internationally. International trade in energy materials is overwhelmingly in oil, so such a tax would be barely distinguishable from the international oil tax that has already been considered.)

Technical Features

Administering a tax on coal, oil, and natural gas would be fairly complicated, since detailed rules would have to be developed for quite different extractive processes. Establishing the minehead value for coal would be particularly difficult. Frequently, coal is not sold before it is used; it is transferred within a single firm to a coke oven or a boiler. This would require constructing a price for the coal based on actual sales by comparable mines. It would probably be most efficient to establish a uniform price based on British thermal unit (Btu) content, such as $50 for the equivalent of a metric ton of bituminous coal. This would permit application of the tax to various forms of lignite, manufactured gas, and so on, without getting into the complexities of the price data.

Quite clearly, collection of this tax would have to rely on national tax administrations. The burden of enforcement could be reduced by exempting some small producers, but such an exemption would create more disparities among different countries.

Incidence of the Tax

In both the long and the short run, the incidence of a tax on all oil, natural gas, and coal would be mostly on consumers. In contrast to a tax on oil alone, this tax would also apply to the most important current substitutes for oil. It would in fact be close to a tax on all energy. In the short run, the demand for energy must be highly inelastic, since it is dictated by custom and energy-using equipment. In the long run, the importance of energy sources other than hydrocarbons—for example, nuclear power and solar energy—will probably increase, and more efficient methods of using energy may be adopted. Demand for hydrocarbons will therefore become somewhat more elastic, forcing producers to absorb more of the tax and to pass some of it back to owners of oil, gas, and coal deposits.

Distribution of the Tax Burden

Table 3-5 presents for more than fifty selected countries estimates of the burden of a 1 percent ad valorem tax on each of the hydrocarbon fuels (natural gas, coal, and oil) and an estimate of the total burden of such a tax on all three fuels. The pricing of the fuels in question posed a difficult problem in making these estimates. Prices differ from country to country, partly because of governmental controls. The decision was made to price coal at $50 a metric ton and to assign prices to the other fuels on the basis of their relative heat content.[13] This approach yields an oil price of $10.50 a barrel and a gas price of $1.85 per thousand cubic feet.

As table 3-5 indicates, extending the tax on oil to gas (but not to coal) would significantly increase the burden on several countries, including the United States, the Soviet Union, Canada, Libya, and the Netherlands. The political acceptability of the overall distribution of the burden would not, however, be much greater than that of a tax on oil alone. Many developing countries would still bear heavier burdens than many developed countries.

Taxing all three sources of energy would produce a distribution of burden that might be viewed as more equitable. For most of the developed countries, the burden would be between 0.05 percent and 0.09 percent of GNP, and for most of the developing countries it would fall between 0.01 percent and 0.05 percent. The burden on most of the oil-exporting countries would be at the upper end of the range for developing countries, and a few developing countries (most notably Chile, Nicaragua, Colombia, India, and Pakistan) would have burdens similar to those of the developed nations.

The heaviest burdens would be borne by the countries with centrally planned economies. All of these countries are heavy users of coal, and reducing the tax rate on coal (but not on oil and gas) would reduce the

13. In early 1975, the average price of coal in Europe was close to $50 a metric ton. See *Energiestatistik—1975* (Brussels: Statistical Office of the Economic Community, 1976).

disparity between the burdens of these countries and those of countries with market economies.

Tax on International Trade in Mineral Raw Materials

If the international community desired to impose a tax on a component of international trade other than fuels, mineral raw materials might be given serious consideration. The trade in these materials is quite large, and virtually all nations are involved, either as exporters, or as importers, or in many cases as both. A low tax rate could therefore generate substantial revenue, and the burden of the tax would not fall on a small number of countries.

Technical Features

In the case of a tax on internationally traded mineral raw materials, defining the tax base poses both conceptual and practical problems. The source of difficulty is the fact that iron, for example, can be exported as ore, as steel, or as finished products such as automobiles. The problem is where and how to draw the line between commodities that are subject to the tax and those that are not. On the one hand, taxing the mineral content of everything from unprocessed ores to finished manufactures would be an extremely complicated procedure. On the other hand, going to the other extreme and taxing only mineral ores would sharply reduce the tax base. Moreover, it would be difficult to justify taxing minerals if they were exported as ores and exempting them from taxation if they were exported in the form of ingots.

One possibility would be to use the Standard International Trade Classification (SITC) in defining the tax base. For example, the tax might be applied to international trade in the following SITC categories: ores, basic metals (ingots), wrought metals, and semimanufactures. This approach would, however, involve serious problems, especially with respect to semimanufactures. In the case of some items in this category, the value that is added when it is manufactured is greater than the value of the mineral component that is supposedly the object of taxation. Also, the line between manufactures and semimanufactures is far from clear, and numerous controversies could arise over whether or not particular commodities were subject to the tax.

A more workable approach might be to devise a qualitative definition of taxable trade. Qualitative descriptions of goods taxable at different rates are at the heart of any tariff schedule. The national customs officials who would presumably have to collect an international tax on mineral raw materials would therefore find a qualitative description of taxable items quite consistent with their established procedures.

One possibility would be to say that an item would be taxable if at least a specified percentage of its invoice value was accounted for by its principal mineral content, valued at the world market price. Table 3-6 presents illustrative data for several items fabricated from iron and for several made of copper. If the specified percentage were set at 30 percent, all of the items containing copper shown in the table would be taxable, but steel wire and some steel hoop strips would be exempted from the tax.

As a practical matter, the value of the mineral content, and hence the percentage of the invoice price that it represented, could not be recalculated every time the world price of the mineral changed. Customs officials would have to be provided with standard lists of taxable and nontaxable items that would be revised periodically. Unlisted items could be judged on the basis of average mineral prices from some past period. New base prices would also be calculated periodically.

In principle, the tax would be applied to the value of the mineral content of each taxable item—not to the total invoice value of the item. The need to use base prices, rather than up-to-date market prices, would involve some departure from this principle, but recalculation of base prices, say, every three months would reduce the difference between this tax and a strict ad valorem tax on mineral content.

Incidence of the Tax

The incidence of a tax on internationally traded minerals would vary from mineral to mineral in both the long run and the short run. The determining factors in the case of each mineral would be the elasticities of demand and supply, the amount of competition among producers internationally, and in some countries competition between foreign and domestic suppliers.[14]

14. See appendix A for a fuller discussion of the incidence of this tax.

Table 3-6. *Comparison of the Value of Resource Content with the Total Value of Various Categories of Iron and Copper Products*
Prices in U.S. dollars per metric ton

Product	Price of first refined product	Price of semimanufacture	Resource content as percent of price
Pig iron	60	. . .	. . .
Steel ingots	. . .	90	67
Steel slabs	. . .	100	60
Iron and steel shapes	. . .	150	40
Universals, plate, sheet	. . .	150–200	40–30
Hoop strip	. . .	200–400	30–15
Wire	. . .	300	20
Copper	1,100	. . .	. . .
Bars, wire	. . .	1,300–1,400	85–79
Plate, sheet strip	. . .	1,400–1,600	79–68
Foil	. . .	2,000–3,000	55–37
Tubes, pipe	. . .	1,500	73

Source: Data derived from United Nations Statistical Office, *World Trade Annual 1971*, vol. III (New York: Walker and Co., 1972).

How much of the tax on a particular mineral material would be shifted by producers to consumers would depend on the elasticities of demand and supply. Generally speaking, the less elastic the demand for the material, the larger the portion of the tax that would be paid by consumers. This would be the case because producers could recoup a large part of the tax by raising prices before losses in sales exceeded gains from higher receipts on each unit sold. Producers whose supply was also inelastic, however, would be restricted in their ability to take advantage of elastic demand. A producer in this situation would find that his marginal costs changed sharply with the volume of output and that, if he raised his price more than a small fraction of the tax, he would have to cut output below the level at which profits would be maximized.

It seems reasonable to assume that the demand for minerals is relatively inelastic, since they are essential in many important industrial processes. It also appears likely that the supply of these materials is not particularly inelastic. If these judgments are correct, the larger part of the tax would be shifted forward to consumers in the form of higher prices.

In the short run, the remainder of the tax would tend to be absorbed by the producers; over the long run, however, some producers would shift their part of the tax backward to the owners of mineral deposits in the form of reduced royalty payments. The only producers that could continue to absorb part of the tax would be those that were able to earn above-normal profits (that is, greater profits than were required to attract and retain needed capital). Producers in an industry in which substantial competition prevailed would be unable over the long run to earn more than normal profits, and therefore they could not absorb any of the tax.

The above discussion has proceeded implicitly on the assumption that there is a single world market for mineral raw materials. In fact, because the transport costs of marketing these materials are a substantial portion of their value, a number of separate markets exist in different countries and regions. How much of the tax would be shifted to consumers globally would depend upon the overall elasticities of demand and supply for the taxed commodity. How much of the tax would be shifted to consumers in a given country would depend upon these factors and also upon the effect the tax had on the division of the local market between foreign and domestic producers, where the latter exist.

From the point of view of the domestic producers, the international tax and the resultant increase in the international price would operate like an import duty and permit them to take over a larger share of the domestic market. How much market the domestic producers would be able to take over would depend upon their elasticity of supply (that is, how much increase in production could be supported at the new, higher price). Domestic output would, of course, not be subject to the tax. Thus, to the extent that domestic producers increased their share of the local market, the tax would not be shifted to consumers in that particular country. This circumstance would make little difference to the individual consumer who would in any case pay the higher price on both domestic and imported material, but the distinction is relevant to the question of how the burden of the tax would be distributed among countries.

Whether this distinction has much practical importance appears questionable, particularly if the tax is levied at a very low rate. The possibility exists, however, that some small firms dependent on export markets in only a few countries could suffer if the tax enabled domestic producers to take over larger shares of those markets.

Distribution of the Tax Burden

Because a tax on internationally traded mineral raw materials would normally be collected at the point of importation, this tax—like the general trade tax—would probably be perceived as falling on consumers in the importing country. As was brought out in the analysis of incidence, this perception would more or less correspond to the facts. For purposes of estimating the distribution of the tax burden, it therefore appears justi- fied to assume that all of the tax would be shifted to consumers, at least in the short run.

Table 3-7 presents for thirty-two selected countries estimates of the revenue that a 1 percent ad valorem tax on internationally traded mineral raw materials would have produced in 1970–71. In making these esti- mates, it was assumed that the tax would be applied to the value of the mineral content of internationally traded goods if that value was one-third or more of the total price. Because it was necessary to rely upon a variety of sources, these estimates are only approximate.

Table 3-7 also shows the burden of the tax as a percentage of the GNP of each of the selected countries, on the assumption that the entire tax would be shifted to consumers. As would have been expected, the burden of the tax is affected by both a country's size and its level of economic development. Thus, the burdens of developing countries are relatively low, but so are the burdens of the two largest developed countries, the United States and the Soviet Union, which obtain a large share of their mineral raw materials from domestic sources.

Representatives of developing countries have charged that the duties imposed by industrialized countries on primary commodities give an un- fair competitive advantage to synthetic substitutes produced in the import- ing countries. The same charge could logically be made against inter- national taxes on the same commodities. It appears, however, that the competition of synthetic substitutes is more serious in the case of agri- cultural products, such as rubber and fibers, than it is in the case of min- eral raw materials. In fact, the lack of satisfactory substitutes is a major reason for assuming that the demand for such materials is relatively in- elastic.

Table 3-8 shows how much revenue would be provided by each of the taxed metals and metal ores imported by the group of thirty-two selected countries. Iron and steel in both crude and processed forms account for 53.5 percent of the total revenue. Zinc produces the next highest amount of revenue, followed by copper and aluminum.

At 1971 trade levels for the entire world (not just for the thirty-two selected countries), the tax would have yielded about $0.5 billion. This

Table 3-7. *Distribution of the Burden on Selected Countries of a Tax on International Trade in Mineral Raw Materials,*
Assuming Full Shifting to Consumers, 1970–71
Money amounts in U.S. dollars

Country	GNP 1972 (billions)	Revenue (in millions) from 1 percent ad valorem tax on				
		All ores	Metals	Other crude minerals (except fuels)	Total	Percent of GNP
		DEVELOPED MARKET ECONOMIES				
United States	1,167.4	37.90	139.50	2.80	180.20	0.015
Sweden	36.4	0.64	4.85	...	5.49	0.015
Canada	97.1	1.70	4.00	0.80	6.50	0.007
United Kingdom	145.0	21.50	30.10	1.60	53.20	0.037
France	187.4	17.00	13.20	2.10	32.30	0.017
Germany, Federal Republic of	209.0	32.20	26.40	3.30	61.90	0.030
Australia	38.7	0.05	0.62	0.57	1.24	0.003
Japan	247.9	69.20	9.50	3.20	81.90	0.033
Italy	107.0	8.21	10.46	1.54	20.21	0.019
Greece	13.0	0.21	0.65	0.17	1.03	0.008
Spain	41.5	3.02	1.63	0.56	5.21	0.013
Netherlands	37.9	5.54	6.11	1.84	13.49	0.036
		CENTRALLY PLANNED ECONOMIES				
Soviet Union	377.7	3.83	2.64	0.11	6.58	0.002
Poland	49.6	3.75	1.62	0.01	5.38	0.011
Yugoslavia	16.8	0.14	2.37	0.45	2.96	0.014

Per capita GNP 500–1,000						
Panama	1.3	...	0.05	0.18	0.23	0.018
Chile	8.0	...	0.17	0.04	0.21	0.003
Portugal	7.6	0.07	0.74	0.23	1.04	0.014
Brazil	52.0	0.19	1.07	0.26	1.52	0.003
Lebanon	2.0	...	0.26	0.03	0.29	0.014
Per capita GNP 200–500						
Turkey	13.7	0.61	0.68	0.01	1.30	0.010
Nicaragua	1.0	...	0.04	0.01	0.05	0.005
Ivory Coast	1.8	...	0.13	0.08	0.21	0.012
Ghana	2.7	...	0.04	...	0.04	0.001
Morocco	4.3	0.02	0.10	0.02	0.14	0.003
Philippines	8.6	0.10	0.82	0.02	0.94	0.011
Per capita GNP below 200						
India	61.9	0.10	1.64	0.16	1.90	0.003
Kenya	2.1	...	0.18	0.01	0.19	0.010
Uganda	1.6	0.03	0.22	...	0.25	0.016
Chad	0.3	...	0.01	...	0.01	0.003
Central African Republic	0.3	...	...	...	...	...
Senegal	1.1	...	0.04	0.01	0.05	0.005

Sources: Basic data for GNP in 1972 from *World Bank Atlas 1974*, pp. 12–20. The revenue estimates for a tax on international trade in mineral raw materials were pieced together from a number of sources. The principal source for the developed market economies was data on imports by SITC classification in United Nations Statistical Office, *1971 World Trade Annual*, vols. 1 and 3. For other countries, mineral imports were taken from U.S. Department of the Interior, Bureau of Mines, *1971 Minerals Yearbook*, vol. 1 (GPO 1973). In general, shipments were recorded in tons and prices of the metal or mineral were estimated from data in the *1971 Minerals Yearbook*. It was assumed that the tax would be imposed on the content at the first marketable product of refined mineral. For example, imports of semimanufactured steel shapes were recorded by tonnage and taxed on the basis of the pig iron price.

In some cases, data for particular countries were reported only in terms of dollars and these had to be converted to weight measures by dollar/weight relationship for other countries. Some difficulties were encountered from the circumstance that some ore weight figures were reported as gross weights and some by weight of contained metal. Most data were given in terms of contained metal, except aluminum ores and iron ore. For iron ore, the average metal content of U.S. imports was used. For aluminum, the dollar values of ore imports was used directly, because the tax rate is fairly uniform in relation to the price of bauxite and alumina, even though the metal content is very different. For nonmetals, the 1 percent tax rate applied directly to the import values.

Table 3-8. *Estimated Revenue for Selected Countries from a 1 Percent Tax on International Trade in Metals, by Type of Resource, 1970–71*
Millions of U.S. dollars

Resource	Developed market economies	Centrally planned economies	Developing countries with per capita income of			Total	
			500–1,000	200–500	Below 200	Amount	Percent
Metal ores							
Aluminum	19.3	2.48	0.01	0.003	...	21.793	4.7
Copper	2.7	0.06	0.03	0.004	...	2.794	0.6
Iron	86.4	0.08	0.07	0.001	0.003	86.554	18.7
Lead	2.4	0.19	...	0.001	...	2.591	0.5
Nickel	7.4	...	...	...	...	7.400	1.6
Manganese	9.1	0.48	...	0.004	0.003	9.587	2.1
Tin	2.4	0.09	...	0.148	...	2.638	0.6
Zinc	62.4	4.95	...	...	0.102	67.452	14.6
Other	5.5	...	0.15	...	...	5.650	1.2
Subtotal	197.6	8.33	0.26	0.161	0.108	206.459	44.6
Metals							
Aluminum	12.2	0.21	0.31	0.157	0.225	13.102	2.8
Copper	29.6	0.45	0.78	0.038	0.665	31.533	6.8
Pig iron	3.9	1.07	0.02	0.072	...	5.062	1.1
Steel	149.6	3.61	1.03	0.963	1.029	156.232	33.7
Lead	2.4	0.20	0.05	0.030	0.124	2.804	0.6
Nickel	7.9	0.06	0.02	0.024	0.012	8.016	1.7
Tin	4.6	0.16	...	0.118	0.001	4.879	1.1
Zinc	24.8	0.82	0.02	0.360	0.129	26.129	5.6
Silver and platinum	5.9	...	...	...	...	5.900	1.3
Other	3.1	0.03	0.02	0.023	0.005	3.178	0.7
Subtotal	244.0	6.61	2.25	1.785	2.190	256.835	55.4
Total	441.6	14.94	2.51	1.946	2.298	463.294	100.0

Source: Table 3-7.

suggests that, at 1976 levels of world trade, total revenue would have been $1.2 billion.[15]

Tax on International Investment Income

All of the possible international taxes considered thus far in this chapter are similar to import duties or excise taxes, which have been criticized as regressive because they do not vary with taxpayers' incomes. A tax on incomes would, of course, not be vulnerable to this kind of criticism. A general income tax for international purposes must probably be ruled out of consideration, however, because it would infringe on the major source of revenue of many governments. An effort to construct such a tax would, moreover, encounter many difficult problems arising from differences in the definitions of taxable income used by various governments. A more promising kind of income tax would be one limited to international investment income, that is, earnings received by residents of one country from investments in another country.

Technical Features

International investment income arises from: (1) direct private foreign investment; (2) private portfolio investment abroad; (3) bilateral intergovernmental loans; and (4) loans by international financial institu-

15. The 1971 estimate was obtained by multiplying the tax revenue obtained from each of the five country categories in table 3-7 by the ratio between the total GNPs of all countries in each category and the GNPs of the countries listed under the same category in table 3-7. Data used were from the *World Bank Atlas 1972.*

The 1976 estimate was obtained by assuming that the increase in the trade in mineral raw materials (and therefore the increase in tax revenues) from 1971 to 1976 would bear the same relationship to the increase in total imports over those years as the increase in raw material imports (except food) bore to the increase in total imports over the period 1971–74. Between 1971 and 1976 the value of total imports in current dollars rose 154 percent in the developed market economies, 214 percent in the developing market economies, and 160 percent in the centrally planned economies. Between 1971 and 1974, raw material imports (except food) rose 90 percent as much as total imports in the developed market economies, 196 percent as much in the developing market economies, and 86 percent as much in the centrally planned economies. Data used were from United Nations, *Monthly Bulletin of Statistics,* vol. 31 (January 1977), p. 110. In most cases, 1976 figures were extrapolated from data for the first nine months of the year.

tions. The first question to be faced is whether the tax should be imposed on all of these kinds of international investment income.

A strong case can be made for exempting interest payments received by the World Bank and other international financial institutions. The lending activities of these institutions do not yield private profits but help borrowers—in most cases poor countries—to meet their development goals or to cope with other financial problems. Taxing the interest paid on loans made by international financial institutions would appear to place a burden on activities that the international community should be encouraging. The result of such an action could be to force an increase in interest rates, which many borrowers could ill afford. Alternatively, funds that might have been lent for constructive purposes might have to be diverted to support the institutions in question. Apart from these important considerations, applying an international tax to institutions such as the World Bank would appear incongruous since the purposes of the tax would include raising money to expand the kind of programs already financed by those institutions.

Similar arguments might be advanced for exempting interest payments on bilateral intergovernmental loans. The force of such arguments is greatly weakened, however, by the fact that such loans often serve narrow national interests, or they are perceived as doing so by nations other than the two countries directly involved. A more compelling reason for exempting the interest earned on bilateral intergovernmental loans is the virtual certainty that taxing such interest would be viewed by many national governments as an intolerable infringement on their sovereignty.

Exempting interest on intergovernmental loans would, however, have the undesirable consequence of including the countries with centrally planned economies in the coverage of the tax to only a limited extent. Those countries do make intergovernmental loans, but their citizens are not involved in either direct foreign investment or portfolio investment. The only transactions involving this group of countries that might be subjected to the tax are the repatriation of earnings on the various commercial activities of their governments in other countries. Such activities would include banks, trading firms, and joint manufacturing ventures.

All taxes have deficiencies, and the fact that the centrally planned economies would be touched very little by a tax on international investment income must be accepted as a major shortcoming of this particular tax. It does not necessarily follow that such a tax must be ruled out of consideration. An alternative in this and other cases in which tax burdens appear to be distributed inequitably is to make compensating adjustments on either the revenue-raising side or the disbursing side of the international fiscal system.[16]

Apart from the fact that the centrally planned economies would not be touched, there would appear to be no particular reason not to tax the remaining two categories of foreign investment income: earnings from direct foreign investment and portfolio investment. It can be argued that these forms of private investment contribute to the development of the poorer nations of the world by transferring capital to them and that it would be as inappropriate to tax the income produced by such investment as it would be to tax the interest earned on loans by international financial institutions. Some observers would counter this line of argument by asserting that, at least in the case of direct foreign investment, the benefits received by host countries are reduced, if not eliminated, by the restrictive and exploitative practices of the investing corporations.[17] For purposes of this study, however, it is not necessary to pass judgment on the activities of multinational corporations. The relevant fact—which can scarcely be disputed—is that private foreign investment is made for profit. There would appear to be nothing inappropriate about taxing that profit, whether or not private foreign investment confers net benefits on host countries.

A general decision to tax income from private foreign investment does not settle several subsidiary questions. One question is whether to tax patent royalties and management fees as well as dividends and interest payments. If the tax is defined strictly as one on net earnings from invested capital, the former two kinds of payments should be exempted.[18] To make such an exemption, however, would be to open the way to tax evasions through disguising dividends as royalties or management fees. As a practical matter, all payments received by foreign investors should probably be taxed.

Another question that arises in connection with direct foreign investment is whether to tax the total income of companies with some minimum

16. The problem of sharing the tax burden is considered in detail in chapter 7.

17. See, for example, Constantino Vaitsos, *Intercountry Income Distribution and Transnational Enterprises* (Oxford: Clarendon Press, 1974); and Richard J. Barnett and Ronald E. Müller, *Global Reach* (Simon and Schuster, 1974).

18. Patent royalties cover development costs as well as net earnings, and management fees cover compensation for personal services.

percentage of international ownership, or only that part of investment income that is transmitted from the country in which it was earned to a resident of another country. The latter alternative is clearly preferable. The places of residence of the owners of a company have little to do with the percentage of the company's income that comes from foreign investment. Taxing all of the income of companies with a specified minimum of international ownership would therefore be quite arbitrary. An effort to sort out the part of the income of such companies that had been earned in countries other than the countries of residence of individual stockholders would encounter virtually insuperable complications.

Imposing a tax on dividends and other payments to foreigners would, however, be both quite feasible and consistent with the concept of a tax on international investment income. Nearly all income tax systems have a procedure for imposing a withholding tax on dividends payable to foreigners. The same procedure could be used to collect the international investment tax. For reasons of administrative convenience, local definitions of which kinds of payments—including royalties—were subject to the withholding tax should probably be followed. This, however, would result in some differences in the application of the international investment tax from country to country. For example, many countries do not impose withholding taxes on the transfer of branch profits to a foreign corporation. Again, some countries do not tax the international transfer of interest payments. These circumstances could lead to tax avoidance. At a minimum, they would pose administrative problems.

In the case of income from portfolio investments, it may sometimes be difficult to identify payees as residents of another country. One possible solution to this problem would be to withhold the tax on all dividend and interest payments and permit local residents to claim a refund. Another possibility in countries with exchange controls would be to collect the tax when the firm making payments to foreigners applies for permission to buy foreign exchange.

Incidence of the Tax

Some governments now grant tax credits for taxes paid to foreign governments. To the extent that this precedent is followed in the case of a tax on international investment income, the incidence of the tax would—by their choice—fall on the treasuries of the governments concerned. For purposes of the present analysis, this possibility will be ignored.[19]

In the short run, the incidence of an international investment tax on portfolio investments would fall entirely on lenders-investors, since the terms of their outstanding loans or equity investments would be fixed. The case of direct foreign investment is somewhat different. The tax would not immediately affect the supply and cost of capital in the countries in which international investment income is earned. The profits before taxes of firms earning the investment income would therefore not be affected. Firms that were pursuing a profit-maximizing strategy—which would probably be the majority of all firms involved—would therefore absorb the full amount of the tax.

Firms that were pursuing some other strategy, such as achieving a target rate of return or limiting profits to a level that would not attract competition, would be able, in the short run, to shift a large part of the tax to consumers in the form of higher prices for their products. Their ability to do so would be facilitated by the fact that their international competitors would be subject to the same tax. Some of the part of the tax that was shifted would fall on consumers in the host country and some on consumers elsewhere in proportions that would depend on the marketing practices of the firms concerned.

In the long run, the tax would make it more attractive for investors-lenders to place their funds at home rather than abroad. Because of the tax, capital-importing countries would have to provide a higher rate of return to maintain any given level of flow of loans and equity investments. How much higher rate of return would be required would depend on the elasticities of supply and demand for capital. If demand is quite inelastic and supply quite elastic, the cost of capital would rise by an amount equal to a large portion of the tax levied. That is, investors-lenders would have to absorb very little of the tax. Most of the tax would be shifted to the firms dependent on imported capital. Those firms would in turn absorb part of their increased capital costs and pass part on to consumers of their products in the host country and elsewhere.

The actual elasticities of supply and demand for capital can only be a matter for speculation. There are reasons, however, for suspecting that, at least for direct foreign investment, demand is moderately elastic and sup-

19. See appendix A for a fuller analysis of the incidence of a tax on international investment income.

ply moderately inelastic.[20] If so, something more than half of the tax would be absorbed by investors-lenders, and there would be only a modest reduction in the flow of capital. This, of course, would be viewed favorably by capital-importing countries.

Distribution of the Tax Burden

Making even rough estimates of the distribution of the burden of a tax on international investment income among different countries is an impossible task. Comprehensive, reliable information on the international flow of investment income simply does not exist. As demonstrated above, even if such information did exist, it would be difficult to determine what assumption should be made, country by country, concerning the incidence of a tax on international investment income. The best that can be done is to speculate about the order of magnitude of the revenue that might be raised by such a tax and about how the burden that this revenue represents might be divided between developed and developing nations.

A very crude estimate of the tax base, using partial data for 1975, is presented in table 3-9. The tenuous and arbitrary nature of some of the components of this estimate is explained in the note to the table. If it is accepted, however, that private international investment income approaches $50 billion annually, it follows that a 1 percent tax on such revenue would bring in roughly $500 million a year.

In the short run, as was explained above, the burden of providing this amount of revenue would fall largely on investors-lenders, who in most cases are residents of, or firms based in, the developed countries. Over the long run, more of the burden would be borne by firms using the capital on which international investment income is earned and by customers of those firms. The firms in question, however, are typically based in developed countries, and many of their customers are also in developed countries. It therefore appears reasonable to conclude that in the long run, as well as in the short run, the tax burden would fall principally on the developed countries. This conclusion would be reinforced to the extent that the

20. This judgment rests on the fact that profits on foreign investment vary widely, which suggests that considerations other than the rate of return explain much of such investment. The evidence is not conclusive, however, and some observers believe that the supply of capital is elastic and that a tax on investment income would cause a moderately large reduction in capital flows. The supply of capital for portfolio investment should be more elastic than that for direct investment.

Table 3-9. *Estimated Private Income from International Investments, 1975*
Billions of U.S. dollars

Description	United States	Rest of world	Total
Profits from direct foreign investment	9.1	9.1	18.2
Other income from direct foreign investment	3.4	1.7	5.1
Income from portfolio investment	7.6	15.0	22.6
Total	20.1	25.8	45.9

Sources: Figures on U.S. income from private foreign investment are from the *Survey of Current Business*. See vol. 55 (October 1975), p. 32, for U.S. profits from direct foreign investment and vol. 56 (March 1976), p. 40, for other U.S. income from direct foreign investment (that is, fees and royalties from affiliated foreigners) and for U.S. income from private portfolio investment. The United States accounts for about one-half of direct foreign investment in the developing world. See *Multinational Corporations in World Development*, UN Doc. ST/ECA/190 (New York: 1973), p. 139. Thus, income from such investment in the rest of the world was assumed to be the same as that received by the United States. Other income received by the rest of the world from direct foreign investment was arbitrarily set at one-half the U.S. figure, and income from private portfolio investment at twice the U.S. figure. The latter assumption is to some extent justified by the fact that non-U.S. portfolio investment appears to be significantly higher than that of the United States. See *World Bank Annual Report 1974* (Washington, D.C.: World Bank, 1974), pp. 98–99.

governments of developed countries granted tax credits for payments made under an international revenue tax.

This conclusion refers only to the monetary burden. If—contrary to the view expressed above—the tax caused an appreciable decline in foreign investment, the developing countries would bear the burden of a lower level of labor productivity than would have been possible without the tax.

Evaluation of Possible International Revenue Taxes

In the course of describing and analyzing the various possible taxes considered in this chapter, some of the advantages and disadvantages of each tax were noted. It appears useful, however, to conclude the chapter with a more complete evaluation in which the relative merits of the various taxes can also be brought out.

Criteria for a Good International Tax

The various characteristics that are usually considered in deciding whether a tax is good can be taken up under four headings: economic effects, fairness, administrative convenience, and revenue-raising potential.[21]

ECONOMIC EFFECTS. Much of the public debate about taxes is devoted to their economic effects, but there is great disagreement about why the effects of one tax may be better than those of another tax.

Historically, the text books about public finance suggested the standard that taxes should be "neutral"; that is, a good tax is one that brings about the least changes in relative prices. This position assumed that, in the absence of a tax, the public would have made a rational allocation of resources on the basis of prevailing market prices. Any tax reduces purchasing power, but one that distorts relative prices imposes an additional burden by forcing consumers away from the most efficient combination of goods.

Perfect price-neutrality in taxes is impossible to achieve. (The most neutral tax would be a per capita or poll tax which is hardly acceptable as a major source of revenue.) Moreover, it cannot even be proved that a more neutral tax is better than a less neutral tax. A tax that is not neutral may introduce distortions which just offset market defects.[22] From the public viewpoint, this kind of distortion of market decisions would be regarded as a net improvement.

In recent literature about public finance, considerable attention has been given to the notion that an optimum tax is relatively output-neutral, rather than price-neutral. From this point of view, an optimum tax is one that, despite its price effects, causes a minimum distortion in the income-earning and the income-using decisions of individuals and businesses.[23] This is a refinement of a very old notion in taxation—that taxes should fall on windfall incomes. The economic characteristic of a windfall income is that the recipient would do the same thing even if his income from doing it was very much reduced.

---

21. For another brief contemporary summary of goals and principles of taxation, see George F. Break and Joseph A. Pechman, *Federal Tax Reform: The Impossible Dream?* (Brookings Institution, 1975), pp. 4–10. Their categories were: equity, economic efficiency, fiscal efficiency, simplicity, and certainty. For other accounts, see Carl S. Shoup, *Public Finance* (Aldine, 1969), pp. 21–45; and James Buchanan and M. Flowers, *The Public Finances,* 4th ed. (Irwin, 1975), pp. 94–104.

22. See R. G. Lipsey and Kelvin Lancaster, "The General Theory of Second Best," *Review of Economic Studies,* vol. 24 (1956), pp. 11–32.

23. See Peter A. Diamond and James A. Mirrlees, "Optimal Taxation and Public Production," *American Economic Review,* vol. 61 (1971), pp. 8–27 and 261–78.

An international tax is unlikely to be judged on the basis of either its price-neutrality or its output-neutrality, as those concepts are applied to domestic taxes. Within a single nation, a consensus might be reached on the deliberate use of a tax that is not output-neutral, that is, a tax that would increase some outputs and reduce others. Such agreement would be much less likely internationally for two reasons: differences among cultures would result in differing views concerning what changes in output were desirable, and a deliberate policy of changing outputs is likely to result in net burdens for some countries and net gains for others. In the case of an international tax that changed prices but not outputs, the focus of international discussion would probably not be the distorting effect of the tax on relative prices, but the effect of changed prices on the burdens of different countries.

FAIRNESS. Public debates on domestic taxes often give much attention to the question of whether the ratio of tax payments to income rises, falls, or is constant as the income of taxpayers rises. If the ratio rises, the tax is progressive; if the ratio falls, the tax is regressive; if the ratio is constant, the tax is proportional. Although there is no scientific way of proving that one distribution of income is better than another,[24] progressive taxes are generally regarded as more fair than regressive taxes.

Trying to apply the principle of progressivity internationally at the level of individual taxpayers would be quite difficult. Detailed information on income distribution does not exist for many countries, and cultural differences would complicate the task of comparing the relative progressivity of various possible international taxes. In any event, national governments are certain to judge progressivity in terms of the burdens imposed on countries relative to their gross national products—not in terms of the burdens on individual taxpayers with different incomes.

Progressivity is, of course, not the only criterion of fairness. When a taxpayer complains of being treated unfairly, he often means that he is being required to pay more taxes than other, similarly situated taxpayers. Differences in the tax treatment of nations, as well as individuals, should not be based on trivial circumstances.

ADMINISTRATIVE CONVENIENCE. Simplicity and ease of administration are desirable attributes of any tax, whether national or international. Simplicity tends to hold down administrative costs, which of course makes a

24. See Walter J. Blum and Harry Kalven, *The Uneasy Case for Progressive Taxation* (University of Chicago Press, 1953), pp. 49–68.

tax more efficient as a means of raising revenue. Simplicity must, however, sometimes be sacrificed in the interest of greater fairness.

Simplicity is especially desirable for international taxes since they will in all probability have to be administered by national revenue-collecting officials with differing experience and technical competence. Also, any international body charged with monitoring an international tax and making necessary adjustments in its application is more likely to carry out its duties successfully if the tax is not too complicated.[25]

REVENUE-RAISING POTENTIAL. Everything else being equal, a tax that can produce a large amount of revenue at a low rate of taxation (that is, a tax with a large base) is better than a tax that must be levied at a higher rate to yield the same results. This rather obvious principle is especially important for international taxes since such taxes are more likely to be acceptable to the governments involved if they can generate substantial amounts of money at low tax rates.

International taxes are not likely to be used to check excessive swings in economic activity (that is, to be countercyclical), as are some national taxes. Thus a good international tax should yield fairly stable (or better still, rising) revenues from year to year. Long-term commitments to program expenditures cannot be made if revenues fluctuate unpredictably.

Another desirable attribute in any tax is that it be able to be collected. Taxpayers should not find the tax too easy to evade. In the case of international taxes, in which the cooperation of a large number of governments is essential, a tax that can be collected in more than one jurisdiction has an important advantage over a tax that cannot.

Comparison of Possible International Revenue Taxes

If international taxes are not likely to be judged on their economic effects, except to the extent that those effects influence the relative burdens of different countries, the taxes presented in this chapter need be compared only in terms of fairness, administrative convenience, and revenue-raising potential.

FAIRNESS. The fairness of all of the taxes in question could be challenged—and probably would be challenged—by asking: Why tax these particular transactions? Why not tax something else? There are no entirely

25. See chapter 7 for a discussion of possible legal and administrative arrangements.

convincing answers to this challenge, but the same questions might be raised about most national taxes, and no better answers would be forthcoming. The starting point has to be the agreement that *some* tax, or taxes, must be levied. The fairness of specific taxes can then be judged in terms of how well they avoid trivial distinctions concerning what is to be taxed and what is not, and in terms of the way in which their burdens would be distributed.

None of the taxes considered in this chapter can be said to distinguish between taxable and exempt transactions on trivial grounds. Once the concept of taxing international trade has been accepted, however, it is easier to defend a general trade tax than a tax on even broad categories of trade, like fuels or mineral raw materials. Similarly, within categories, it may be difficult to justify taxing only oil, rather than all energy materials, or taxing only ores, metals, and some semimanufactures, rather than all products made from metals, including finished goods. Much the same problem arises with a tax that is applied only to international investment income and not to the many other kinds of income.

Defining tax bases on grounds of practicality and political feasibility is standard practice in all nations, and there is no reason to expect the choice of international taxes to be approached in any different spirit. The relative fairness of different possible international taxes will be judged not so much on the basis of abstract logic as on the way in which their burdens are distributed among various countries or groups of countries.

The burdens of the taxes discussed in this chapter are distributed in quite different ways:

—A general tax on international trade would favor large countries, including the United States and the Soviet Union, and would impose relatively heavy burdens on small countries. Much, but not all, of this disparity could be eliminated by automatic application of a formula permitting small countries to retain a larger proportion of tax collections than large countries.

—A tax on internationally traded oil might well fall principally on the relatively small numbers of countries that export oil. If the tax were shifted to consumers in oil-importing countries, tax burdens would be erratic. Some of the countries with relatively heavy burdens would be developed countries, some would be developing countries. The burden on the United States would be relatively low, and the Soviet Union would pay almost no tax.

—A tax on both domestic and internationally traded oil—if it were shifted fully to consumers—would not be biased in favor of countries with substantial domestic oil production. Some countries would, however, bear relatively heavy burdens because they are unusually dependent on oil in comparison with other fuels. If, as appears likely in the long run, the incidence of the tax fell more heavily on oil producers and the owners of oil deposits, the burden of the tax would be borne disproportionately by the oil-exporting countries.

—A tax on all hydrocarbon fuels, both internationally traded and domestic, would produce a distribution of burden that (assuming, again, that the tax would be shifted to consumers) might be viewed as more equitable than taxing oil alone. In most cases, developed countries would bear heavier burdens than developing countries. There would be problems, however, the most notable being the fact that the heaviest burdens would be borne by the countries with centrally planned economies.

—A tax on international trade in mineral raw materials would, in most cases, fall more heavily on developed than on developing countries. The burdens of the United States and the Soviet Union would be relatively low, however, because they obtain substantial shares of their mineral raw material requirements domestically.

—A tax on international investment income would be borne largely by the developed countries with market economies. There probably would be no politically feasible way to structure the tax to impose any significant part of the burden on the countries with centrally planned economies.

The major conclusion to be drawn from this review of the distribution of the burden of various possible international taxes is that none of the taxes, standing alone, would be perceived to be entirely fair. It must be emphasized, however, that even a tax whose burden varied from country to country exactly with GNP would not be regarded as fair by most developing countries. Proportionality would not be enough. The poorer countries would be certain to insist on a high degree of progressivity. It follows that some compensatory adjustments, on either the revenue or the expenditure side, would be necessary in connection with virtually any conceivable international tax. How such adjustments might be made is considered in chapter 7.

ADMINISTRATIVE CONVENIENCE. All of the taxes considered in this chapter involve some administrative problems, but it would be difficult to conceive of a tax that did not. The tax that would probably be the easiest to administer would be a general trade tax applied to the declared gross value of imports. The most difficult would probably be a tax on internationally traded minerals. The other taxes would fall in between, with a tax on international investment income being relatively difficult and a tax on oil relatively easy to administer.

REVENUE-RAISING POTENTIAL. In gross terms, the revenue-raising potential of a tax depends upon the size of the tax base. It is therefore interesting to compare rough estimates of the bases of the taxes discussed in this chapter:

	Tax base *(billions of U.S. dollars)*
General trade tax	1,000
Tax on internationally traded oil	100
Tax on all oil	180
Tax on all hydrocarbon fuels	380
Tax on internationally traded minerals (except fuels)	120
Tax on international investment income	50

The most striking feature of this comparison of tax bases is of course the way in which the general trade tax overshadows all the other taxes. Nevertheless, all of the taxes in question possess respectable bases and could generate substantial revenue.

In terms of collectibility, the various trade taxes share a major advantage: they can be collected at either the point of importation or the point of exportation. The taxes on all oil and on all hydrocarbons possess this advantage in part, but the portion of these taxes levied on domestic oil and other hydrocarbons would have to be collected in their countries of origin or not at all.

Collection of a tax on international investment income could prove quite difficult. In theory, this tax, like the trade taxes, could be collected at either of two points, but whether facilities for doing so would exist in all cases may be questioned. Moreover, the possibilities for evading this tax would appear to be much greater than in the case of the trade taxes. Transfers of funds can be concealed more easily than shipments of physical goods.

Conclusions

All of the taxes under consideration have deficiencies and pose a variety of problems. All things considered, however, the general trade tax is probably the best of the lot. It scores first in administrative convenience and in revenue-raising potential, and the distribution of its burden is not any more of a problem than that of the other taxes. The least attractive of the taxes considered is clearly the tax on international investment income. Although its base is substantial, it is not as large as that of some other taxes. Also, the tax on international investment income would be relatively difficult to administer and to collect.

CHAPTER FOUR

Taxes on Polluters
of the Marine Environment

THIS CHAPTER examines possibilities for international taxes on pollutants which enter the marine environment as a result of various human activities. The principal purpose of the taxes discussed here is to modify the behavior of polluters—that is, to induce them to reduce polluting emissions. These taxes would not necessarily yield large revenues which could be turned over to the international community. It is important to note, however, that some of the pollution taxes examined here would mobilize substantial additional amounts of money for international purposes because polluters would be given an economic incentive to spend considerable sums on abatement technologies.

Oil in the Marine Environment

Before considering possible taxes on oil emissions from various sources, including tankers, other merchant ships, and offshore drilling operations, it may be useful to examine briefly what is known about the problem of oil in the marine environment. Scientific research on the impact of oil spills on the marine environment has been expanding rapidly since the late 1960s. Appendix B contains a summary of the principal findings of the studies as of late 1975.

One of the chief sources of marine pollution is oil, which is transmitted into the oceans from a number of natural and human activities, including offshore production of crude oil, coastal refineries, municipal and industrial wastes, shipping, river runoff, and aerial fallout. Because pollution is frequently discussed in emotional terms, it is important to analyze the scientific evidence with respect to damage suspected or known to be associated with emissions of petroleum hydrocarbons into the oceans. This will provide a basis for judging whether the damage is sufficient to warrant the imposition of some kind of international control, such as a tax.

There appears to be considerable agreement among marine scientists that the potential for harmful effects from oil spills varies greatly, depending on where in the ocean the oil is spilled.[1] It is generally thought that oil spills in the Arctic—for example, in Alaskan waters and in some Canadian offshore waters—may be more serious than in some other areas because biological processes are very slow in these waters and the ecosystems are fragile because of the climate. Enclosed or protected seas such as the Mediterranean, the Baltic, and the Sargasso are regarded as more vulnerable than the open ocean. In these seas, oil emissions do not disperse rapidly, as they are not subjected to the turbulence (high winds and waves) characteristic of much of the Atlantic, Pacific, and Indian oceans.

Another area of more or less general agreement is that the immediate effects of a large, catastrophic spill—such as from a tanker accident or a drilling blowout—are different from the possible effects of low-level chronic spills. (Even with large catastrophic spills, the locational factor is an important variable.) Another important factor appears to be timing. For example, if an accidental spill occurred in or near fish breeding grounds during spawning periods, the results could be more serious than at other times. Finally, some marine scientists believe that there is a difference in impact, depending on the type of oil that is spilled.

Scientists have reached no consensus on the ultimate long-run impact of low-level chronic spills either in the open ocean or in nearshore areas. There is considerable evidence from research that crude oil and some fractions of refined products can be harmful to various forms of marine life. As yet, however, there is no proof that the world's fish harvest has been reduced, or even that the annual rate of increase has been lowered, as a result of oil pollution in the ocean. Although annual harvests from ocean fisheries are generally regarded as considerably lower than would be possible with good management, the explanation generally offered is that

1. Council on Environmental Quality, *OCS Oil and Gas—An Environmental Assessment,* vol. 5, *Potential Biological Effects of Hypothetical Oil Discharges in the Atlantic Coast and Gulf of Alaska* (GPO, 1974), pp. 19–29 and 73–110.

overfishing has reduced fishery productivity.[2] It is by no means certain, however, that the only cause of the declining world output of fish is over-fishing. Numerous studies conducted over a period of nearly ten years under the auspices of the Woods Hole Oceanographic Institution suggest that the impact of oil spills on coastal nursery and fishery areas may indeed be serious.[3]

In addition to the oil that is spilled into the ocean from human activities, oil enters the ocean from seeps in the ocean floor. The fact that crude oil is a natural part of the ocean ecology does not mean that additional inputs of oil into the ocean are not harmful. Presumably, there are limits on the total quantity of oil which is not harmful to the environment. The presence of indigenous crude oil, however, indicates that the marine environment can tolerate some amount of oil. These observations about crude oil do not necessarily apply to refined products, which have different chemical characteristics than crude oil.

Given the present state of scientific research on this matter, there are at least two basic and opposing viewpoints about the impact of petroleum from human activities on the marine environment. One view argues that petroleum in the marine environment has the potential to destroy various forms of marine life in the open ocean. Even though it is not known how much marine life is being damaged by chronic oil spills, the fact that both crude oil and various fractions of refined products are known to be toxic to various forms of marine life and that some oil is degraded only slowly and can persist in the environment for long periods of time suggests that over time, as more and more petroleum is spilled in the ocean, the earth's genetic resources may be in danger of depletion. Another view is that the ocean is enormous, its absorptive capacity is immense, and there is no evidence that marine life in the open ocean is being harmed by oil spills. This school of thought recognizes that fish and other marine life have been damaged by acute, massive spills. According to this view, however, in these cases death is usually caused by direct contact (for example, smothering), and that it does not follow that low-level chronic spills in the open ocean would have the same effect.

2. Francis T. Christy, Jr., and Anthony Scott, *The Common Wealth in Ocean Fisheries* (Johns Hopkins Press for Resources for the Future, 1965), pp. 74–152.

3. See, for example, Max Blumer and others, "The West Falmouth Oil Spill," WHOI-70-44 (Woods Hole Oceanographic Institution, 1970; processed); Howard L. Sanders and others, "The West Falmouth Oil Spill," WHOI-72-20 (Woods Hole Oceanographic Institution, 1972; processed).

A study by the U.S. National Academy of Sciences summarized the present status of knowledge about petroleum hydrocarbons and their relationship to the marine environment as follows:

> In general, much more research regarding the fates and effects of petroleum hydrocarbons in the marine environment is needed. We know that the quantity of floating tar in the open ocean and of tar along coastlines has been increasing, that major spills and localized continuous discharges of petroleum hydrocarbons have damaged various species of marine life, and that low levels of petroleum may affect the behavior patterns of certain species. Studies to date indicate that areas polluted with petroleum hydrocarbons "recover" within weeks or years . . . ; however, composition of the local biological communities may be altered. The oceans have considerable ability to purify themselves by biological and chemical actions. A basic question that remains unanswered is, "At what level of petroleum hydrocarbon input to the ocean might we find irreversible damage occurring?" The sea is an enormously complex system about which our knowledge is very imperfect. The ocean may be able to accommodate petroleum hydrocarbon inputs far above those occurring today. On the other hand, the damage level may be within an order of magnitude of present inputs to the sea. Until we can come closer to answering this basic question, it seems wisest to continue our efforts in the international control of inputs and to push forward research to reduce our current level of uncertainty.[4]

Possible Use of Taxes to Deal with Oil Discharges into the Marine Environment

The imposition of taxes on firms which discharge petroleum hydrocarbons into the ocean is one approach to reducing oil emissions. In theory, the most suitable type of tax for present purposes is the effluent tax, which has been developed by various economists as a means of changing the behavior of individual economic entities responsible for discharging pollutants into the environment. Most concrete efforts to adopt effluent taxes, however, have met with limited success thus far. The difficulties have been not only political (nobody likes to pay taxes) but also practical. In general, it has not been found easy to transform the theoretical effluent tax into a workable tax system.[5]

As will be brought out below, applying a pure effluent tax to pollution

4. National Academy of Sciences, *Petroleum in the Marine Environment* (Washington, D.C.: NAS, 1975), pp. 106–07.
5. The European Community (EC) has adopted the "polluter pays principle" as a chief policy instrument for dealing with air and water pollution. Although the EC has not yet adopted a broad action plan for implementing the polluter pays

of the marine environment is not feasible. It is useful, however, to examine briefly the theoretical basis for effluent taxes and then to consider a more practical alternative approach.

The Theoretical Basis for Effluent Taxes

The effluent tax was developed within the framework of welfare economics. In traditional Western economic theory, the competitive market is viewed as a decentralized decision-making mechanism in which firms and individuals make decisions on levels of production of various goods and services on the basis of economic advantage. Each productive resource is used up to the point where the cost of an additional unit equals its contribution to the value of output. In a market economy that is functioning perfectly, maximum output is achieved at the lowest cost.

This, of course, represents an idealized model of the competitive market economy. In practice, even if such a system were to be fully implemented without alterations or exceptions, there are problems with such a system. One problem, which is of prime concern in the environmental area, is the failure of the private market to reflect the full costs that each unit of economic activity imposes on society. These costs are usually referred to as external costs, and the question of who should bear these costs is one of the issues addressed in welfare economics. An example of an external cost in the environmental area is the injury that industries which dispose of their wastes in streams may cause to subsequent users of the same water.

In order to compensate for this kind of market failure, the effluent tax was devised.[6] In principle, an effluent tax is based on the costs that are imposed on others because of pollutants that are emitted into the environment by a unit of economic activity. In this way, these costs are "internalized" and they will influence the unit's decisions as other costs do.

---

principle on a community-wide basis, a number of European countries have had some experience with a pollution tax. Because of the practical difficulties involved in devising a true effluent tax, each of these countries has adopted some sort of pragmatic variation of the classical effluent tax.

6. For a thorough treatment of the effluent tax, see Allen V. Kneese and Blair T. Bower, *Managing Water Quality: Economics, Technology, Institutions* (Johns Hopkins Press for Resources for the Future, 1968), pp. 75–141; and Karl-Göran Mäler, *Environmental Economics: A Theoretical Inquiry* (Johns Hopkins University Press for Resources for the Future, 1974), pp. 200–61.

Ideally, anyone devising an effluent tax should know two things: the money cost of the damage caused by each successive increment of pollution per unit of time and the cost of cleaning up the pollution.[7] (The first of these relationships is referred to in the literature as a damage function; the second can be thought of as an abatement function.) In most situations, the amount of damage attributable to each successive increment of pollution rises as the amount of pollution increases,[8] and the abatement of increments of pollution becomes more costly as the degree of abatement increases. There will therefore be a level of pollution at which the cost of abating one more increment of pollution equals the damage caused by that increment. In theory, the level of the tax should be set so that polluters will reduce pollution to just that level.

Effluent taxes are, of course, not the only tool available to a public authority for reducing the level of polluting emissions into the environment. One of the most common tools is the setting of compulsory effluent standards.[9] For example, an upper limit might be set on the amount of a material toxic to fish that can be emitted into a stream or a body of water. Standards of this type are common in the United States.

A system based entirely on the setting of standards has a number of practical disadvantages. A basic problem with the use of emission standards as the mainstay of pollution control is that the approach relies on administrative and judicial enforcement, which can be a very lengthy process, rather than on economic incentives. Also, policies which impose uniform limitations on emissions or require use of a specific technology are usually very inefficient and therefore wasteful. This is because they ignore the fact that different polluters have different capabilities and therefore experience different costs in achieving specified pollution abatement goals. The main theoretical advantage of an effluent tax over reliance on standards is that the effluent tax provides a constant incentive to polluters to reduce emissions (in order to lower the tax burden). A system of standards does not provide this continuous incentive. Once a polluter has achieved the specified standard, there is no motivation for further reduction of polluting discharges.

7. See Kneese and Bower, *Managing Water Quality,* pp. 109–29.

8. The amount of damage attributable to pollution will not necessarily rise smoothly as the quantity of pollution increases.

9. For a fuller treatment of the subject, see Kneese and Bower, *Managing Water Quality,* pp. 131–72. See also Allen V. Kneese and Charles L. Schultze, *Pollution, Prices, and Public Policy* (Brookings Institution, 1975), pp. 22–25 and 85–109.

In principle, effluent taxes on oil emissions into the oceans should be based on the damage and abatement functions. In practice, it will not be possible to impose a true effluent tax. One problem is the absence of information upon which to develop a damage function.[10] The current status of scientific research does not provide adequate data on the effects of persistent hydrocarbons in the ocean, and no market prices exist for most of the biological harm which is suspected to be caused by chronic oil spillage. Another problem is the difficulty of proving the level of discharge that is coming from each polluter.

Alternative to Effluent Taxes

An alternative approach is to use taxes to induce polluters to buy pollution-abating equipment. Polluters buying such equipment would be granted reductions in their tax bills that would be slightly larger than the cost of the equipment. This result could be achieved by setting the tax per ton of oil emitted annually a bit above the figure obtained by dividing the annual equipment cost by the average annual reduction (in tons) of oil spillage that would be brought about by using the equipment.

In deriving the tax rate in this way, the following question must be asked: Is reduction of oil discharges into the ocean worth $10 a ton (or whatever the tax rate happens to work out to be)? In other words, is it reasonable to assume that the damages to the marine environment— whether to marine life, beaches, fisheries, or anything else—from chronic oil spillage total at least $10 per ton of oil spilled? Given the present state of knowledge about the damage caused by the emission of oil into the marine environment, there is no direct way of answering this question. Various tests of plausibility will, however, be used in order to assess the reasonableness of the illustrative taxes presented below.

Although there are several types of technology for reducing oil emissions from the chief source of tanker emissions and numerous possibilities for reducing emissions from offshore petroleum development, the illustrative taxes presented here will be based on only one technological alternative. However, because other technological alternatives are possible, it is recognized that the individual polluter, faced with a tax rate per ton of spillage, could choose the technology that was most economic, given his

10. Obtaining information about the abatement function is a less serious problem, since the results of different tax levels could be learned through trial and error.

particular production costs and processes, and receive credit for it in the form of a lower tax bill.

In calculating the tax rates for the various taxes considered in this chapter, all polluters are assumed to emit the same level of discharges into the ocean until they switch to another technology. All firms using similar new technology are then assumed to emit a uniform (but obviously lower) level of pollutants. Each polluter would, however, be allowed to pay a lower tax if he could prove that his emissions were consistently below average.[11] The burden of proof would be on the polluter. This provision should stimulate the development of reliable devices to measure oil emissions from individual ships and from offshore oil exploration and production installations. (The technology for monitoring emissions from individual sources is not very advanced.) From a practical point of view, this approach appears to hold obvious advantages over one that would require the administrative or tax authorities to prove the level of discharge emanating from each source.

The provision for allowing the individual polluter to pay less tax if his discharges are reduced below the average level is the feature that distinguishes the tax outlined here from a standard investment credit. This component allows the tax to perform an important function of the classic effluent tax, in that the provision constitutes a constant incentive to polluters to reduce emissions.

The possible use of taxes to reduce oil discharges into the ocean will be developed most fully in the case of chronic oil spills by tankers. Illustrative taxes on other sources of oil pollution of the marine environment will be considered more briefly.

Tax on Chronic Oil Spillage from Tankers

According to estimates by the National Academy of Sciences, oil spills from marine transportation account for about one-third of the petroleum

---

11. Precedents for basing a tax on an assumed average level of discharges (as opposed to actual discharges from each polluter) may be found in taxes now in force in Norway and the Netherlands. These countries levy taxes on industrial discharges of sulphur dioxide based on the sulphur content of the fuels burned by the various industries. See Organisation for Economic Co-operation and Development, "A Case Study of Norwegian Measures," OECD Doc. AEY/ENV/73.191, 1973; and OECD, "A Case Study of Dutch Measures," OECD Doc. AEU/ENV/73.20, 1973.

hydrocarbons entering the ocean from all sources.[12] Chronic emissions from routine tanker operations are the single most important cause of discharges from shipping. Spills from tankers occur in connection with waste disposal, during various terminal operations including bunkering, during cleaning and inspection, and, most importantly, during ballasting operations. After tankers unload oil in port, they are too light for the return voyage. The common practice is to fill some tanks with sea water to add weight (or ballast) to the vessel. In the process of discharging ballast water in preparation for taking on new cargo, a significant amount of oil (which had been clinging to the walls of the tanks) is released with the ballast water.

Current Efforts to Deal with Chronic Oil Emissions from Tankers

Efforts to deal with chronic emissions from tankers have concentrated on ballasting operations, partly because they are the chief culprit and partly because the other sources of chronic emissions appear at present to be less amenable to control. The chief methods for eliminating or reducing oil spills from ballasting that are in use, under development, or under discussion, include: "load on top" (LOT), crude oil washing of tanks, and various technologies for separating ballast water from oil cargo tanks (normally referred to as segregated ballast).

LOT is a method for separating oily water from sea water before emptying ballast tanks at sea. The crude oil floats on top of the sea water, which settles to the bottom of the tank and is pumped out into the ocean. The oily ballast water is collected in a special tank. Crude oil washing, a relatively new process, involves washing out tanks with crude oil cargo (instead of with water) during cargo discharge. The solvent action of the crude oil reduces sludge buildup and the clinging of oil particles to tank walls. This helps to clean tanks before ballasting. Segregated ballast can be accomplished by incorporating various changes in the design of new tankers, including double bottoms, double hulls, and separate wing tanks reserved for carrying ballast only. All of these design features would greatly reduce or eliminate the need to put sea water for ballast into cargo tanks.

Any approach to the problem of chronic tanker emissions must be international in scope if it is to have much impact. The main forum for

12. NAS, *Petroleum in the Marine Environment,* p. 6.

international efforts to deal with oil emissions from ships has been the Inter-Governmental Maritime Consultative Organization (IMCO), a specialized UN agency concerned with many aspects of world shipping. Under IMCO auspices, a number of working parties have studied pollution from shipping and have produced various recommendations.

In response to efforts by IMCO and others, the major oil companies, which own a considerable proportion of the world tanker fleet, have instituted LOT technology on their crude oil tankers. A number of independent tanker companies have also instituted LOT. In recent years, a few companies have begun to utilize crude oil washing, but they still practice LOT on the same ships because water is needed in the final rinse.

Although these two methods have contributed considerably to reducing oily ballast discharges, they are not universally regarded as satisfactory solutions to the problem. Both of these procedures depend heavily on crew motivation and attentiveness, and they are subject to human error. In addition, LOT cannot be utilized effectively on short hauls and in certain weather conditions. Finally, neither method is much use on tankers carrying refined products.

Because of dissatisfaction in some quarters with existing methods for tackling the problem, a treaty, the International Convention for the Prevention of Pollution from Ships, was drawn up under IMCO auspices in 1973.[13] The key provision of this treaty sets oil discharge limits from tankers—namely, 60 liters per mile, not to exceed 1/15,000 of cargo capacity for vessels in the present fleet and 1/30,000 of cargo capacity for new vessels.[14] Emissions are absolutely prohibited in the Mediterranean, Baltic, Black, and Red seas, and in the Persian Gulf and the Sea of Oman. In addition, segregated ballast tanks are required for new tankers that are more than 70,000 deadweight tons. This convention, which was not in effect as of early 1977, requires only twelve ratifications to go into force. The twelve countries, however, must meet certain requirements regarding their participation in world shipping.[15]

13. An earlier IMCO treaty, the International Convention for the Prevention of Pollution of the Sea by Oil (12 UST 2989; 327 UNTS 3), was drawn up in 1954 and has been in force for the United States since 1961. This treaty, which has been amended several times, provides for standards for intentional discharges of oil.

14. These standards are much more stringent than those stipulated in the 1954 treaty and in subsequent amendments.

15. As of early 1977, only three countries—none of which meet the requirements —had acceded to the treaty. For a text of the convention and analysis of its provisions, see Charles S. Pearson, *International Marine Environment Policy* (Johns Hopkins University Press, 1975), pp. 84–124.

If the 1973 convention were to go into force, it could be an effective tool for reducing oil emissions from ships. There are, however, a number of problems with some of the treaty provisions. The principal drawback is that the convention requires the installation of segregated ballast tanks, rather than permitting shippers to select the method of control that costs the least—whether it be segregated ballast technology, shipboard retention of wastes to be deposited in shore reception facilities, or equipment for "load on top" and/or crude oil washing (combined with reliable shipboard monitoring devices). Another problem is that the requirement for segregated ballast technology applies to new tankers only; this would encourage tanker owners to hang on to old vessels as long as possible in order to avoid the cost of acquiring the abatement technology.

Calculation of Illustrative Tax on Chronic Oil Spillage from Tankers

In order to show how a tax on chronic oil spillage from tankers might work, it is necessary first to estimate total spillage, assuming a continuation of present technology, in some future year. The year chosen for illustrative purposes is 1985. Second, the tax rate must be derived in the manner described above. Finally, possible future revenue from the tax can be calculated.

The first step—estimating future spillage—is quite complicated. The amount of spillage depends principally on the number of trips made each year by tankers of different sizes. The number of trips depends in turn on the amounts of crude oil and refined products to be shipped over various ocean routes. And shipments of crude oil and products vary largely with the amounts needed by the oil-importing countries.

Appendix C sets forth the basis for an estimate of the chronic oil spillage from tankers in 1985. Table C-1 shows rough forecasts of trade in crude oil and products for 1985. Table C-2 shows major oil shipping movements for 1985. Table C-3 shows the number of tankers required in each of three representative size categories to carry the projected oil shipments and the amount of oil spillage from all tankers operating in 1985. The underlying assumptions for all of these forecasts are explained in the appendix and in the footnotes to the tables. Briefly, the total volume of oil imports in 1985 is estimated at about 1.6 billion metric tons, based on an assumed price for crude oil of about $88 a ton (about $12 a barrel) in 1975 dollars, f.o.b. (free on board) the Persian Gulf. Total spillage from routine tanker operations (usually referred to as "chronic spillage") is estimated at about 3.5 million tons.

On the basis of statements of intent by governments of various OPEC countries to expand exports of refined products and on the basis of recent construction of refineries in these countries, it is assumed that about 12 percent of all oil exports from OPEC countries (except Venezuela) will be in the form of refined products.[16] (In 1974, OPEC countries excluding Venezuela exported almost 4 percent of their total oil exports in the form of refined products.)[17] The environmental implications of the rise in the proportion of world oil trade in refined products and the increased distances over which products appear likely to be hauled are twofold. First, many tankers carrying products do not practice LOT because a number of products cannot tolerate being mixed with sea water. Thus, in practice, many tankers that carry products normally dump their oily ballast water into the ocean. Second, a number of fractions of refined products are regarded by many marine biologists as vastly more damaging to marine life than most crude oils.[18]

Continuation of present practices with regard to chronic emissions—namely, relying on load on top and crude oil washing systems to reduce emissions from tankers carrying crude oil and ignoring, by and large, the problem of emissions from tankers carrying refined products—does not appear to constitute an adequate response to the potential environmental harm caused by discharge from ballasts. The introduction of technologies and/or operating practices that eliminate the need for using cargo tanks in ballasting operations should result in a substantial reduction in oil discharges into the ocean from tankers.

The cost of representative alternative technologies to achieve this result is the basis for the tax rate presented here. Table 4-1 shows the annual cost per vessel of installing segregated ballast tanks on new tankers. The costs are estimated for double bottoms on vessels in the categories of very large crude carriers (VLCCs) and intermediate tankers and for double hulls on

16. Venezuela has been exporting a considerable proportion of its oil shipments to the United States in the form of refined products for years. Venezuela is assumed to continue to export about half of its oil in the form of refined products.

17. *World Energy Supplies, 1950–1974,* UN Doc. ST/ESA/STAT/SER.J/19, 1976, pp. 193 ff. and 280 ff.

18. See Donald F. Boesch, Carl H. Hershner, and Jerome H. Milgram, *Oil Spills and the Marine Environment* (Ballinger, 1974), pp. 7–8.

small tankers (known as "handy" tankers). The table also shows the estimated savings in spillage which could be expected as a result of these technological changes.

As noted previously, there are other technologies for achieving segregated ballast. The technologies used here for illustrative purposes were chosen because several tankers under construction or recently built (1975) in the United States have double bottoms or double hulls, and actual cost figures are available. The costs are applicable to new vessels only.

It may be possible for some of the various technological design alternatives to be installed on existing ships. For example, it might be possible to retrofit some existing tankers so that some tanks now used for carrying cargo could be used exclusively for carrying ballast water. Thus, a tanker would not normally use cargo tanks for ballasting operations. The feasibility of retrofitting any particular vessel depends on various considerations, such as whether the converted ship could still meet trim, stress, and draft restrictions.

Retrofitting has been done only rarely, if at all, because a tanker would lose considerable capacity for carrying cargo. Reliable cost estimates for retrofitting are not available, and it is not known how much of the existing world tanker fleet could be converted. Consequently, this technology is not used as an example of how to calculate the tax. However, it should be noted that, if an international pollution tax on tankers were imposed, tanker owners could choose this option for those ships for which it was technically feasible. Indeed, owners might do so if this option proved cheaper than continuing to pay the full tax for the remaining lives of the ships.

The annual cost per vessel of building segregated ballast capacity in double bottoms on a new VLCC is $193,600 over the twenty-year life of the tanker. This design alternative is estimated to produce a reduction in spillage of about 2,100 metric tons a vessel each year (the spillage associated with ballasting is virtually eliminated). This means that the annual cost of reducing oil emissions is about $92 a ton. For the intermediate tanker, the cost of reducing oil emissions works out to about $54 a ton. For the small handy tankers, the cost is higher, about $105 a ton. (See table 4-1.)

If the value of the oil saved is taken into account, the net cost of the

Table 4-1. *Annual Cost per Tanker of Installing Segregated Ballast Tanks on New Tankers and Estimates of Reduction in Spillage*

Description	VLCC (double bottoms)	Intermediate (double bottoms)	Handy (double hull)
Annual cost of technology (U.S. dollars)	193,600	90,600	70,400
Spillage savings (metric tons per year per vessel)	2,104	1,686	668
Continued spillage from non-ballasting tanker operations (metric tons per year per vessel)	886	375	171

Sources: Cost estimates are from U.S. Congress, Office of Technology Assessment, *Oil Transportation by Tankers: An Analysis of Marine Pollution and Safety Measures* (GPO, 1975), pp. 40–43. Spillage estimates are derived from estimates by Joseph D. Porricelli, Virgil F. Keith, and Richard L. Storch, "Tankers and the Ecology," in *Transactions of the Society of Naval Architects and Marine Engineers*, vol. 79 (1971), pp. 169–221; and from National Academy of Sciences, *Petroleum in the Marine Environment* (Washington, D.C.: NAS, 1975), pp. 8–12.

a. The annual cost of the technology is calculated on the basis of average annual cost over the assumed twenty-year life of the ship, with an interst rate of 12 percent.

new technology is much lower. At $12 a barrel, or $88 a ton, the net cost for a VLCC would be only $4 a ton.[19] Intermediate tankers (assuming that they carried crude oil) would realize a net gain of $34 a ton. Handy tankers would also come out ahead, since the value of the refined products that they carry exceeds by varying amounts the gross cost of the technology per ton of emissions saved.

On the basis of these calculations, the question arises why owners of vessels in the intermediate and handy size categories do not, when ordering new tankers, routinely order them equipped with some segregated ballast system. Although some new tankers have been built with these design features, it is not the usual practice. There may be a number of reasons for this. For example, tanker owners may make different assumptions about the future price of oil and therefore about the value of oil saved than those used here. Some owners may calculate that LOT and/or crude oil washing procedures will work more effectively on their vessels than is assumed here for the average vessel. Whatever the reasons may be,

19. The calculation for the VLCC is as follows: 2,104 tons (spillage savings) multiplied by $88 (value of the oil per ton) equals $185,152. The difference between the annual cost of the technology ($193,600) and the value of oil saved by reduced emissions ($185,152) is $8,448, or about $4 per ton of reduced oil spillage.

it can be assumed that the imposition of a tax of the sort discussed here would serve to highlight the desirability of various abatement technologies.

The tax rate per ton of oil emitted annually for each VLCC should be set slightly above the figure obtained by dividing the annual equipment cost by the average annual reduction of oil spillage that would result from using the new equipment, after the value of the oil saved has been taken into account. The need to take the value of the oil saved into account in setting the level of the tax is obvious in the case of tankers owned by oil companies. Reduced spillage also provides an incentive for independent tanker operators to adopt the new technology. This is so because contracts for tanker services require operators to reimburse shippers for the value of oil lost in transit in excess of a certain specified percent of the total cargo.

A tax of $10 per ton of emissions associated with ballasting operations should be sufficient to induce owners of VLCCs to include segregated ballast when they order new tankers to replace their existing vessels. No such inducement would seem to be needed in the cases of intermediate and handy tankers. On grounds of both equity and logic, however, the same tax of $10 per ton should be applied to their ballasting emissions. If the emission of a ton of oil from a VLCC inflicts damage of at least $10 on the marine environment, the same must be true of a ton of oil spilled by an intermediate tanker or a handy tanker.

The spillage from other tanker operations (such as bunkering and other port operations and from engine wastes) should also be subjected to the same tax of $10 a ton. The impacts of discharges from these operations are similar to those associated with ballasting discharges, and the tax should provide an incentive to reduce them. Thus, the tanker with the design alternative for eliminating ballast emissions would still be liable for taxes on other oil emissions. In effect, there would be a two-tier tax structure on tankers, depending on whether they were equipped with the pollution abatement technology.

To recapitulate, in the absence of contrary evidence, all tankers would be presumed to be responsible for the average annual spillage per deadweight ton attributable to tankers of their category, and they would be taxed at the rate of $10 a ton for such spillage. Tankers with segregated ballast, however, would be credited with the average reduction of spillage brought about by that technology in vessels of their category, and their tax would be reduced accordingly. Tankers could also receive reductions in tax liability upon presentation of proof that their emissions were less than average.

Although no abatement technologies applicable to operations other than ballasting appear to be available at present, there are procedures, such as the exercise of greater care during port operations, that could reduce spillage. Also, as was pointed out above, careful execution of LOT and crude oil washing procedures can reduce ballasting emissions. Monitoring devices that are based on the vessel would probably be required to prove lower-than-average spillage. Accurate monitoring devices are not yet available commercially. Alternatively, a system of precisely certified cargo tonnage at points of loading and unloading might provide the proof. In any case, the tax should be expected to stimulate development of some means of measuring emissions by individual vessels.

Table 4-2 shows how the tax would be levied and the resultant revenues. At the end of twenty years, if not before, the entire tanker fleet would be replaced by vessels with segregated ballast, and the revenue from this part of the tax would be phased out. Therefore, table 4-2 shows the average revenue from the tax on ballast spillage. The revenues from emissions other than ballasting were assumed to continue at a constant level, although they, too, could decline if tanker operators reduced their tax liability by proving rates of spillage that were less than average. Average annual revenue would be about $22 million.

The total estimated revenue from the tax on tanker emissions would be quite sensitive to the price of oil. If the price (in 1975 dollars) is assumed to be $8 a barrel, rather than $12, a tax of $35 to $40 a ton might be needed to induce tanker owners to adopt segregated ballast. At a lower price, moreover, oil consumption, oil shipments, and oil spillage subject to the tax would be much greater than has been assumed. Total revenue of considerably more than $100 million a year would then be entirely possible.

As is generally true of pollution taxes, the tax on chronic oil spills by tankers would probably exert its main economic leverage on the expenditures that it would cause polluters to make for pollution-abating technology. Over a twenty-year period, the illustrative tax described above would induce tanker operators to spend between $4 billion and $5 billion on such technology. In a very real sense, those expenditures represent financial resources that are mobilized to achieve an international objective.

Table 4-2. *Tax Rates and Revenues from a Tax of $10 a Ton on Oil Spillage from Tankers*

Description	VLCC	Intermediate	Handy
Ballast spillage			
Average spillage per vessel (metric tons)	2,104	1,686	668
Tax rate per vessel (U.S. dollars)	21,040	16,860	6,680
Average number of vessels[a]	372	120	507
Average annual revenue yield (U.S. dollars)	7,827,000	2,023,000	3,387,000
Other tanker spillage			
Average spillage per vessel (metric tons)	886	375	171
Tax rate per vessel (U.S. dollars)	8,860	3,750	1,710
Average number of vessels	744	240	1,014
Average annual revenue yield (U.S. dollars)	6,592,000	900,000	1,734,000
Total average annual yield	14,419,000	2,923,000	5,121,000

Sources: Same as table 4–1. Numbers of vessels are derived from data in U.S. Department of Commerce, Maritime Administration, *A Statistical Analysis of the World's Merchant Fleets* (1975), pp. 155–56.

a. The actual number of vessels assumed to be in operation has been divided in half on the assumption that on the average over a twenty-year period half of the vessels will be equipped with segregated ballast and therefore not subject to this part of the tax.

Tax on Spillage from Tanker Accidents

In addition to chronic spillage from routine operations, tankers spill oil into the marine environment as a result of accidents. Because these spills are episodic and because they are sometimes massive, their immediate environmental impacts are different from those resulting from low-level chronic spills. For example, a serious tanker accident in a nearshore area can cause considerable, highly visible damage to beaches and to fish, birds, plants, and other marine life.

There are essentially two categories of damages associated with tanker accidents: private and public damages for which there is an identifiable claimant or claimants, and social costs where the injured party is society as a whole. The private and public damages involving identifiable liable parties and claimants can be taken care of by insurance. This section examines existing insurance arrangements and international law pertaining to these kinds of damages from tanker accidents in order to consider whether and how the international community might wish to improve upon the present system. In principle, an adequate system of insurance and liability law would result in the internalizing of these costs of oil spills from tanker accidents. The purpose of insurance is to share risks and, in general, premiums and payments for damage claims should roughly balance. The insurance approach is therefore a means of accomplishing certain objectives, but it should not be thought of as a means of raising revenue.

Social damages from massive spillage from tanker accidents can be both immediate (such as massive killings of birds and other wildlife) and long run. The potential long-run damages are by and large the same as those that may arise from low-level chronic spillage. For these damages, where there are no individual claimants, insurance is not feasible, but a tax might be used to induce tanker operations to adopt safety measures that would reduce the risk of damage to the marine environment.

Until the early 1970s, the obvious costs attributable to major nearshore tanker accidents—such as the costs for cleaning beaches, the losses to resort industries and to fisheries, and the reduced property values—were often not compensated. International law did not adequately cover the problem of liability for pollution damages from tanker accidents, and insurance coverage was spotty. Tankers flying under "flags-of-convenience" (which in 1974 accounted for about 32 percent of the total world tanker fleet)[20] posed (and continue to pose) a particularly difficult problem. These ships often carried little insurance for pollution and other damages resulting from accidents at sea.

The dramatic case of the *Torrey Canyon,* a vessel registered in Liberia, which ran aground in the English Channel outside British territorial waters in 1967, brought the problem to general world attention. After the *Torrey Canyon* ran aground, its hull crashed onto rocks. At the time the accident occurred, it was the largest and most costly oil spill caused by a tanker accident on record. An estimated 100,000 tons of oil escaped, and

20. "Flag-of-convenience" states include a handful of countries (including Liberia, Panama, and Honduras) which have standards for such matters as ship and crew safety, insurance, and crew wages that differ from those in force in some industrialized countries. These countries have become havens for vessel registration as a means of earning income and foreign exchange. For a shipping company based in an industrialized country, registration in these states is usually cheaper than registration in the country which is the headquarters for the company. The calculation of the proportion of the total world tanker fleet comprised by flag-of-convenience vessels is based upon information supplied by the U.S. Department of Commerce, Maritime Administration, and its publication *A Statistical Analysis of the World's Merchant Fleets* (1975), pp. 155–56.

the costs were calculated at more than $33 million, including damage to the ship and cleanup costs. The media covered the accident extensively, and public attention was caught up in the vain seven-day attempt to pull the ship from the rocks, in the containment and cleanup efforts, and in human interest stories. The owners of the tanker refused to acknowledge any responsibility for the disaster, and they were not covered by adequate insurance. The only assets of the tanker company were two sister ships of the *Torrey Canyon*. With no other viable recourse in international law, British naval forces captured one of the sister ships and released the vessel in exchange for a bond as security for damages claimed by the French and British governments against the tanker company. In the end, the two governments were able to recover a fraction of their claim.[21]

The drama of the *Torrey Canyon* and a number of subsequent major tanker accidents that have resulted in sizable damages have served to stimulate further efforts by IMCO to draw up international treaties to deal with the problem of compensation for damages from accidents. (IMCO had been working on treaties in this area since the late 1950s.) Although several conventions have been drawn up under IMCO auspices, as of late 1977 the most important one, which was drawn up in 1971, was not in force.[22]

As an interim measure, pending ratification of the various treaties, a group of tanker companies formed the Tanker Owners Voluntary Agreement Concerning Liability for Oil Pollution (TOVALOP). Organized in response to strong public pressure arising out of the *Torrey Canyon* disaster, TOVALOP went into effect in late 1969. By the mid-1970s more than 90 percent of world tanker tonnage (excluding Communist countries) was covered by TOVALOP.[23]

In essence, TOVALOP was organized to provide compensation for cleanup costs in the numerous circumstances where legal liability for dam-

21. Paul Burrows, Charles Rowley, and David Owen, "Torrey Canyon: A Case Study in Accidental Pollution," *Scottish Journal of Political Economy,* vol. 21 (November 1974), pp. 237–57.

22. For a description of the main provisions of the 1969 International Convention on Civil Liability for Oil Pollution Damage, the 1971 International Convention on the Establishment of an International Fund for Compensation for Oil Pollution Damages, and other international conventions dealing with oil pollution in the ocean, see Pearson, *International Marine Environment Policy,* pp. 41–47.

23. Gordon L. Becker, "A Short Cruise on the Good Ships TOVALOP and CRISTAL," *Journal of Maritime Law and Commerce,* vol. 5 (July 1974), p. 610.

ages from oil discharges either does not exist or is not generally recognized. The distinction between legal liability and voluntary liability is not entirely clear. Some countries have laws pertaining to liability for damages caused by oil discharges into their territorial waters. Where these laws are enforced, damage claims were and are normally settled by standard "protection and indemnity" insurance policies, which are carried by many large shipping companies. There are, however, gaps in insurance coverage with respect to marine oil pollution damage; namely, accidents occur in various parts of the ocean (not just in the recognized territorial waters of various states), many countries do not have pollution liability laws, and not all shipping companies carry adequate insurance. TOVALOP was created specifically to fill these gaps—the insurance provided under the agreement is supposed to pay claims regardless of whether a country's laws state that liability exists.

TOVALOP provides that either tanker owners, or governments, or both acting jointly be compensated for expenditures made to avoid or mitigate pollution damage which occurs or threatens to occur as a result of oil discharges from a tanker. To qualify for compensation through TOVALOP, the spill can occur anywhere, as long as damage or the threat of damage occurs to "coast lines," which are defined as "land and improvements thereon whether the land adjoins the sea, inland waterways, harbours or other bodies of water."[24] Damage includes physical contamination, but ecological damage is specifically omitted from coverage.[25] The liability limit is $10 million or $100 per gross registered ton, whichever is less.[26]

The Contract Regarding an Interim Supplement to Tanker Liability for Oil Pollution (CRISTAL) was organized in 1971 by the major oil companies to supplement TOVALOP.[27] Under the CRISTAL agreement, coverage is provided for cleanup costs in excess of $10 million up to $30 million (or $125 per gross registered ton, whichever is less). Moreover, CRISTAL allows individuals (in addition to governments and tanker companies) to make direct claims for compensation for damages from an

24. Ibid., p. 611.
25. The Tanker Owners Voluntary Agreement Concerning Liability for Oil Pollution, Clause I. The agreement is available from International Tanker Indemnity Association Ltd., Hamilton, Bermuda.
26. Ibid., Clause VI(A).
27. Becker, "A Short Cruise on the Good Ships TOVALOP and CRISTAL," pp. 616–17.

accident. Thus, while the TOVALOP scheme applies entirely to cleanup costs, CRISTAL was designed to provide compensation for economic damages to injured parties ("third parties"), including losses suffered by commercial fisheries, tourist enterprises, and the like.

In the case of TOVALOP, a shipowner takes out insurance through private brokers against his TOVALOP risks. Under CRISTAL, the oil companies which are participants agree to contribute to a fund which can be drawn upon for damage payments. The resources of CRISTAL have seldom been called on.

In two important respects these voluntary insurance agreements can be regarded as positive developments in the effort to provide compensation for pollution damages. First, the very existence of TOVALOP and CRISTAL stimulated the private insurance industry to offer policies covering third-party damages (for example, losses suffered by coastal fisheries and tourist facilities) and oil cleanup costs stemming from tanker accidents. Second, more than 90 percent of the world tanker fleet is covered by TOVALOP. (Participation in CRISTAL is less widespread.) This is significant because most ships registered in "flag-of-convenience" countries, which in many cases would not have been covered otherwise, participate in TOVALOP. Widespread participation in TOVALOP was brought about by the major oil companies. They required adherence to TOVALOP in order for a tanker operator to be allowed to carry oil owned by the major companies.

The effectiveness of TOVALOP and CRISTAL is not entirely clear. An impartial evaluation of the adequacy of payments for cleanup costs and other pollution damages is very hard to come by. Experience undoubtedly varies from case to case and perhaps among countries in whose territorial waters major accidents have occurred.

Since the creation of TOVALOP and CRISTAL, however, some governments have taken measures to establish legal liability for damages from tanker accidents occurring in their coastal waters. This fact suggests that the coverage provided under CRISTAL and TOVALOP may not be totally satisfactory.[28] At the same time, it is apparent that the present sit-

28. For example, on March 1, 1971, the Canadian government passed an amendment to the Canada Shipping Act wherein a Maritime Pollution Claims Fund was established. (Section 746 of Part XIX of the Canada Shipping Act, as amended.) Payments to the fund, which is regarded as a guarantor for a governmental or private claimant, are made either by owners or by shippers of oil imports and oil

uation represents a significant improvement since the days of the *Torrey Canyon*. If it becomes apparent that the present insurance system is not fully adequate, the best recourse would probably be to improve upon TOVALOP and CRISTAL, or similar schemes, and to work through the private insurance industry. The alternative of designating an international agency to engage directly in the insurance business does not appear practical. In order to stimulate expansion of and improvements in the TOVALOP and CRISTAL systems (should this prove necessary or desirable), the international authorities charged with managing various tanker and other shipping taxes (if they are established) could be given power to impose a tax on any tanker operator whose insurance was clearly inadequate for certain kinds of damage claims. Such a tax would be set at a level that would make it financially advantageous for the operator to obtain the needed insurance rather than to pay the tax.

In addition to the question of whether the coverage for damage claims is adequate, there is the issue of whether the international community should try to get tanker companies to take steps to lower the probability of accidents and to reduce their severity. The insurance premiums are apparently not high enough to induce tanker operators to install technology designed to reduce accidents or to undertake additional safety procedures that might involve extra labor or other costs. If additional inducement is desired, imposing a tanker accident tax might be considered. The rate for such a tax would be set slightly above the annual cost per tanker of the improved safety technology (such as specified navigational aids).

Short of setting up a tanker accident tax, it might be possible to encourage the private insurance industry to offer differential rates for protection and indemnity coverage for pollution damages. At present, the International Tanker Indemnity Association and other insurance syndicates charge all members (tanker companies) the same rate per gross registered ton. Differential rates, which would vary according to the safety equipment and vessel design, should encourage tanker owners to adopt additional safety measures and to incorporate advanced safety features and technologies into the design of new ships. The possibility that a tanker accident tax might be imposed, with its proceeds being used to pay damage claims, might be sufficient encouragement to the insurance industry to offer differential rates.

---

exports. In effect, the fund is a source of compensation of last resort that is supposed to fill gaps in insurance coverage.

Tax on Non-Tanker Cargo Shipping

All oceangoing vessels engaged in international commerce are the source of chronic oil spills into the marine environment. As noted previously, tankers present the greatest problem because of the oily ballast water discharges. Nonetheless, other vessels contribute significantly to the annual influx of oil into the oceans. The amount of spillage per vessel is much less for cargo carriers than for tankers. However, freighters and other dry cargo vessels greatly outnumber tankers, so that their total impact on the marine environment is important. The U.S. Maritime Administration estimates that about 70 percent of oil emissions from shipping are from tankers and 30 percent from other cargo vessels.[29]

In principle, it would be desirable to relate the tax on oil spillage from shipping to the amount of quantifiable damage caused by the emissions. As was discussed in the section on tankers, this is not possible in light of the status of scientific research on the impacts of oil pollution on commercial fisheries and other marine life. As an alternative, the method used here to illustrate the tax is to apply the same tax rate to nonpetroleum cargo vessels as was earlier applied to tankers. It can be assumed that the impact on the marine environment of oil is approximately the same, whatever its source. It must be conceded, however, that this approach has a conceptual weakness because the tax rate on tanker spillage is based on the cost of equipping vessels with devices designed to eliminate ballasting emissions. The ballasting problem, of course, applies only to tankers and has nothing to do with ordinary cargo ship operations.

For illustrative purposes, the cargo vessels were divided into three size categories, in order to reflect the fact that the spillage varies with vessel size. The average size of ships in the small class is about 17,800 deadweight tons (dwt); in the medium class it is about 60,350 dwt; and in the large class it is about 150,000 dwt. Thus, although the tax rate per ton of oil spilled is the same, the tax rate per vessel varies among the three categories. As was the case with the tax on tankers, cargo ship owners would be taxed at the average rate per deadweight ton applicable to each size category.

---

29. U.S. Department of Commerce, Maritime Administration, *Maritime Administration Tanker Construction Program* (1973), p. IV-2.

Table 4-3 shows estimates of the average amount of spillage for vessels in each of the three size categories in 1985, the tax rate per ton of spillage and per vessel, and the total revenue yield from each category of vessel. The size and composition of the world cargo fleet were forecast by assuming that the annual net growth in the fleet over the 1974–85 period would be about the same as it had been in the previous decade. The total revenue yield from the tax in 1985 is estimated at about $2.5 million (in 1975 dollars).

The question arises whether it is worthwhile to levy a tax which produces such a low level of revenue. Moreover, the tax by itself would probably do little to reduce emissions from cargo vessels. If the tax were imposed along with the tanker taxes, however, it would enhance the incentive to industry to develop monitoring devices for individual ships. Such devices could be useful to owners of all classes of vessels who wished to prove that their performance was better than average in terms of chronic oil emissions, in order to be eligible for lower tax rates.

Tax on Offshore Petroleum Production

Oil emissions from offshore petroleum exploration and production in the early 1970s accounted for a very small proportion of total petroleum inputs into the oceans, according to various estimates. For example, the National Academy of Sciences estimates that, out of a total of about 6.1 million metric tons of oil introduced into the oceans from all sources in 1971, only about 1 percent was attributable to offshore petroleum exploration and production.[30]

However, offshore production in 1971 accounted for a relatively small percentage (about 18 percent) of total world production.[31] Offshore output is expected to expand rapidly in the late 1970s and the early 1980s, and it may account for as much as one-third of total world production by the mid-1980s.[32] Total world production of crude oil may then be on the order of 4,250 million metric tons a year (about 85 million barrels a

30. NAS, *Petroleum in the Marine Environment*, p. 6.
31. *World Energy Supplies, 1950–1974*, UN Doc. ST/ESA/STAT/SER.J/19, 1976, p. 193.
32. The assumption that one-third of total crude oil production in 1985 will come from offshore areas is based on estimates from industry sources.

Table 4-3. *Tax Rates and Revenues from a Tax of $10 a Ton on Oil Spillage from Cargo Ships, 1985*[a]

Description	Small	Medium	Large
Average spillage per vessel (metric tons)	12	38	100
Tax rate per vessel (U.S. dollars)	120	380	1,000
Average number of vessels	12,600	1,300	500
Average annual revenue yield (U.S. dollars)	1,512,000	494,000	500,000

Sources: Spillage per vessel is derived by assuming that, within each size category, the amount of spillage is equal to that category's proportion of carrying capacity (dwt) of the total fleet, divided by the number of vessels in each category. Total spillage was estimated at 250,000 metric tons in 1985 and proportions of total carrying capacity were 60 percent, 20 percent, and 20 percent for small, medium, and large vessels, respectively. Spillage estimates were made for emissions from bilges, bunkering, leakages, and vessel accidents. The calculations were based on estimates for spillage from cargo vessels in 1970 by Porricelli, Keith, and Storch, *"Tankers and the Ecology,"* pp. 175–76. It was assumed that the 1970 spillage rates per vessel would be the same in 1985; the changes in total spillage from non-tanker cargo vessels are because of assumed changes in the composition and size of the fleet. The forecast of the 1985 fleet was based on the discussion of supply of shipping services and freight markets in Organisation for Economic Co-operation and Development, *Maritime Transport, 1974* (Paris: OECD, 1975), pp. 47–87.

a. This table includes only vessels over 10,000 dwt as it is assumed that smaller vessels, by and large, will not be involved in international trade to a significant degree in 1985. Small = 10,000 dwt–39,000 dwt; medium = 40,000 dwt–99,000 dwt; large = 100,000 dwt and over.

day).[33] If approximately one-third of total production is from wells in the ocean, about 1,400 million metric tons (28 million barrels a day) will come from offshore areas. Given the projected expansion of world off-shore oil exploration and production, it seems reasonable to assume that the volume of oil spills from these activities will also increase.

According to estimates by the National Academy of Sciences, about three-fourths of oil discharges associated with offshore production in 1971 resulted from unpredictable major accidents.[34] (A major accident is defined as one involving a spill of at least fifty barrels.) These spills can occur during both the exploratory drilling phase and the production phase. A common cause of the episodic spill is the "blowout" which results from undetected and unwanted changes in the pressures down in a hole being drilled. Rapid and unexpected changes in the amount and circulation rate of drilling mud can cause eruptions of liquids or gases as a well is being drilled. Blowouts can occur in wells being drilled from conventional plat-

33. This rough estimate is based on forecasts from "Exxon Press Briefing: World Energy Outlook" (December 9, 1975; processed), for noncommunist countries; U.S. Central Intelligence Agency, "China: Energy Balance Projections," A(ER) 75–75 (November 1975; processed), p. 29; "Russia Faces Tightening Crude Oil Supply Situation," *Oil and Gas Journal,* vol. 74 (April 12, 1976), p. 27.
34. NAS, *Petroleum in the Marine Environment,* pp. 6–7.

forms above the sea and from the relatively new subsea production systems that are in use and under development.

Besides the spills from major accidents, low-level chronic spills from minor accidents occur during both exploratory and production operations. A second cause of low-level chronic emissions is disposal of production wastes. A small amount of oil is lost in the course of discharging field brine. Brines are produced in conjunction with oil and gas, and they are dumped into the sea after passing through an oil-water separator. The amount of oil spilled this way varies with the type and the efficiency of the separator system used.

Natural gas is, of course, produced offshore as well as oil. Although blowouts can occur in connection with drilling for natural gas, the blowouts vent to the surface and are dissipated into the atmosphere. Some of the hydrocarbons from blowouts of gas wells may eventually find their way back to the oceans. The environmental impacts of such blowouts are not known, but they do not appear to be as serious as those associated with spillage of crude oil.

World production of offshore petroleum in 1971 was about 435 million metric tons. The amount of spillage from offshore operations that year has been estimated in the range of between 80,000 and 150,000 metric tons.[35] On the assumption that oil spills from offshore petroleum activities in 1985 will occur at the same rate per unit of output that prevailed in 1971, rough projections have been made of chronic and episodic oil spills from offshore operations for 1985. Offshore crude oil production in 1985 was estimated at about 1,400 million metric tons. Taking the lower of the spillage figures, total spillage in 1985 is thus estimated at about 250,000 metric tons. Low-level chronic spills from producing operations and field brine discharges would account for roughly 50,000 metric tons, and spillage from larger accidents about 200,000 metric tons.[36]

This estimate is probably very conservative. If the spillage estimate at the upper end of the range for 1971 (150,000 metric tons) cited in the National Academy of Sciences study were used as the basis for calculation, total emissions from offshore petroleum activities in 1985 could approach 500,000 metric tons. Furthermore, even with improvements in offshore technology the spillage rate per unit of output may rise instead of either remaining stable or declining. As the depth in offshore drilling in-

35. Ibid., p. 6.
36. The calculations for 1985 are derived from 1971 estimates in ibid., pp. 6–7.

creases, production difficulties are expected to increase. Thus, it is possible that the rate of major accidents may rise.

One argument in favor of an international tax on pollution associated with offshore petroleum exploration and production is that the activity does not fall within the scope of any international agreement or authority. Some countries have fairly stringent safety regulations with respect to offshore drilling, but there is considerable variation in this area and some countries have essentially no effective regulation of this activity. Yet, the problem is global. Oil spills are not usually "local" (except when they occur in enclosed or protected seas). Those oil emissions that are carried out to sea are part of the total level of oil pollution in the oceans. The projected rapid increase in petroleum output from offshore wells and the very real possibility of increased rates of spillage suggest the need for some international means of influencing the conduct of offshore activities in order to minimize potential damages, or at least to assure that compensation for damages is available.

In 1975, the oil companies followed the precedent of TOVALOP and CRISTAL, which provide compensation for some of the economic damage caused by tanker accidents, and launched a somewhat similar scheme to cover damage resulting from their offshore activities. More than thirty companies have joined the Offshore Pollution Liability Agreement (OPOL), thereby accepting liability to pay claims up to a ceiling of $16 million per incident. Although the agreement covered only seven European countries in early 1977, it was designed to be extended to other areas.[37]

The creation of OPOL provides grounds to hope that specific public and private damages caused by offshore oil spills will eventually be provided for. As in the case of tanker accidents, however, it is not clear that the compensation will be adequate and it is far less certain that the coverage will be global. Here, too, the most feasible course appears to be to expand and improve upon the private insurance scheme.

In addition, there is a similar question about whether the international community will be satisfied with providing compensation for damages suffered by individual claimants. Because of public concerns about large catastrophic spills and because there appears to be no satisfactory way to compensate society for the potential long-run damage to the marine en-

37. *Petroleum Economist,* vol. 43 (March 1976), p. 108.

vironment (or for the immediate damage to birds and other marine life), the international community may wish to go beyond the compensation route and work toward reducing the probability of major spillage accidents.

One means of pursuing this objective would be to impose a tax on offshore oil production that would be based on the cost per well of some advanced technology for preventing blowouts. Cost estimates are not available for various technologies that some experts regard as highly desirable, such as remote control systems for operating blowout prevention systems or sophisticated monitoring systems (also with remote onshore controls) to detect "downhole" pressures.[38] Thus, it is not possible in this study to provide an estimate either of the tax rate needed to promote adoption of various advanced technologies or of the revenues that would be generated. In a similar vein, if abatement of chronic emissions from offshore drilling were desired, it would be possible to impose taxes on chronic spillage in terms of the cost of improved systems for separating oil and water.

If a pollution tax on offshore drilling were to be imposed, the tax could be collected on offshore output in various ways, depending on the nature and terms of the contract between the host government and the foreign oil company. For example, in cases where the host government owns the oil and the foreign oil company produces the oil and then buys oil from the host government, the tax could be due at the time of the sale of the oil. The host government would collect the tax from the oil company on the company's share of the output (which usually amounts to a large proportion of the total output) and would pay the remainder of the tax on the government's share of the output. The tax would be paid to a designated international authority. To facilitate compliance, if a government refused to pay the tax, it could be collected at the port of importation to which the crude oil was shipped for refining.

As noted previously, the chief source of spills from offshore drilling activity is the catastrophic blowout. Whenever a major blowout occurs, the whole world knows about it. Statistics on drilling accidents are kept by various maritime and other governmental agencies and are available for public scrutiny. It should be relatively easy for an oil company to maintain

---

38. For an excellent discussion of the various possible technologies which could be developed to improve the safety of offshore drilling, see Don E. Kash and others *Energy Under the Oceans* (University of Oklahoma Press, 1973), pp. 113–37.

statistics on blowouts (in terms of frequency and volume of discharge) and to demonstrate that the company's performance over time is better than average for drilling in a particular part of the ocean. (It is assumed that the tax will provide an incentive for a company to install more effective blowout prevention systems than most that are presently in use.) A company with performance that is better than average would obtain a reduction in its tax bill commensurate with the level of reduced emissions. In the case of chronic spillage, the use of improved oil-water separator systems might be accepted as one proof of better-than-average performance. There is a wide variety in the effectiveness of such systems currently in use in different parts of the world.[39]

Plausibility of the Taxes on Oil Polluters of the Marine Environment

The taxes outlined above would not be justified if their respective yields exceeded the damage to the marine environment caused by the emissions taxed. In the absence of good quantitative information on the effect of chronic oil discharges on the marine environment, it is necessary to find other means of testing the plausibility of these taxes. Both total revenue yields and yields per unit of economic activity (for example, per tanker or per oil well) would diminish over a period of time, as the firms adopted various technologies and practices to abate pollution. The plausibility of these taxes should, however, be tested when yields are at their peak.

Beach recreation and commercial fishing are two of many economic activities that depend on the quality of the marine environment. For illustrative purposes these two activities will be used to provide a basis for judging the reasonableness of the taxes analyzed in this chapter.

The Problem of Tar on Beaches

Chronic oil spills in the open ocean are known to have deleterious

39. NAS, *Petroleum in the Marine Environment*, p. 6. See also U.S. Environmental Protection Agency, "Economic Analysis of Proposed and Interim Final Effluent Guidelines of the Offshore Oil and Gas Producing Industry," EPA-230/1–75–063 (A) (July 1975; processed), pp. III-10 to III-13.

effects on beaches. The 1975 study by the National Academy of Sciences notes:

> Perhaps the most obvious effect of marine oil pollution is the residue stranded on beaches, particularly in areas of high recreational use. This occurs not only when local acute oil spills happen but also on a worldwide chronic basis in areas far from tanker lanes and bunkering ports. The loss of aesthetic resources is substantial. . . . The amount of beach tar collected (in Bermuda) . . . for both 1971 and 1972 . . . is 40 times as much as the average amount found on Golden Beach, Florida, during the same period. . . . The chemical composition of beach tar (as determined by gas chromatography) is indistinguishable from that collected at sea in most parts of the Atlantic Ocean. . . . Because of the widespread occurrence of tar on the surface of the ocean, it is not surprising that other oceanic islands have beach tar comparable in amount with Bermuda. For example, a report from Zanzibar in 1972 implies a tar level . . . comparable with that found in Bermuda. Similar anecdotal evidence implies that the entire coast of the Mediterranean, Red Sea, and much of the remaining coast of Africa is heavily polluted with tar.[40]

In addition to the beaches mentioned above, other coastal areas where pelagic tar (that is, tar from the ocean) is accumulating include the Atlantic coast of South America, much of Central America, various Caribbean islands, Japan and other Asian countries along the tanker route from the Middle East to Japan, and various Persian Gulf states. Pelagic tar has been found on the east coast of the United States, but concentrations are relatively low because of the protection provided by the Gulf Stream.[41]

The tar found on beaches comes from the open ocean and is washed ashore by winds and currents. Scientists have collected the tar from the ocean's surface and from beaches. The tar forms lumps of irregular shapes, with the greatest dimension typically varying from one millimeter to ten centimeters. Samples of the tar lumps found both on beaches and at sea have been chemically analyzed by means of gas chromatography by a number of scientists. Virtually all of the samples analyzed contained iron. This indicates that the source is not natural hydrocarbons present in the ocean, because natural hydrocarbons contain no iron. The iron in the lumps comes from oil that has been in contact with ship tanks, bilges, and engines.

Earlier studies suggested that the oil lumps were entirely from the

40. NAS, *Petroleum in the Marine Environment*, pp. 95–96.
41. Byron F. Morris, biological oceanographer, Bermuda Biological Station for Research, personal communication.

residues of crude oil associated with ballasting.[42] More recent studies, however, show that the chemical composition of the tar lumps varies widely. This suggests that various kinds of crude oils and some refined products are the source of the lumps. The lumps are apparently attributable not only to tank washing operations but also to other tanker emissions (for example, from engine wastes and from bunkering) and to oil spills from sources other than tankers.

There is a wide variety of estimates of the amount of pelagic tar in the oceans, both on the surface and in the water columns. Moreover, there is no good estimate of the proportion of the tar that gets washed ashore on beaches. Systematic quantitative monitoring of beach tar has been done in only a few places—the east coast of the United States,[43] southern California,[44] and Bermuda.[45] Anecdotal evidence in the literature provides the basis for the above listing of the other coastal areas which are polluted with the tar.

Tar is already an important problem from the standpoint of recreation at some beaches, and it could well pose a problem with respect to future development of unutilized coastal areas (for example, much of the Atlantic Coast of South America) for recreational purposes. The major negative impacts of the tar on human beach users are aesthetic. The tar is very unattractive and can easily spoil the appearances of an entire beach area. Moreover, tar tends to cling to human skin when contact is made, either while swimming or while walking along the shore.

The tar lumps do not weather rapidly, either on the shore or at sea. One report notes:

> On high-energy sandy beaches, such as Bermuda's south shore, the self-cleaning action of high surf and offshore winds can remove virtually all the tar

42. Byron F. Morris and James N. Butler, "Petroleum Residues in the Sargasso Sea and on Bermuda Beaches," in *Proceedings of Joint Conferences on Prevention and Control of Oil Spills,* sponsored by the American Petroleum Institute, the Environmental Protection Agency, and the U.S. Coast Guard, March 13–15, 1973 (Washington, D.C.: API, 1973), pp. 521–29.

43. See, for example, J. V. Dennis, *Oil Pollution Survey of the United States Atlantic Coast,* American Petroleum Institute Publications no. 4054 (Washington, D.C.: API, 1959).

44. H. F. Ludwig and R. Carter, "Analytical Characteristics of Oil-Tar Materials on Southern California Beaches," *Journal of Water Pollution Control Federation,* no. 33 (1961), pp. 1123–39.

45. J. N. Butler, B. F. Morris, and J. Sass, *Pelagic Tar from Bermuda and the Sargasso Sea,* Special Publication no. 10 (Bermuda Biological Station for Research, 1975).

in one tide cycle. In rocky areas, even with high wave energy, removal by natural means may be essentially negligible. One tar globule stranded on a rock on Bermuda's south shore was sampled periodically for 16 months. Similar samples were obtained from Martha's Vineyard for 13 months. Both were analyzed by gas chromatography and were found to degrade primarily by evaporation of the more volatile components. Even after a year of weathering, the basic composition of the original paraffinic crude oil was retained.[46]

Another study dealing with the weathering of the tar lumps at sea reports:

In the absence of substantial amounts of nutrients, degradation of crude oil residues occurs on a time-scale of the order of many years: that the normal paraffins of lower molecular weight are the most easily degraded, that the isoprenoids may remain longer, and that many of the components forming the unresolved background of our chromatograms may remain undegraded for many years.

This result is in sharp contrast to the extrapolations frequently made from laboratory experiments on the biodegradation of crude oil by high population microbial cultures in the presence of adequate nutrients. Under such favorable conditions, crude oil may be emulsified and dispersed in a matter of days to weeks. We cannot emphasize too strongly, however, that the rate of microbial degradation in the open ocean is certainly very low, and, except for the normal paraffins, may be essentially negligible compared to other processes which disperse the petroleum residue but do *not* degrade it to carbon dioxide.[47]

It appears that pelagic tar on certain types of beaches does not readily degrade and wither away by natural processes, but tends to accumulate. Therefore, either the tar must be removed (not an easy task, as the lumps get mixed up in the sand and in beach vegetation) or the harm to the beaches must be tolerated.

In Bermuda, which is the best documented case, complaints of tourists and the threatened loss of tourism at resort areas, where the problem was worse than on other local beaches, resulted in the initiation in 1970 of a program to clean the beaches. The estimated annual cost of removing the tar from the public beaches in Bermuda provides the basis for the calculations of harm to beaches presented below. It has seemed reasonable to assume that many other beaches polluted with tar (either beaches which are already developed or future beaches which can be expected to be developed to meet future recreational demands of an expanding world population) will have to institute tar removal programs in order to satisfy

46. NAS, *Petroleum in the Marine Environment*, p. 96.
47. Butler, Morris, and Sass, *Pelagic Tar from Bermuda and the Sargasso Sea*, pp. 103–04.

local needs and to maintain or launch tourist industries. This will be the case particularly if the pollution worsens.

However, it may not always be possible to decide at some future time to develop a beach on a vacant strip of coastline. The concepts of "irreversibility" and "option value" may apply here.[48] When the environment undergoes more or less permanent damage as a result of various human activities, the damage can be regarded as irreversible. Option value, briefly, refers to the value of retaining the opportunity of benefiting from a good or service for which future demand and supply are uncertain. For example, the argument is made that in considering whether to construct a hydroelectric power plant weight should be given to the possibility that benefits from leaving the river in its natural state will, over time, be greater than the benefits from the power plant.[49] A similar type of analysis can be applied to problems of pollution control.[50]

Technically, an irreversible development is one for which the costs of reversal are infinite. At present, it is by no means certain that pollution by pelagic tar—even on rocky, sheltered beaches where the tar does not weather well—is irreversible. It is clear, however, that from a practical standpoint reversal is not certain. If, one generation hence, society wanted to remove several decades' worth of accumulated tar from a strip of coastline, at a minimum the removal would be extremely difficult and costly.

The various taxes on oil spills are, at best, only a partial answer to the problem of pelagic tar on beaches. The tax on chronic spillage from tankers could be expected gradually over a period of twenty years to stop almost all oil emissions associated with ballasting. The effect of the taxes on nonballasting emissions from tankers and from other cargo vessels is less certain, but it would also be gradual. However, even if the taxes alone would not necessarily prevent irreversible damage to beaches, they might still be justified as a means of charging oil users the social costs of chronic oil spillages that their consumption imposes on others. The immediate question is whether the revenue raised by the taxes is a reasonable, or at least not excessive, proxy for those costs.

48. For a thorough discussion of these concepts, see John V. Krutilla and Anthony C. Fisher, *The Economics of Natural Environments* (Johns Hopkins University Press for Resources for the Future, 1975), pp. 39–75.

49. Ibid., pp. 79–150.

50. See Kenneth J. Arrow and Anthony C. Fisher, "Environmental Preservation, Uncertainty, and Irreversibility," *Quarterly Journal of Economics,* vol. 88 (May 1974), pp. 312–19.

Based on rough estimates supplied by the Bermuda Ministry of Agriculture and Fisheries, the annual cost of removing tar from one mile of beach is about $13,600.[51] The average annual revenues from the tanker tax were estimated in table 4-2 at $22.5 million. If the tax were to be justified solely on damages to beaches, approximately 1,650 miles of beach would have to require regular cleaning each year. This distance amounts to not much more than 1 percent of the coastlines of countries along major tanker routes mentioned earlier which are known to be heavily polluted with tar. The estimated revenues from the taxes on cargo shipping are considerably less than $2.5 million a year, so that even fewer miles of beach would have to be cleaned to justify this tax. Therefore, the taxes do not appear to be implausibly high; indeed, they may be too low, in terms of compensating for the full social costs of their operations. This conclusion is reinforced by the strong possibility that beach pollution will prove to be only one of the ways in which chronic oil emissions from ships and offshore petroleum development damage the environment.

Potential Damage to Ocean Fisheries

As noted above in the excerpt from the summary section of the National Academy of Sciences report, *Petroleum in the Marine Environment,* it is possible that a species (either a fish or a part of the food chain upon which a fish depends) may be eliminated as a result of oil pollution damage. It is by no means certain that this is happening; if it occurs, however, the loss of the genetic resource would be irreversible.

There is also the possibility that the productivity of fisheries may be reduced by oil pollution. This subject has received relatively little attention from marine scientists and fishery experts. The latter generally regard overfishing as the chief threat to expanding production from ocean fisheries. Annual growth rates of the world ocean fish catch have been in the

51. Letter to the authors from the Bermuda Ministry of Agriculture and Fishing, August 28, 1975. When the beaches are cleaned, trash and other debris are also removed. However, if the tar were the only item removed, the costs of labor and equipment would still be roughly the same. It was not possible to obtain estimates of how much of the beach-cleaning costs are assignable to tar and how much to litter. We arbitrarily assign three-fourths of the cost to the removal of tar and one-fourth to the removal of other debris because (a) the frequent (sometimes daily) cleaning program was initiated because of the tar problem and (b) tar removal requires special machinery which is not required for litter removal.

range of between 6 percent and 7 percent since World War II. However, one leading expert has forecast a decline in the growth rate to about 3.5 percent or lower in the late 1970s because of overfishing.[52]

Some studies have been undertaken of fisheries along the Louisiana coast in the United States, where oil is constantly discharged into near-shore areas from offshore petroleum production and from refineries. Although these studies have shown no decline in fishery output over the years, the fishing area has been expanded substantially in order to maintain yields.[53] If continued and increasing emissions of oil into the ocean are in fact a cause of diminishing rates of increase in fishery output, they are making it more difficult to provide proteins for an expanding world population.

If productivity from an ocean fishery is found to be diminished because of oil pollution, it is of course possible that the fishery will recover when the pollution is reduced. The record with respect to fisheries damaged by major oil spills from tanker accidents is that most of the fisheries appear to have recovered within two years or less. However, recovery was not complete twelve years after the *Tampico Maru* accident off the coast of southern California and Mexico. Also, scientists have reported that oil deposits in bottom sediments continue to repollute the fishery seven years after a tank barge accident resulted in a catastrophic spill in the area of West Falmouth, Massachusetts.[54] These cases suggest that recovery is sometimes uncertain. Moreover, it is not possible to propose that, if a fishery does not recover, the problem can be solved by cultivating a new fishery elsewhere in the ocean. One expert has discussed the limitations on fish supply:

> With only a few exceptions, marine species of fish are wild stocks not susceptible to cultivation. For these species, the yield of a particular stock can be increased only to a certain point—the maximum sustainable yield (MSY). . . . With regard to increasing the yields of marine fisheries through cultivation practices, there appear to be few opportunities, at present, that are significant.

52. Francis T. Christy, Jr., "Distribution Systems for World Fisheries: Problems and Principles" in National Science Foundation, *Perspectives on Ocean Policy: Conference on Conflict and Order in Ocean Relations* (GPO, 1975), p. 184.

53. NAS, *Petroleum in the Marine Environment*, p. 89.

54. Howard L. Sanders, "Some Biological Effects Related to the West Falmouth Oil Spill" in "Background Papers for a Workshop on Inputs, Fates, and Effects of Petroleum in the Marine Environment," vol. 2 (National Academy of Sciences, 1973; processed), pp. 778–800.

It is extremely difficult and costly to control the necessary elements in an eco-system as wide open as the oceans.[55]

The annual production costs (not including profits) of world fishery output has been estimated at roughly $12.5 billion.[56] This estimate is based on an assumed world fish price of 10 cents to 12 cents a pound, landed, and on an assumed world output of 65 million metric tons. From the point of view of society as a whole, the cost of the pollution abatement technology can be regarded as an additional cost of production in order to preserve the fish. The total annual revenue from the taxes on tankers and other ships—about $25 million—is relatively small (around 0.2 percent of the annual value of world ocean fishery production). This low charge would appear to be not an unreasonable amount to pay to bring about some reduction in chronic pollution of the oceans by oil emissions from ships.

Incidence of Taxes on Polluters of the Marine Environment

The estimated yield of the tax on merchant ships other than tankers is so small as to make any effort to determine its incidence virtually mean-ingless. The tax on chronic oil emissions by tankers could, however, pro-duce significant revenues, particularly if the price of oil were to fall con-siderably below its current level. The extent to which this tax was thought to be absorbed by producers or shifted to consumers could influence the attitudes of different governments toward its imposition.

It is quite possible that the effect of the tanker tax would be submerged by other factors influencing the behavior of the Organization of Petroleum Exporting Countries, with the result that it would be impossible to deter-mine how much of the tax was being absorbed by producers and how much was being passed on to consumers. In all probability, however, the burden of the tax in the short run would fall largely on consumers. With the passage of time, owing to the greater elasticity of demand for petro-leum products in the long run, more and more of the tax could be expected to be absorbed by producers.[57]

55. Christy, "Distribution Systems for World Fisheries," p. 183.

56. Richard N. Cooper, "The Economics of the Law of the Sea Debate" in NSF, *Perspectives on Ocean Policy*, p. 149, and letter to the authors from Cooper, De-cember 19, 1975.

57. See appendix A for a fuller discussion of the incidence of the tanker tax.

Summary

The primary purpose of the taxes examined in this chapter is to give polluters of the marine environment an incentive to reduce the level of their pollution. Ideally, this goal could best be achieved by levying effluent taxes that would vary with the damages caused by pollutants, in this case oil emissions into the ocean. However, scientific knowledge concerning the impact of petroleum on the ocean is inadequate, and market prices cannot be established for some of the suspected damages associated with oil pollution.

An alternative approach is to concentrate on giving polluters a financial incentive to adopt a less polluting technology. This can be done by granting to polluters that adopt such technology a tax credit that is somewhat greater than the cost of the technology. The tax rate would then be related to the cost of the technology and the amount of pollution abatement attributed to it.

This approach could be used to reduce oil spills from routine tanker operations, tanker accidents, and offshore oil production. For example, a tax of $10 a barrel on oil emitted in the course of normal tanker operations should be sufficient to induce operators to buy tankers with some form of segregated ballast when they replace their present vessels. A major source of oil emissions into the ocean would thereby be greatly reduced. The same tax rate might logically be applied to oil emissions from other merchant ships on the ground that the damage caused by a ton of oil is the same, irrespective of its source. A tax at this low rate does not appear unreasonable when its total burden of about $25 million a year is compared with either the cost of cleaning beaches polluted by oil or the total value of the world fishery catch that may be adversely affected by continued oil emissions into the ocean.

CHAPTER FIVE

Revenue from Nonliving Ocean Resources

IT WAS pointed out in chapter 2 that most nonliving resources of the ocean lie close to shore and that the only major exceptions to this rule appear to be hydrocarbons and manganese nodules. Whether these two resources will in fact yield revenue for international purposes depends upon future developments in international law, the economics of their exploitation, and the nature of any international regime established to regulate such exploitation.

National and International Rights to Nonliving Ocean Resources

At the present time, the international community has no legal claim to any part of the ocean or its resources. The ocean areas that lie beyond national jurisdictions do not belong to anyone. The legal problem is therefore one of delineating national rights to the ocean and its resources. Whatever remains might or might not someday be placed under some kind of international regime.

Under existing international law, the ocean—moving outward from the coastline—is divided into five zones: internal waters, the territorial sea, the contiguous zone, the continental shelf, and the high seas.[1] For

1. For a concise summary of the current state of the relevant law of the sea, see R. M. Logan, *Canada, the United States and the Third Law of the Sea Conference* (Montreal: Canadian-American Committee, 1974), pp. 5–18.

present purposes, the first two zones may be treated as one, since in both national control over nonliving resources is complete and unqualified.[2] The contiguous zone, which has been defined in various ways by different nations, overlaps at least in part with the continental shelf. The high seas are what remains outside any national jurisdiction and in the present discussion will also be referred to as the deep ocean.

Unfortunately, the nations of the world have been unable to agree on the geographical extent of any of these zones. Greater or lesser disputes also remain unresolved concerning the nature of national rights within various zones.

With respect to the first two zones (internal waters and the territorial sea), the disagreement that most affects prospects for obtaining revenue from nonliving ocean resources is that over the breadth of the territorial sea. Before World War II, a 3-mile territorial sea was generally accepted. Today, claims range from 3 miles to 200 miles.[3] Most nations would probably now accept 12 miles, but the First and Second Law of the Sea Conferences, held in 1958 and 1960, were unable to resolve this question.

The concept of contiguous zone is not well defined. Various nations have claimed jurisdiction beyond the territorial sea for differing special purposes, including the prevention of smuggling, the exclusion or regulation of foreign fishing boats, pollution control, and the assertion of an exclusive claim to the resources of part of the ocean floor. The geographical extent of such claims has also varied, reaching in some cases as far as 200 miles from shore and into waters that would otherwise be part of the high seas.

One of the achievements of the First Law of the Sea Conference was the 1958 Geneva Convention on the Continental Shelf.[4] Under this convention, coastal states are granted exclusive rights to resources of the adjacent seabed to a depth of 200 meters "or beyond that limit, to where the depth of the superjacent waters admits of the exploitation of the natural resources." Rapid technological advances since 1958 have made

2. Internal waters lie shoreward of the inner boundary of the territorial sea, which is defined by the low tide mark or in some cases by straight base lines. The principal legal difference between these two zones is that foreign ships are generally regarded as having the right of innocent passage through the territorial sea, but not through internal waters.

3. All references to miles in this chapter are nautical miles, which equal 1.15 statute miles.

4. 15 UST 471; 499 UNTS 311.

possible the exploitation of resources lying under deeper and deeper waters. The boundary set by the convention on the rights of coastal states has therefore been moving farther out to sea. It may in fact be argued that the convention, taken literally, now confers on coastal states rights extending well beyond the continental margin into the deep seabed or abyssal plain.[5]

The Third Law of the Sea Conference has among its most important task the delimiting of the various zones of the ocean and the defining more precisely of the rights of coastal and other states in each zone. Although the conference has made progress on some of these issues, formal agreement has not yet been reached on any of them.[6] Some indication of how the conference may come out on these issues is provided by the "informal single negotiating text" that the chairmen of the conference's three main committees prepared during the final weeks of the 1975 session in Geneva and revised during the first New York session in May 1976.[7] It must be emphasized that this text has no legal status. The text was prepared solely as a means of focusing consideration of the large number of complicated issues that the conference is trying to resolve.

Concerning the various zones of the ocean, the negotiating text takes the following key positions:

—Coastal states are given the right to establish territorial seas with a breadth not exceeding 12 miles measured from baselines drawn in accordance with specified rules. (Waters on the landward side of the baselines are defined as "internal waters," which represents no change from established international law.)

—The term "contiguous zone" is applied narrowly to an area extending no more than 24 miles from the baseline from which the breadth of the territorial sea is measured. The coastal state is given the right within the contiguous zone only to prevent or punish "infringement of its customs,

5. The continental margin begins at the point at which the seabed begins to rise toward the land. The margin includes the continental shelf, which slopes gently downward from the shoreline, the continental slope, which inclines more steeply, and the continental rise, which rises gradually from the deep ocean or abyssal plain.

6. The first substantive session of the conference opened in Caracas, Venezuela, on June 20, 1974. Further sessions were held in Geneva in the spring of 1975 and in New York in 1976 and 1977. Another session is scheduled for March 1978 in Geneva.

7. United Nations, Third Conference on the Law of the Sea, *Informal Single Negotiating Text,* UN Doc. A/CONF.62/WP.8, May 17, 1975, and *Revised Single Negotiating Text,* UN Doc. A/CONF.62/WP.8/Rev. 1, May 6, 1976.

fiscal, immigration, or sanitary regulations within its territory or territorial sea."

—Coastal states are given the right to establish an "exclusive economic zone" that can extend no more than 200 miles from the baseline from which the breadth of the territorial sea is measured. Within the economic zone, the coastal state is given (among other rights) "sovereign rights for the purpose of exploring and exploiting, conserving and managing the natural resources, whether living or non-living, of the bed and subsoil and the superjacent waters."

—Coastal states are given similar, and in part overlapping, sovereign rights over the natural resources on or under the continental shelf, which is defined as the natural prolongation of national territories beyond the territorial sea to the continental margin, or for a distance of 200 miles from the baselines from which the breadth of the territorial seas are measured, whichever distance is greater.[8]

—A subzone is in effect established for those parts of the continental shelf that lie more than 200 miles from the baseline. Within that subzone, the coastal state is required to pay to an international authority an unspecified percentage of either the value or the volume of nonliving resources extracted from the continental shelf. (The authority is to distribute these payments in accordance with undefined "equitable sharing criteria.")

If the above definitions of oceanic zones are accepted by the conference, and if—as would almost certainly happen—coastal states then exercise their rights fully up to the specified geographical limits, there would be no prospect whatsoever of deriving revenues for international purposes from the exploitation of ocean resources within 200 miles of land. In the parts of the continental shelf that extend more than 200 miles from land, only an unspecified, but presumably small, portion of the resources extracted from the seabed and the subsoil might conceivably be available for international purposes. In fact, considerable doubt exists concerning the willingness of coastal states to give up any part of the resources of the continental shelf. They may well insist on reserving all such revenues for themselves. This would limit the possibilities for international revenues to the deep ocean areas beyond the continental margin and at least 200 miles from land.

8. This definition seems to give a different meaning to "continental shelf" than is customary (see footnote 5 above). The definition can be interpreted to include everything from the outer edge of the territorial sea to the abyssal plain.

Hydrocarbons

The seabed committee of the United Nations estimates that the equivalent of 284 billion barrels of oil or 13 percent of total offshore resources of oil and gas may ultimately be recoverable from the ocean area more than 200 miles from land.[9] The U.S. National Petroleum Council (NPC) estimates that the same area contains 5 percent to 20 percent of the offshore oil and gas that may ultimately be recoverable, but believes that a quantitative estimate of the resources of that area cannot be made, given the present state of knowledge.[10] Both the seabed committee and the NPC believe, however, that most of the hydrocarbon resources lying seaward of 200 miles are on the continental margin. The committee allows for no such resources on the abyssal plain, and the NPC estimates that at most 2 percent of all offshore oil and gas lies beyond the continental margin.

A potentially important question is whether significant deposits of oil and gas will be found on the part of the continental margin that may remain outside the control of coastal states, that is, on the continental slope and the continental rise more than 200 miles from land.[11] The NPC assigns 5 percent to 18 percent of all offshore oil and gas resources to this area.[12] The seabed committee makes no comparable estimate, but notes that the upper part of the slope holds promise for hydrocarbons and that opinions differ concerning the potential of the lower part of the slope and the rise.

The most that can be concluded from the above brief survey is that some oil and gas resources of uncertain importance may remain outside national jurisdictions. As was noted earlier, it is also possible that a fraction of the revenue from any future exploitation of hydrocarbon deposits on the part of the continental shelf lying more than 200 miles from shore

9. See "Economic Significance in Terms of Sea-bed Mineral Resources, of the Various Limits Proposed for National Jurisdiction," UN Doc. A/AC.138/87, June 4, 1973, especially pp. 37–39.

10. National Petroleum Council, *Ocean Petroleum Resources* (Washington, D.C.: NPC, 1975), p. 17.

11. Posing the question in this way assumes that any future international convention on the continental shelf will define the shelf in geological terms. This is not, however, a foregone conclusion. As was pointed out earlier, the shelf could conceivably be given a legal definition that would include the slope and the rise, thereby preempting all of the continental margin for the coastal states.

12. NPC, *Ocean Petroleum Resources,* p. 17.

would be available for international purposes. But neither of these possibilities has practical significance unless the resources in question can be found, extracted, and brought ashore at acceptable cost. Whether or not this will prove to be the case depends on the international prices of oil and gas and on the special factors that influence the cost of offshore exploration and production.[13]

Among these factors are distance from shore, water depth, and climatic conditions. All of these factors work with special force against the early exploitation of hydrocarbon resources located more than 200 miles from land. By definition, moving oil and gas to shore is a problem. (This is especially serious in the case of gas, since it must be moved by pipeline.) Also, most of the area more than 200 miles from shore is in fairly deep water; only a small part of the area is even on the continental shelf. The NPC report cited above estimates that under moderate climatic conditions (for example, in the Gulf of Mexico) development and production expenses in 1,000 meters of water would be nearly five times as great as they would be in water only 200 meters deep. Costs are even higher in regions subject to severe climatic conditions, such as the Arctic, where a substantial part of the continental margin that extends farther than 200 miles from land happens to be located.

Because of these special cost factors, the economic feasibility of exploiting hydrocarbon deposits in deep water more than 200 miles from land would depend on the availability of the economies of scale provided by large reservoirs and high productivity per well. The NPC estimates that, even under favorable assumptions concerning the price of oil and the size of the government take,[14] oil production at a water depth of 1,000 meters would not provide an adequate return on invested capital (defined as 20 percent) unless the reservoir being exploited contained at least 100 million barrels of oil. Thus, the question is not simply whether oil can be found, but whether it can be found in large reservoirs.

All things considered, there would appear to be little basis for optimism concerning prospects for deriving revenues for international purposes by exploiting hydrocarbon deposits under the seabed. The amount of such resources lying beyond the continental shelf is uncertain and may turn out

13. Ibid., pp. 24–38.
14. Ibid., p. 35. The NPC assumes the price of oil to be $11 to $13 a barrel in 1974 dollars and "no royalties or bonus and tax provisions similar to those applying to U.S. federal offshore leases."

to be quite small. Substantial deposits of oil and gas may exist in the part of the continental shelf that extends more than 200 miles from land, but whether such deposits will provide any revenues for international purposes is open to serious question. The Law of the Sea Conference may in the end fail to require coastal states to give up any part of the proceeds of exploiting nonliving resources in the outer part of the continental margin.

Even if the resources are there and international access to them is not foreclosed, it does not follow that either governments or private enterprises will be prepared to invest substantial sums in the search for oil and gas 200 miles and more from land. If they do, future prices may not cover the costs of developing and producing oil and gas from such deposits as may be located. Because of these uncertainties and technological limitations,[15] the more accessible offshore areas, closer to land and in shallower water, will be explored and developed first. Such areas will almost certainly be under the control of coastal states and therefore will not produce revenues for international purposes.

Of course, prospects may improve with time. Continued advances in the technology of exploring for and exploiting oil and gas resources in deeper and deeper water appear likely, and exhaustion of lower cost sources of hydrocarbons on land and close to shore may make those far from land more attractive. It is even possible (although not very likely) that oil and gas deposits will be discovered beneath the floor of the deep ocean about whose geology much remains to be learned.[16] Even though oil and gas

15. Although recent technological advances have made research drilling possible in water depths exceeding 3,000 meters, the petroleum industry is not expected to become capable of conducting petroleum development operations in water as deep as 500 meters before 1980. NPC, *Ocean Petroleum Resources,* pp. 20 and 30.

16. The fact that "the geology of the deep ocean floor is fundamentally different from that of the continents and their continental shelves . . . can be used as an argument for and against the probability of discovery of large oil fields beneath the oceans. Since the geological regime is quite different from that on land, it could be hoped that some new type of oil deposit might be found in the sediments of the sea floor. However, one should not be very optimistic, since the deep sea sediments, which on any supposition are needed to provide sources of oil accumulation, are probably only a few thousand feet thick beneath the oceans. On the other hand, the history of oil discovery shows that unexpected discoveries do occur, and therefore, there may be some rich fields on the ocean floor, and also on the continental slope." T. T. Gaskell, "Oil and Natural Gas: Evaluation, Exploration and Exploitation of Deep Water Petroleum," in *Symposium on the International Regime of the Deep Sea-Bed* (Rome: Accademia Nazionale dei Lincei, 1970), p. 94. The Deep Sea Drilling Project (1968–75) failed to locate oil in the deep basins of the South Atlantic, but it did reveal the existence of large deposits of black shale. See Walter Sullivan, "Atlantic Oil Drilling Yields Shale," *New York Times,* November 14, 1975.

deposits beneath the ocean floor are not likely to provide revenues for international purposes for many years, and may in fact never do so, it would not be prudent to exclude this possibility entirely. The possibility should be taken fully into account in working out the nature and functions of any international regime to regulate the exploitation of ocean resources beyond national jurisdictions.

The legal status of Antarctica provides an additional reason for keeping open the possibility of international regulation of hydrocarbon resources beneath the ocean floor. As was noted in chapter 2, the waters surrounding Antarctica do not necessarily fall under the jurisdiction of any nations, and the establishment of an international regime over the area is by no means out of the question. In that event, substantial hydrocarbon resources might become available for exploitation under international auspices. The U.S. Geological Survey has reportedly estimated that 45 billion barrels of oil and 115 trillion cubic feet of natural gas could be recovered from the continental shelf of west Antarctica.[17]

Manganese Nodules

Manganese nodules are potato-sized objects consisting principally of iron, manganese, silica, and lime in varying proportions, plus smaller amounts of nickel, copper, and cobalt.[18] These nodules are found on the surface of the seabed in many parts of the world, principally in deep ocean areas that appear destined to remain outside any national jurisdiction.[19] A number of large firms (mostly American, but also Japanese and European) have shown an interest in mining the nodules for their nickel, copper, and cobalt content, and in the case of some firms also for their manganese content. Several of these firms have invested substantial amounts of money in the development of mining and processing techniques. None of them, however, has thus far begun actual mining opera-

17. For discussion of possible hydrocarbon resources near Antarctica, see Jonathan Spivak, "Frozen Assets?" *Wall Street Journal,* February 21, 1974; and "Talking About Antarctica," *The Petroleum Economist,* November 1975, pp. 411–13.

18. Even smaller amounts of vanadium, molybdenum, and zinc are also typically present.

19. "Economic Significance, in Terms of Sea-bed Mineral Resources, of the Various Limits Proposed for National Jurisdiction," UN Doc. A/AC.138/87, June 4, 1973, pp. 18–26.

tions on a commercial scale.[20] Therefore, whether manganese nodules can be mined profitably remains an open question. And if they can, the magnitude of any margin above the normal return on investment in industries with similar risks (that is, the economic rent) that might be diverted to international purposes cannot easily be estimated.

Both the economics and the politics of the problem are complicated by the physical properties of the nodules. Depending upon the process used, either three (nickel, copper, and cobalt) or four (nickel, copper, cobalt, and manganese) of the commercially interesting components of the nodules are joint products; that is, it is not possible to separate out one mineral without simultaneously getting the others. In the process in which manganese is not a joint product, it can be derived as a by-product through additional processing steps.[21] Since the proportions in which nickel, copper, cobalt, and manganese occur in the nodules differ by wide margins from the proportions in which those minerals are used, large-scale mining of nodules could have a disproportionate impact on the prices of some of the minerals extracted from them. Understandably, the countries that export these minerals see this possibility as a potential threat to their foreign exchange earnings. Before attempting to weigh the seriousness of this threat, however, it is necessary to inquire more generally into the economic prospects of the nodule mining industry.

Early assessments of the profitability of nodule mining were rather pessimistic. One widely quoted analysis concluded that nodule mining would be unprofitable even at current (1968) prices of the minerals extracted from the nodules.[22] Since nodule mining would increase the supply and, it was assumed, depress the prices of those minerals, prospects were seen as even more bleak. Another analysis, using different assumptions concerning metallic content of nodules, transport requirements, and

20. See Arnold J. Rothstein and Raymond Kaufman, "The Approaching Maturity of Deep Ocean Mining—the Pace Quickens," in *Mineral Resources of the Deep Seabed,* Hearings before the Subcommittee on Minerals, Materials and Fuels of the Senate Committee on Interior and Insular Affairs, 93 Cong. 1 sess. (1973), pt. 1, pp. 201–21. See also Allen L. Hammond, "Manganese Nodules (II): Prospects for Deep Sea Mining," *Science,* vol. 183 (February 15, 1974), pp. 644–46.

21. See Hammond, "Manganese Nodules (II)," pp. 645–46; and "Economic Implications of Sea-bed Mineral Development in the International Area: Report of the Secretary General," UN Doc. A/CONF.62/25, May 22, 1974, p. 33, n. 64.

22. Philip E. Sorensen and Walter J. Mead, "A Cost-Benefit Analysis of Ocean Mineral Resource Development: The Case of Manganese Nodules," *American Journal of Agricultural Economics,* vol. 50 (December 1968), pp. 1611–20.

processing costs, concluded that nodule mining would be marginally profitable only if the entrepreneur did not have to provide the substantial development capital required.[23]

These early assessments were made in the absence of much directly relevant information concerning the capital requirements and operating costs of a nonexistent nodule mining industry. Of necessity, arbitrary assumptions were made concerning the extent to which nodule mining might resemble existing economic activities. The industry still does not exist on a commercial scale, but much research and development work has been done and some of the results have been made public.[24] A somewhat better basis therefore exists for estimating the economic prospects of the industry.

One of the most thorough analyses of this subject was conducted by the United Nations staff charged with preparing for the Third Conference on the Law of the Sea.[25] The UN staff attempted to determine the profitability of two kinds of nodule mining operations that are in fact under consideration by commercial interests: a "four-metal" operation that would mine and process 1 million tons of nodules a year and extract all four of the principal metals present (manganese, nickel, copper, and cobalt) plus several minor metals; and a "three-metal" operation that would mine and process 3 million tons of nodules a year and extract all metals except manganese. The conclusion, which was reached on the basis of rather complicated assumptions, was that the four-metal operation might return 43 percent to 109 percent annually on total investment and the three-metal operation might return 54 percent to 94 percent. The return on investment in the UN study's medium case was 69 percent for the four-metal operation and 73 percent for the three-metal operation.

These estimates of the profitability of nodule mining depend upon a number of critical assumptions, including the scale of the mining and processing operations, the metallic content of the nodules, the capital investment required, the operating costs, and the prices of the various metals extracted from the nodules. There is no reason to depart from the assump-

23. Commission on Marine Science, Engineering and Resources, *Marine Resources and Legal-Political Arrangements for Their Development,* vol. 3 (GPO, 1969), pp. VII-179 to VII-186.

24. Comprehensive information is still not available because the firms in possession of such information regard it as proprietary.

25. "Economic Implications of Sea-bed Mineral Development in the International Area," UN Doc. A/CONF.62/25, May 22, 1974, pp. 26–44 and 64–70.

tions made by the UN staff with respect to the scale of operations (1 million tons and 3 million tons for four-metal and three-metal operations, respectively), since these assumptions are based securely on statements by industry representations. All of the other assumptions made by the UN staff are also quite reasonable in light of the evidence available, but it is worthwhile considering possible variations in each of them and asking how such variations might affect the profitability of the industry.

The metallic content of nodules varies from place to place on the ocean floor. All other things being equal, firms interested in mining nodules will try to concentrate their efforts on areas with the richest nodules. They might not, however, achieve this objective. It is therefore interesting to compare the assumptions of the UN study concerning the metallic content of nodules with the range of economically acceptable percentages presented by Wayne J. Smith of the Woods Hole Oceanographic Institution. (See table 5-1.) Since the UN study deliberately presented estimates for "high grade nodules," it is not surprising that the UN percentages (except for cobalt) are at the upper end or in the middle of Smith's range.

If Smith's low figures are substituted for the percentages assumed by the UN staff in its medium case (and no other changes are made in the UN staff's assumptions), the net annual revenue of a four-metal operation producing 1 million tons of nodules in 1985 would fall from $104 million to $75 million, and the annual rate of return on investment would fall from 69 percent to 50 percent. A similar substitution would reduce the net annual revenue of a three-metal operation producing 3 million tons of nodules from $193 million to $148 million, and its rate of return on investment from 73 percent to 56 percent.[26]

A variety of estimates of both capital requirements and operating costs have been made by industry sources and independent analysts. Nina W. Cornell has presented these different estimates in a well-organized form.[27] Cornell shows that estimates of the capital cost of a four-metal operation producing 1 million tons may range from $110 million to $250 million, and that similar estimates for a three-metal operation producing 3 million tons may range from $220 million to $400 million. The medium estimates

26. Since the UN study used 1972 industry data, all estimates of costs and revenues of nodule mining are in 1972 dollars.
27. "Manganese Nodule Mining and Economic Rent," *Natural Resources Journal* (October 1974), pp. 519–31.

Table 5-1. *Metallic Content of Dry Nodules*
Percent

Metal	UN study	Smith study
Manganese	24.0	20.0–25.0
Nickel	1.6	1.2–1.6
Copper	1.4	1.2–1.6
Cobalt	0.2	0.2–0.5
Other metals	0.3	not given

Sources: "Economic Implications of Sea-bed Mineral Development in the International Area: Report of the Secretary-General," UN Doc. A/CONF.62/25, May 22, 1974, p. 28; Wayne J. Smith, "Economic Considerations of Deep Mineral Resources" (Woods Hole Oceanographic Institution, October 1972; processed), p. 3.

used in the UN study ($150 million and $265 million, respectively) lie in the lower part of these ranges.[28]

It is instructive to substitute Cornell's maximum capital cost figures in the UN study's calculations of the possible profitability of the nodule mining industry.[29] In the case of the four-metal operation, this substitution reduces net annual revenues from $104 million to $94 million and the rate of return on invested capital from 69 percent to 38 percent. A similar substitution in the case of the three-metal operation reduces net annual revenues from $193 million to $180 million and the rate of return on invested capital from 73 percent to 45 percent.

The range of operating costs shown by Cornell is $55 to $74 per ton of nodules for a four-metal operation and $21 to $54 for a three-metal operation. The UN study in its medium case used $66 and $25, respectively, for total costs. If Cornell's high figures are substituted in the UN study's calculations, net annual revenues of a four-metal operation are reduced from $104 million to $96 million and the rate of return on investment falls from 69 percent to 64 percent. Making a similar substitution in the case of a three-metal operation cuts net annual revenues from $193 million to $156 million and the rate of return from 73 percent to 59 percent.

The most difficult set of decisions that must be made in trying to estimate the profitability of the nodule mining industry is assigning prices to

28. "Economic Implications of Sea-bed Mineral Development in the International Area," UN Doc. A/CONF.62/25, May 22, 1974, p. 71.

29. Somewhat arbitrarily, the differences between Cornell's maximum capital costs and those of the UN study are amortized over a period of ten years, thereby increasing annual costs of the four-metal operation by $10 million and those of the three-metal operation by $13 million.

each of the metals that are to be extracted from the nodules. Applying current prices to projected output in 1985 would almost certainly be wrong, but estimating what prices will prevail almost a decade from now is all but impossible. Probably the best that can be done is to follow the approach adopted by the UN staff and other analysts. That approach is to adjust current (or recent) prices for the impact on metals markets of the output of the new nodule mining industry.

The first problem to be faced in assessing this impact is forecasting entries into the still nonexistent nodule mining industry. On the basis of what is known about the plans of the interested firms, the UN study forecasts that mining operations by the first firm will begin in mid-1979 and that 15 million tons of nodules will be mined in 1985. Again, on the basis of known plans, the UN study estimates that manganese will be extracted from only 4 million tons of nodules.[30] (That is, 11 million tons will be mined by three-metal operations.)

Using the assumptions concerning metal content that were noted earlier, the UN study calculates that in 1985 the nodule mining industry will produce the following amounts of metal from nodules (in metric tons) :[31]

Manganese	920,000
Nickel	220,000
Copper	200,000
Cobalt	30,000
Other metals	38,000

The UN study notes that this estimate of manganese production could prove to be low if more firms engage in four-metal operations, and that the estimates for cobalt and other metals could also be on the low side since some nodule deposits are richer in these metals than was assumed.

The effect of these projected production levels on prices would depend on complex interactions among a number of factors, including the rate of growth of the market for a given metal at existing prices, the price elasticity of demand for the metal (which would depend in part on the technical feasibility of substituting one metal for another), and the reactions of land-based producers to the invasion of their market by the new nodule mining industry. These factors are different in the cases of each of the four principal metals that can be extracted from manganese nodules.

30. "Economic Implications of Sea-bed Mineral Development in the International Area," UN Doc. A/CONF.62/25, May 22, 1974, p. 31.
31. Ibid., p. 32.

A rough indication of the probable size of the price effect of projected production of the nodule mining industry can be obtained by estimating the share of the world market for each metal that the new industry will have to take over in 1985 if it is to sell its output. This has been done in table 5-2, using assumptions concerning the rates of growth of the metal markets in question drawn from the UN study.

As table 5-2 indicates, copper from nodules is not likely to occupy more than an insignificant fraction of the total world market for this metal in 1985. This prospect, along with the fact that the demand for this versatile metal is relatively elastic, makes it unlikely that nodule mining will have much effect on the price of copper.

At first sight, a somewhat similar conclusion might appear to be warranted in the case of manganese, but this line of reasoning would ignore two important facts. First, manganese is used almost exclusively in the production of steel, and the demand for manganese is determined by the level of production of the world's steel industry. Thus, the price elasticity of demand for manganese is relatively low. Second, most manganese is used in the form of ferromanganese; the market for pure manganese metal, which will be the product of the nodule mining industry, is quite small.[32]

Manganese metal is priced much higher than ferromanganese in terms

Table 5-2. *Possible Penetration of Metals Markets by Output of Nodule Mining Industry, 1985*

Metal	Estimated world demand (thousands of metric tons)	Estimated production from nodules (thousands of metric tons)	Share of nodule mining industry (percent)
Manganese	16,400	920	5.6
Nickel	1,220	220	18.0
Copper	14,900	200	1.3
Cobalt	60	30	50.0

Source: "Economic Implications of Sea-bed Mineral Development in the International Area," UN Doc. A/CONF.62/25, May 22, 1975, pp. 33–41. Estimates of world demand (not including Communist countries) in 1985 were derived by assuming the following annual growth rates: manganese, 5 percent, 1972–85; nickel, 6 percent, 1972–85; copper, 5 percent, 1972–85; cobalt, 6 percent, 1972–80, and 8 percent, 1981–85. See the text for derivation of estimates of production from nodules.

32. In 1972, consumption of pure manganese metal in the United States was only about one-thirtieth as great as consumption of ferromanganese. U.S. Department of the Interior, Bureau of Mines, *Minerals Yearbook 1973,* vol. 1 (1975), p. 747.

of manganese content.[33] The only way that the manganese metal extracted from nodules could be marketed would be as a replacement for ferromanganese in the making of steel. As a consequence, it is likely that the price of manganese metal would fall at least to the same level as the implicit price of the manganese content of ferromanganese. The increased total availability of manganese for steelmaking could cause a further, presumably modest, fall in the prices of both manganese metal and ferromanganese.

As table 5-2 suggests, nodule mining is likely to have the greatest impact on the price of cobalt. Land-based mining of this metal is likely to increase along with the mining of copper and nickel of which cobalt is a by-product. The projected output of the nodule mining industry could probably be marketed only if prices fell substantially from present levels.[34] The fall in the price of cobalt might not be checked until it reached the price of nickel. At that price, it could be substituted for nickel in some uses. Since projected cobalt production is only about 2.5 percent of the estimated nickel market in 1985, such substitution would have little effect on the price of nickel.

The amount of nickel that may be extracted from nodules in 1985 would, however, exert strong downward pressure on the price of that metal, unless land-based producers made compensatory adjustments in the level of their output. In a competitive industry, there would be no reason to expect this to happen. But in the case of nickel mining, which is an oligopoly dominated by one firm, it is quite possible that the growth of land-based production would be slowed down sufficiently to permit the new nodule mining industry to market its output without causing a fall in the price of nickel.[35] An alternative market strategy for the nickel oligop-

33. During most of 1973, the U.S. price of standard high-carbon ferromanganese was $200 a long ton, or about 11.5 cents a pound for its manganese content of 78 percent. The price of manganese metal was 32.25 cents a pound. U.S. Department of the Interior, *Minerals Yearbook 1973*, p. 749.

34. Land-based production of cobalt in 1972 was already nearly 25,000 metric tons. (U.S. Department of the Interior, *Minerals Yearbook 1973*, p. 419.) If, as projected in table 5-2, the total market in 1985 is 60,000 tons and if half of the total is taken over by the new nodule mining industry, the land-based producers would be able to expand output by only 5,000 tons—an annual rate of growth of only about 1.5 percent, which is implausibly low.

35. This could be done fairly easily. In 1973, world smelter production was 740,000 short tons, or 670,000 metric tons. (U.S. Department of the Interior, *Minerals Yearbook 1973*, p. 869.) If, as table 5-2 projects, the market for nickel is

oly would be to depress prices sufficiently to make nodule mining unprofit-able. This course would, however, expose the oligopoly to substantial political risks. To the extent that the oligopoly did not make way for nickel extracted from nodules, the price would be forced down. The rate of decline would probably be fairly gentle, however, since the uses of nickel are growing, and increasing amounts of the metal can be sold at any given price.

Deriving specific prices from the above general analysis of the possible impact of nodule mining on metals markets is obviously very difficult. Prediction of future prices is out of the question. The best that can be hoped for is to arrive at illustrative prices that will throw some light on the economic prospects of the nodule mining industry. Table 5-3 compares three sets of prices: those used in the UN study, those used by Cornell in the article cited above, and an alternative set developed in the course of this study.

Some of the differences between the UN study and Cornell resulted from the use of different starting points. The UN staff began with December 1973 or January 1974 prices; Cornell used 1974 prices for all metals except manganese, for which she used 1971 prices. A case can be made for beginning with average 1972 prices, which do not reflect the 1973–74 upsurge in the prices of many primary commodities. The alternative set of prices has been developed on this basis.[36]

The UN staff cut the price of manganese in half to allow for the impact of nodule mining on the small market for manganese metal. Cornell went further and reduced the price of manganese metal all of the way to that of the manganese contained in ferromanganese. Given the low elasticity of demand for manganese in all forms, we believe that Cornell's position is the more plausible one. In fact, it would not be unreasonable to postu-late an additional fall in the price of both manganese metal and ferro-manganese of, say, one cent per pound of metal content.

In her basic analysis, Cornell assumes no fall in the price of nickel, but she also considers an alternative case in which the price of nickel is arbi-

---

1,220,000 metric tons, the land-based producers could make way for 220,000 metric tons from the nodule mining industry and still expand their output at an annual rate of about 3.5 percent. (From 1971 to 1973, output grew at an annual rate of 4 percent.)

36. The source used was U.S. Department of the Interior, Bureau of Mines, *Minerals Yearbook 1972*, vol. 1 (1974).

Table 5-3. *Alternative Prices of Metals Extracted from Manganese Nodules*
U.S. dollars per metric ton

Metal	UN study	Cornell	Third alternative
Manganese	350	243	220
Nickel	3,300	3,374	3,043
Copper	1,760	1,499	1,125
Cobalt	4,400	3,374	3,043
Minor metals	3,300	2,844	2,646

Sources: "Economic Implications of Sea-bed Mineral Development in the International Area," UN Doc. A/CONF.62/25, May 22, 1974, p. 66. Nina W. Cornell, "Manganese Nodule Mining and Economic Rent," *Natural Resources Journal* (October 1974), pp. 519–31 (Brookings Technical Series Reprint T-010). The third alternative was developed by the authors of this study; see the text for its explanation.

trarily assumed to fall 40 percent. The UN staff, starting with a higher base price, assumed that nodule mining would reduce the price of nickel about 8 percent. If the nickel oligopoly is assumed to be tightly organized, either of Cornell's cases are more plausible than the assumption made by the UN staff. (That is, the oligopoly might be expected either to defend the current price or to try to destroy the emerging nodule mining industry by cutting prices drastically, but not to let prices slip downward only slightly.) But if there is some slack in the market discipline imposed by the oligopoly, the UN staff's position becomes more realistic.

There is no way to determine which view is right. However, given the long lead times in mining enterprises and the uncertainty concerning the output of the nodule mining industry, the nickel oligopoly might find it difficult to adjust land-based nickel production exactly to the emerging production from nodules. If adoption of a strategy of predatory price cutting is ruled out because of the political risks, it does not seem unreasonable to project a fall of, say, 10 percent in the price of nickel as the result of nodule mining.[37]

Neither the UN staff nor Cornell expect nodule mining to have an appreciable effect on the price of copper, and that position seems to be virtually unassailable for reasons that have been explained above. The differences in their price assumptions depend on their starting prices. Cornell began with the December 1973 price of $1.05 a pound and arbi-

37. Starting with the 1972 price for electrolytic nickel of $1.53 a pound, this produces a price of $3,043 a metric ton. Most of the difference between this price and the price of $3,300 used in the UN study results from the differences in starting prices.

trarily reduced it by about 25 percent on the ground that it seemed abnormally high, but ended with a price well above the 1974 level. The 1972 price of 51 cents a pound used without adjustment in the third alternative is substantially lower than Cornell's 1974 price of 68 cents a pound. Which price is most nearly "right" is impossible to say. The important point to be made is the susceptibility of the copper market to fluctuations over a fairly wide range of prices.

The UN staff assumed that nodule mining would cause the price of cobalt to fall to about two-thirds of the December 1973 level. Cornell argued that the price of cobalt would fall to the price of nickel, a position with which we agree. A somewhat lower price, however, has been assigned to cobalt in the third alternative on the assumption that the price of nickel would fall by about 10 percent as a result of nodule mining.

The differences in the prices of minor metals in the three cases presented in table 5-3 reflect principally the fact that price data were drawn from different time periods.[38] In none of the three cases have adjustments been attempted for the possible impact of nodule mining on prices. This procedure is justified by the fact that the amounts of these metals in nodules are so small that considerable variation in their prices would have little effect on total revenues.

If Cornell's prices are substituted for those actually used in the UN study and if all other assumptions of the UN study are left unchanged, the estimated gross revenues (in the UN study's medium case) of a four-metal operation producing 1 million tons would be reduced by 18 percent and those of a three-metal operation producing 3 million tons would be reduced by 6 percent. As a consequence, the return on investment in the four-metal operation would fall from 69 percent to 49 percent and in the three-metal operation it would fall from 73 percent to 67 percent.

Substitution of the third alternative set of prices presented in table 5-3 would reduce estimated gross revenues of the four-metal operation by 27 percent and those of the three-metal operation by 18 percent. The fall in the return on investment would be correspondingly greater: to 39 percent for the four-metal operation and to 54 percent for the three-metal operation.

38. The minor metals are principally molybdenum, vanadium, and zinc. The UN study also includes silver. None of the three cases include platinum, which is present in some nodules.

What conclusion can be drawn from the above exploration of some-what more pessimistic alternatives to the various key assumptions made in the UN study? Certainly, that study has not been discredited in any way, and its estimates of the profitability of nodule mining operations may prove as close to the mark as any that can be devised. All that has been demonstrated is the sensitivity of any estimates of profitability to variations in the metal content of nodules, capital requirements, operating costs, and prices.

The impact on net revenues of each of the alternatives explored above is set forth in table 5-4. None of the alternatives by itself comes close to eliminating net revenues entirely. In fact, it would require the combined impact of all of the more pessimistic assumptions used, including the lower of the two price assumptions, to push the four-metal operation even close to the break-even point. And the combined impact of those assumptions would still leave the three-metal operation with a net annual revenue of $47 million. If capital requirements are assumed to be $400 million (rather than the $265 million used in the UN study's medium case), the return on investment would then be about 12 percent. Whether the prospect of a rate of return this low would be sufficient to induce any firms to invest heavily in a new and risky industry is questionable. Certainly, such a rate of return would not leave any economic rent that might be appropriated to meet international needs.

This outcome, however, is only one of a wide range of possibilities. There is nothing inevitable about any of the alternative assumptions explored here. No one can be sure about the economics of nodule mining, not even the firms that have been working on the problem, until mining operations have been carried out for a number of years on a commercial scale. The value of the exercise that has been gone through above is not in the firm answers that it provides, for there are none, but in the light that it sheds on the key variables that will determine the profitability of nodule mining. The most that can be concluded from this exercise is that, while circumstances can easily be conceived in which nodule mining would not be profitable, there are other possible circumstances in which it would be very profitable indeed.

The prudent course in the face of the wide range of possible outcomes is to avoid either great optimism or great pessimism. The profit rates projected by the UN study may be high, since, as was brought out above, more pessimistic alternatives to that study's key assumptions are worthy of con-

Table 5-4. *Impact of Alternative Assumptions on Estimated Net Annual Revenues of Nodule Mining Enterprises*
Millions of U.S. dollars

Alternative	Four-metal operation (1 million tons a year)	Three-metal operation (3 million tons a year)
UN medium case[a]	104	193
Lower metal content of nodules[b]	75	148
Higher capital requirements[c]	94	180
Higher operating costs[d]	96	156
Lower prices for metals extracted from nodules[e]	58–74	144–177

Sources: See notes below.

a. "Economic Implications of Sea-bed Mineral Development in the International Area," UN Doc. A/CONF.62/25, May 22, 1974, p. 71.

b. Using the lower end of the range of metal content given in Smith, "Economic Considerations of Deep Ocean Resources," p. 3.

c. Using the upper end of the range of capital requirements (amortized over ten years) given in Cornell, "Manganese Nodule Mining and Economic Rent," p. 528.

d. Using the upper end of the range of operating costs given in ibid.

e. Based on table 5-3. The lower figures shown result from using the third alternative set of prices shown in that table; the higher figures result from using Cornell's prices.

sideration. On the other hand, several considerations appear to justify at least moderate optimism concerning the economic feasibility of nodule mining. First, several firms have devoted considerable effort and large financial resources to the tasks of exploring the seabed for nodules and developing technologies for extracting metals from them.[39] These firms would presumably not have persisted in these efforts if they did not believe that the prospects for making profits from nodule mining were favorable. Second, the cost estimates that these firms have made public are quite likely very conservative (that is, on the high side). It can reasonably be assumed that firms that have already invested heavily in research, development, and exploration would not want to encourage other enterprises to prepare to engage in nodule mining. But whether or not the cost estimates in the public domain are realistic, actual costs should decline as greater experience is gained and as mining and processing technologies are refined. Finally, it must be remembered that all the discussion of the economics of nodule mining has been in terms of estimated average costs and revenues. Even if average rates of return prove to be low, some firms

39. See "Economic Implications of Sea-bed Mineral Development in the International Area," UN Doc. A/CONF.62/25, May 22, 1974, pp. 12–25, for a summary of seabed mining activities. Also, see Rothstein and Kaufman, "The Approaching Maturity of Deep Ocean Mining—the Pace Quickens," pp. 201–21.

will do better than the average and their return on capital invested will include some economic rent.

If it is assumed that the average nodule mining enterprise in 1985 will do half as well as was projected in the UN study's medium cases, the average operation would return about 35 percent on capital invested. If it is further assumed that for both kinds of operation, a 20 percent return will be required to induce the needed investment in a new, risky activity, the economic rent produced annually would be 15 percent of total investment. For each million tons of nodules mined and processed, a four-metal operation would yield about $22 million of rent annually and a three-metal operation about $13 million.

If, as the UN study assumes, four-metal operations will mine and process 4 million tons of nodules in 1985, and three-metal operations 11 million tons, the total economic rent theoretically available for international purposes would be roughly $230 million.[40] Larger sums might become available in subsequent years if the nodule mining industry continued to expand. The size of any increase in economic rents would depend upon future prices of the metals extracted from nodules and on the future course of operating costs and capital requirements.[41]

Possible International Regimes over Ocean Resources

In December 1970, The United Nations General Assembly passed by an overwhelming vote a resolution declaring that "the sea-bed and ocean floor and the subsoil thereof, beyond the limits of national jurisdiction . . . , as well as the resources of the area are the common heritage of mankind." The resolution further stated that all activities regarding exploration and exploitation of the defined area "shall be governed by the international regime to be established," and that no state or person "shall claim, exercise or acquire rights with respect to the area or its resources incompatible with the international regime to be established and the prin-

40. It might be noted that if the rates of return projected by the UN study in 1985 are actually realized, the amount of economic rent will rise to about $800 million a year.

41. On the cost side, the question is whether cost-reducing improvements in the technology of mining and processing nodules will keep pace with the increase in costs as the industry expands into areas of the seabed that contain less rich deposits and provide more difficult operating conditions.

ciples of this Declaration." Among the principles proclaimed by the resolution was the injunction that exploitation of the resources of the area "shall be carried out for the benefit of mankind as a whole . . . taking into particular consideration the interests and needs of the developing countries."[42]

One of the most difficult tasks of the Third United Nations Conference on the Law of the Sea has been to give substance to the 1970 resolution by agreeing upon the organizational structure and powers of the international regime called for in the resolution. The outcome of this part of the conference's deliberations will have a decisive influence on prospects for gaining revenues for international purposes from the exploitation of the nonliving resources on and under the ocean floor. Several outcomes are still possible, and each has a different bearing on revenue-raising prospects.

Legal and Administrative Alternatives

A very real possibility exists that the Conference on the Law of the Sea will be unable to agree on an international regime. If so, exploitation of the resources of the deep ocean floor may continue to be free to all on a first-come first-served basis. Nodule mining might, however, be postponed indefinitely, unless the home governments of the interested firms provide a firm legal basis for the firms' planned operations, thereby facilitating their efforts to raise capital.

Various interested governments might act unilaterally in either of two general ways to influence the exploitation of those resources. They might assert national claims to the ocean floor at various distances from the outer edge of the continental margin. Or, they might merely seek to regulate firms based within their own territories that wish to explore or exploit nonliving ocean resources beyond the limits of national jurisdictions. Legislation to the latter effect has been before the U.S. Congress for several years.

It is conceivable that governments whose nationals plan to engage in the exploitation of deep ocean resources would agree to tax them for international purposes. In this way, the governments concerned might demonstrate their support for the doctrine that ocean resources beyond the limits of national jurisdictions are the common heritage of mankind.

42. GA Res. 2749 (XXV), December 17, 1970.

Deliberations at the Conference on the Law of the Sea have brought out a sharp divergence of views between the developing and the developed nations. The developing nations favor a regime under which an international enterprise would directly or indirectly engage in the exploitation of nonliving ocean resources and would also have broad authority to establish the rules under which private firms might participate in such exploitation.[43] The United States and other industrialized nations prefer a regime that would provide broad scope and stable ground rules for private exploitation of those resources. Efforts to find a mutually acceptable compromise between these two positions have thus far been unsuccessful.[44]

If a compromise solution is found, it may involve agreement by the industrialized countries to the establishment of a powerful international ocean authority with an operating arm. In return, the industrialized nations would get voting arrangements that would, in effect, give them a veto over fundamental changes in the terms under which private firms might participate in the exploitation of nonliving ocean resources. Private participation would most likely take the form of joint enterprise agreements with the ocean authority's operating arm.

It should be noted that, although the jurisdiction of the international ocean authority would be restricted to deep ocean areas, the authority would presumably possess through its operating arm rights of ownership (in whole or in part) over chemical-processing facilities within the territories of coastal states. Moreover, the international ocean authority could, if its charter so provided, tax the total profits of joint enterprises engaging in nodule mining, even though some of the activities and assets of such enterprises would be located on land.

Means of Raising Revenues for International Purposes

If, as was suggested above, the international regime over deep ocean resources proves in fact to be a mixed public-private system, more than

43. This position is substantially reflected in the negotiating text prepared by committee chairmen at the Geneva session of the Law of the Sea Conference. (*Informal Single Negotiating Text,* UN Doc. A/CONF.62/WP.8/Part I, May 7, 1975, pp. 9ff.)

44. The differing positions on how the nonliving resources of the deep ocean should be exploited are set forth in the "Report by Mr. Paul Bamelo Engo, Chairman of the First Committee on the Work of the Committee at the Fifth Session of the Conference," UN Doc. A/CONF.62/L.16, September 16, 1976.

one means of raising revenues for international purposes will be required. In the case of extractive operations carried out by the operating arm of the international authority without private participation, the problem is not difficult. The authority would simply require its operating arm to turn over all revenue above a certain percentage return on invested capital. The percentage return that the operating arm would be permitted to keep need not be equated with the normal return that private enterprises must earn to remain in business over the long run. The authority could appropriate not only any economic rent earned by the operating arm, but also part or all of the normal return on equity capital.[45]

In the case of private firms engaging in mining operations under joint enterprise agreements, the problem of the international ocean authority would be to get at two kinds of revenue over and above the normal return on capital: (1) the economic rent created by the scarcity value of high-grade nodule deposits and favorable mining conditions, and (2) profits produced by the superior technological and managerial skills of some of the firms interested in engaging in nodule mining. The international ocean authority, it might be noted, could influence the magnitude of the first of these two kinds of revenue by restricting the area within which nodule mining would be permitted.

A system of auctioning rights to participate in the exploitation of specified parts of the ocean floor would be the best means of diverting the first kind of revenue to international purposes. If prospective miners possessed full knowledge of the resources and other physical characteristics of the area in question, and if they were able to predict accurately the costs and gross revenues of the joint enterprise, they would be willing to pay an amount that would approximate the present discounted value of the stream of future economic rents that they would expect to receive from the area. Bids for participation rights could also be expressed in terms of the percentage of profits that the bidder would agree to turn over to the ocean authority or its operating arm. In the absence of collusion—which could be made more difficult through the use of secret sealed bids—exploitation rights would always go to the firm that anticipated the highest rents.

The auction system should not be relied on to get at the second kind of revenue. To achieve this objective, imposing a percentage tax on the share of profits going to private participants in joint enterprises would be the

---

45. The interest on borrowed capital would, of course, be a fixed charge against the gross revenues of the mining operation.

best approach. In order to avoid an uneconomic distortion of the proportions invested in land-based and oceanic mining, the rate of such a tax should be set at the average rate applied by national governments to land-based mining enterprises.[46] Problems of double taxation would undoubtedly arise in connection with a tax on profits, but these problems could probably be solved through a system of tax credits, as has been done in the case of overlapping national taxes.[47] Since the chemical processing of nodules to extract their metallic content would presumably take place on land, both the international authority and the government of the country in which the processing plant was located could assert tax jurisdiction.

Different approaches might be taken to the revenue shares accruing to the private and public (international) interests represented in joint ventures. Private revenues could be subjected to the profits tax, but the same share of public revenues might be diverted to international purposes as would be taken from wholly public mining operations.

Competing Claims to International Revenues

It cannot be assumed that any of the revenue that an international ocean authority may derive from nonliving resources of the deep ocean will be available to finance international programs. A first claim on such revenues will undoubtedly be meeting the administrative expenses of the international ocean authority, including the costs of monitoring mining operations to ensure observance of environmental standards.[48] Especially in the early years, a large part of total revenues might be devoted to meeting the capital requirements of the international authority's operating arm. A case can also be made for giving high priority to financing any research needed to facilitate the operations of the authority.

46. If the tax rate differs from the standard tax rate for corporate profits, there will be a distorting incentive to invest too much (low tax) or too little (high tax) relative to other sectors of the world economy.

47. In the absence of tax credits, mining companies would reduce their bids for mining privileges to compensate for the effect of double taxation.

48. It is not clear whether or not nodule mining will create serious environmental problems. One recent assessment suggests that the impact of mining operations on ocean flora and fauna will not be great, unless chemical processing of nodules is also done at sea, which does not now seem likely. See Marine Board, Assembly of Engineering, National Research Council, *Mining in the Outer Continental Shelf and the Deep Ocean* (Washington, D.C.: National Academy of Sciences, 1975), pp. 114–18.

But this is not all. As was noted earlier in this chapter, the mining of manganese nodules—which is the only promising major source of revenue from nonliving ocean resources for the foreseeable future—is seen as a threat to land-based producers of manganese, copper, nickel, and cobalt. Insofar as production of these metals is located in industrialized countries, the possible losses of producers would be balanced by gains for consumers who benefit from lower prices. The economic and political problem is therefore concentrated in those developing countries that depend heavily on exports of one or more of these metals as a source of foreign exchange. Such countries can be expected to press hard for restrictions on nodule mining to limit its impact on their foreign exchange earnings. To the extent that such restrictive measures are not fully effective, these countries will almost certainly demand financial compensation. An obvious source of compensation would be the revenues received by the international ocean authority from the nodule mining industry.

A more logical source of compensation would be the industrialized nations that would be the major beneficiaries of the lower metal prices brought about by nodule mining. The agreement of those nations to such a scheme, however, appears quite unlikely, except possibly as an adjunct to broader agreements designed to stabilize the prices of commodities that are important to the economic welfare of the developing nations.[49] For purposes of the present discussion, it will be assumed that any payments to compensate developing countries for losses incurred because of nodule mining will have to come out of the revenues of the international ocean authority.

The size of any such payments is a matter for international negotiations in which political considerations may have more weight than economic ones. It is desirable, however, to try to obtain at least a rough idea of the size of the payments that might be justified on economic grounds a decade from now, if the nodule mining industry develops in the manner projected earlier in this chapter. The possible impact of nodule mining on the foreign exchange earnings of land-based producers of copper, nickel, manganese, and cobalt will be examined in turn. It will be assumed that only nations

49. The international ocean authority might become a party to agreements to stabilize the prices of some of the metals extracted from nodules and help finance either a buffer stock scheme or a fund to compensate land-based producers that could prove damage from nodule mining operations.

able to show substantial damage from nodule mining have any chance of making good their claims for compensation.[50]

Although copper is one of the most important exports of the developing countries, nodule mining does not appear to pose a threat to land-based copper producers for many years, if ever. As was brought out earlier, nodule mining will occupy only an insignificant share of the world copper market in 1985, and the output of the nodule mining industry will have no appreciable impact on the price of copper.

Nickel is a bit more of a problem, despite the fact that most of this metal is produced by industrialized countries. In 1973, developing countries accounted for only 16 percent of world nickel production.[51] (If New Caledonia, a territory of France, is included, the share of the developing countries rises to 31 percent.) Among the developing countries, only Cuba, the Dominican Republic, and Indonesia derive a significant share of their foreign exchange earnings by exporting nickel.

Nodule mining might decrease the prospective foreign exchange earnings of these three countries both by lowering the price of nickel and by reducing their share of the world market. It was argued earlier that effective action by the nickel oligopoly might hold the price decrease to 10 percent if the oligopoly gave up, say, 15 percent of what its market would have been to the new nodule mining industry. If so, the combined impact of a lower price and reduced sales (assuming that the reduction was shared proportionally by all producers) would cause Cuba to earn about $48 million less from nickel exports in 1985 (in 1972 dollars) than might otherwise have been the case. The corresponding losses for the Dominican Republic and for Indonesia would be about $39 million and $29 million, respectively.

---

50. The analysis that follows draws upon three UN studies but does not conform to them in every respect: "Possible Impact of Sea-bed Mineral Production in the Area beyond National Jurisdiction on World Markets, with Special Reference to the Problems of Developing Countries: A Preliminary Assessment," UN Doc. A/AC.138/36, May 28, 1971; "Additional Notes on the Possible Economic Implications of Mineral Production from the International Sea-bed Area," UN Doc. A/AC.138/73, May 12, 1972; and "Economic Implications of Sea-bed Mining in the International Area: Report of the Secretary-General," UN Doc. A/CONF.62/37, February 18, 1975.

51. U.S. Department of the Interior, *Minerals Yearbook 1973*, p. 868. Estimates of potential losses to Cuba, the Dominican Republic, and Indonesia are based on nickel prices in this volume.

As was brought out earlier, the principal effect of the extraction of manganese from nodules will be on the price of ferromanganese, very little of which is produced in the developing countries. The price of the metal contained in manganese ore was projected to fall by less than 10 percent by 1985 as a result of nodule mining. This lower price would have a significant effect on the foreign exchange earnings of only a few developing countries. Only Gabon would suffer substantial damage.[52]

In 1973, Gabon accounted for about 9 percent of total world production of manganese ore.[53] If Gabon retained the same share of the world market projected for 1985, the assumed fall in price would cost the country about $35 million (in 1972 dollars) in foreign exchange earnings. The damage would be somewhat greater if Gabon indirectly lost some of its market share to the nodule mining industry through displacement of ferromanganese by manganese metal. The additional damage suffered in this way would be difficult to prove, however, and would probably not be large in view of the relatively small manganese output of the nodule mining industry and the likelihood that the great fall projected for the price of ferromanganese would be associated with some increase in its use.

The most severe impact of nodule mining would be on the price of cobalt. The analysis above projected a fall of 44 percent in the price of this metal. However, the only developing country that would suffer substantial damage as a consequence is Zaire.[54] If it is assumed that Zaire holds the same share of the projected world cobalt market of 60,000 metric tons in 1985 as it held in 1973 (that is, about 66 percent), the assumed fall in the price of cobalt would cost Zaire about $94 million in foreign exchange earnings (in 1972 dollars).[55] This estimate may, however, be too high. If, as has been assumed here, the price of cobalt falls to the same level as the price of nickel, cobalt would replace nickel in some uses. The market for cobalt would therefore expand and Zaire could make up in greater volume of sales part of the loss caused by lower price.

52. In 1969, manganese accounted for 21.2 percent of the value of Gabon's exports. "Possible Impact of Sea-bed Mineral Production in the Area beyond National Jurisdiction on World Markets," UN Doc. A/AC/138/36, May 28, 1971, p. 33.

53. U.S. Department of the Interior, *Minerals Yearbook 1973*, p. 752.

54. In 1969, cobalt accounted for 5.2 percent of the value of Zaire's total exports. "Possible Impact of Sea-bed Mineral Production in the Area Beyond National Jurisdiction on World Markets," UN Doc. A/AC.138/36, May 28, 1971, p. 36.

55. Based on cobalt prices listed in U.S. Department of the Interior, *Minerals Yearbook 1973*, vol. 1, p. 403.

If these very crude estimates are added up, the total claims in 1985 from countries suffering substantial damage as a result of nodule mining could be of the general order of $245 million a year (in 1972 dollars). This calculation is a rough measure of the gross damages suffered by these countries annually in the short run. It ignores the fact that some of the labor and capital that would have been engaged in land-based mining would in fact be shifted to other activities that may produce either export goods or substitutes for imports. How large this offset would be by 1985 cannot easily be estimated, and the countries claiming compensation are certain to minimize its importance. Even over the longer run, the offset might not be complete, because some of the revenues from metal mining presumably reflect rents derived from the special properties of the deposits being exploited. Whether equivalent rents could be earned by shifting labor and capital to other pursuits cannot be determined in the abstract. The maximum net damage over the long run, however, would be only the loss of some economic rents from mining the metals in question.

Entirely by coincidence, the rough estimate of total damage claims is only slightly larger than the equally rough estimate of the economic rent that the international community might be able to extract from the nodule mining industry. This circumstance argues fairly strongly against the small number of injured nations being able to make good a demand for full compensation in the face of other claims on the revenues of the international ocean authority. The nations most threatened by nodule mining will probably have to rely more on measures to restrain the growth of the new industry than on the hope of financial compensation.

If, contrary to what has been argued above, land-based metal miners are able to collect compensation from the revenues of the international ocean authority, prospects for using any of those revenues to finance environmental or other international programs would indeed be bleak. But even if the revenues in question are not used to compensate the land-based miners, it does not follow that they would be turned over to any international agency to pay for agreed upon international programs. If the developing countries have their way, the revenues of the international ocean authority will go directly to governments on the basis of some mechanical formula. These countries oppose turning over such revenues to the World Bank or any other agency on the ground that this would lead to a net reduction in the contributions of the industrialized countries to development assistance. If, despite the opposition of the developing countries, some of the revenues of the international ocean authority are used for international purposes, development assistance would almost certainly be given top priority.

Conclusions

For the next ten years, and possibly longer, prospects for deriving substantial revenues for international purposes from the exploitation of nonliving ocean resources are, at best, fair.

The most promising nonliving ocean resources are relatively close to land and are already subject to the jurisdiction of coastal states, or will soon fall under the control of those states if current trends, including developments at the Third United Nations Conference on the Law of the Sea, continue. Some oil and gas deposits of uncertain size may remain outside national jurisdictions, but their exploitation will almost certainly be deferred until after more accessible areas on land and in coastal waters closer to land have been more fully explored and developed.

The only major nonliving resource that appears to be ready for early exploitation and that is located almost entirely beyond the probable limits of any national jurisdiction are the manganese nodules that are found on the surface of the deep ocean floor. The profitability of the still nonexistent nodule mining industry is uncertain. It is possible, however, that by 1985 the industry might earn more than $200 million a year above the rate of return on investment required to attract and hold the capital needed in this high-risk activity.

Prospects for tapping this revenue for international purposes will be poor, unless an international regime is established over the nonliving resources of the deep ocean. If an international regime is established, it might consist of an international ocean authority with an operating arm that could engage in nodule mining both directly and indirectly by forming joint enterprises with private firms. Profits accruing to the operating arm would be at the disposal of the international ocean authority. The authority could tap the economic rents earned by private firms by auctioning off rights to participate in the exploitation of specific plots on the ocean floor. A tax on the profits earned by private firms might also be desirable.

First priority in the disposition of any revenues from deep ocean resources would be given to covering the expenses of the international ocean authority and probably also to meeting the capital requirements of its operating arm. Land-based producers of nickel, manganese, and cobalt (copper is no problem) could be expected to attempt to obtain compensation for damage suffered as a result of nodule mining. However, since the number of nations able to show substantial damage would be very small, their leverage would be weak and their chances of receiving full compensation do not appear to be good. They are therefore more likely to concentrate on restricting the output of the nodule mining industry.

Any remaining revenues might well be distributed directly to governments. If some revenues were set aside to finance agreed upon international programs, the most likely beneficiaries would be programs designed to further the economic development of the poorer nations.

CHAPTER SIX

Legal and Administrative Arrangements

NONE of the major new means of financing environmental and other international programs discussed in this study could be put into effect without new legal arrangements. In most cases, new administrative arrangements would also be necessary. The present chapter will consider what would have to be done to tap several of the larger sources of financing identified in previous chapters and to put the resulting funds to good use in support of international programs. For convenience in exposition, problems associated with the generation of funds will be treated separately from those involved in the management of funds.

Generation of Funds

Attention will be focused on two possible new sources of financing (revenue taxes and pollution taxes) and one established source (funds borrowed from capital markets). Legal and administrative arrangements for obtaining revenues from the exploitation of nonliving ocean resources were discussed in chapter 5. Other possibilities either are less promising (for example, the International Monetary Fund's Special Drawing Rights, gold sales, and revenues from telecommunication channels) or pose only minor legal problems (for example, private contributions and the sale of technical services), and they are not examined here.

Revenue Taxes

The revenue taxes analyzed in chapter 3 could be put into effect only by means of an international agreement. Such an agreement, moreover, would almost certainly have to be a formal treaty. Anything less would seem inappropriate for so revolutionary a step as taxing private firms and individuals for the benefit of an international organization.

A single treaty might conceivably provide the legal basis for a broad range of international taxes. In view of the novelty of the concept, however, it seems more likely that initial authority would be limited to a single tax. For purposes of the present discussion, it will be assumed that that tax would be a general ad valorem trade tax. With minor modifications, the following discussion of a treaty creating such a tax could be applied to other international taxes, such as taxes on selected components of international trade or on the international transmission of profits from international investments.

A treaty levying a tax on international trade would, at a minimum, have to deal with: (1) the definition of the tax base, (2) the setting of the tax rate, (3) the method of collecting the tax, (4) the initial disposition of proceeds, (5) the conditions that must be satisfied before the treaty could come into force, (6) the sanctions against treaty violators, and (7) the procedures for withdrawing from the treaty. Provision might also be made for review of the treaty after a specific period, or for its automatic termination at a fixed date, unless states adhering to it reaffirmed their ratifications.

The treaty might attempt to deal with all of these subjects in a definitive way. Alternatively, some subjects might be treated only in general terms. The filling in of details might then be left to a continuing body representing the states adhering to the treaty. This continuing body, which might be named the executive council, might also be given the authority to handle specified procedural and administrative problems and even to adjust tax rates within stated guidelines.

The advantage of trying to settle everything in the treaty is that signatories would then feel that they knew exactly what they had agreed upon. It is unlikely, however, that all problems could be anticipated and disposed of successfully in the treaty. Some means short of renegotiating the treaty should therefore be provided for resolving the many questions that are likely to arise after the treaty goes into effect. Also, it would be useful to provide a mechanism for making some adjustments in response to changing circumstances. The best way to bring out the merits of a treaty that leaves some decisions to a continuing executive council is to consider in somewhat greater detail each of the subjects that must be covered.

In the case of a general trade tax, defining the tax base would appear to be a fairly straightforward matter. Even here, however, there could be problems. National differences in evaluating imports and exports would have to be reconciled or lived with. Whether credits or exemptions would be granted for goods that were reexported would have to be determined and, if such credits or exemptions were to be granted, the circumstances would have to be determined. Even what constitutes international trade, as opposed to domestic trade, might not always be self-evident when the trading partners belong to a common market or even to a customs union. The treaty could, and indeed should, provide the general principles whereby problems such as these might be settled, but detailed definitions and the resolution of specific controversies could best be handled by a continuing executive council.

Governments adhering to the treaty would no doubt want to include a ceiling on tax rates in the treaty itself. Otherwise, the tax liability of their citizens would be too open-ended. Giving the executive council some authority to vary tax rates would, however, be useful. In gross terms, this would make it possible to increase tax yields to meet changing requirements. This authority would be most useful if—as is quite possible—different rates were applied to different classes of countries (or to different classes of goods), in order to produce a distribution of burdens that might be more acceptable politically than would be possible with a single tax rate. The executive council might be authorized to determine periodically what class each country fell in and what tax rate, within specified limits, should apply to each class. Alternatively, burdens might be adjusted through a system of tax rebates that might be administered by the executive council.

The precise burden of an international trade tax on various countries could not be easily calculated, since it would depend on the proportions of the tax on different commodities that were shifted to consumers or absorbed by producers. The burden of the tax would probably be perceived, however, as falling entirely on consumers, who would have the tax added to the prices of imported commodities. That perception will be made a working assumption for the purposes of the present discussion. Under this assumption, the burden of the tax on a given country would vary directly with the value of the country's imports.

A trade tax could be collected by the customs authorities of either the exporting or the importing country in the same way that they administer national duties. The proceeds from the tax would then be forwarded periodically to the international receiving agency specified in the treaty. Some means of monitoring the operation of the revenue system would be necessary, and that task might appropriately be assigned to the executive council.

Because import duties are more common than export levies, the international trade tax would, under most circumstances, be most easily collected (or its prior payment confirmed) at the point of importation. If, however, a country that has adhered to the treaty fails to carry out its obligations in this regard, shipments destined for that country could be taxed at the localities from which they are exported.[1] The determination of when this shift in collection points should be made could also be made by the executive council.

Shifting the point of collection would not change the incidence of the tax. Under either method of collection, the shares of the tax borne by producers in the exporting country and consumers in the importing country would be the same and would depend on the elasticities of demand and supply for the goods taxed.

The shift in collection points could be coupled with an increase in the tax rate on goods destined for countries in violation of the treaty. The executive council could determine the amount of this increase, subject to guidelines provided by the treaty. The council might also be empowered to apply the additional sanction of denying violators the benefits of programs supported by the international trade tax.

A shift in collection points might also be used to reduce the proportion of tax proceeds that would be paid in inconvertible currencies.[2] There

1. There might be some difficulty in collecting the tax at the exporting end in the case of the United States, which is prohibited by its constitution from taxing exports. It might still be possible for the tax to be administered, if necessary, at the point of export but still be regarded as a tax on another country's imports. The U.S. customs officials would, in effect, be administering the import tax on behalf of the international agency; they would not be collecting the tax on U.S. exports for the U.S. Treasury.

2. A currency is inconvertible if it cannot readily be exchanged for other currencies.

would be an obvious advantage in taxing shipments to countries with inconvertible currencies at the points of exportation, if they originated in countries whose currencies were convertible. It is, of course, possible that some countries with inconvertible currencies would agree to remit the tax on imports in a convertible currency. Again, the council could be authorized to handle this problem.

The fact that an international trade tax could be collected at either the point of import or the point of export raises an important policy question that would have to be settled in the treaty itself. This question is whether to tax both exports to and imports from countries that have not adhered to the treaty. Failure to do so would in theory have an undesirable distorting effect on world trade. Of greater practical importance is the fact that failure to tax imports from non-treaty countries would give them an unwarranted competitive advantage in the markets of the importing countries. The practical consideration in favor of taxing exports to non-treaty countries (apart from the revenue that such an action would produce) is that it would impose a burden on citizens and firms in those countries and would reduce somewhat the advantages of not adhering to the treaty. This effect would, however, have to be weighed against the competitive disadvantage that treaty countries would suffer in the markets of non-treaty countries. By taxing exports, treaty countries would be making their goods more expensive, and therefore harder to sell, in the countries for which the exports were destined. This disadvantage would not be great, however, if the tax rate were quite low, as would be likely.

A policy of taxing both exports to and imports from non-treaty countries would, in fact, make it possible to put the treaty into effect with fewer adherents than would be the case if the trade of non-treaty countries were exempted. This is so for two reasons. First, such a policy would extend the reach of the tax and therefore its yield. Second, as has been pointed out, countries remaining outside the treaty would probably gain little advantage, so they might be disposed to join in order to have some influence on the operation of the system. A stronger inducement to join could be provided if non-treaty countries, as well as treaty violators, were denied the benefits of programs supported by the international trade tax. It is, of course, quite possible that countries adhering to the treaty would not want to risk offending non-treaty countries by taxing their trade or applying other pressures on them to join. This reluctance would be all the greater if nonadherents included major powers, such as the Soviet Union or China.

The actual content of a treaty imposing an international trade tax would be determined by negotiation among the governments prepared to consider so radical a means of raising money to pay for international programs. There would be little point in presenting a draft of such a treaty here. It might be useful, however, to set forth in general terms the major points that might be included in such a treaty.

First, governments adhering to the treaty would agree to tax all goods imported into their territories at rates set by the executive council established to administer the treaty. They would also agree to tax all goods exported from their territories destined for countries designated by the executive council at rates set by the council. This might apply to countries that had not adhered to the treaty, or were in violation of it, or insisted on remitting the tax in the form of inconvertible currencies. Governments collecting these taxes would also agree to transmit the proceeds to a designated international agency.

Second, the treaty would establish several classes of countries, rank the classes in order of the relative tax rate that would be applied to each, and set forth criteria for determining which countries would fall in the various classes. The treaty would set ceilings on the rates applicable to each class, but actual rates would be determined by the executive council. The council might also be authorized to rebate taxes collected from firms and individuals in countries with low per capita GNPs. (See chapter 7 for a full discussion of means of adjusting the burden among countries.)

Third, the treaty would provide penalties to be applied to participating countries found by the executive council to be in default of their treaty obligations.

Fourth, an executive council, consisting of representatives of participating governments, would be established with power to resolve questions concerning what goods were subject to the tax, to establish principles for evaluating taxable goods, to set tax rates for imports into (or exports destined for) each class of countries, to monitor enforcement of the tax, and to determine whether any governments were in violation of the treaty and therefore subject to the specified sanctions. In order to keep the council from becoming too large to function efficiently, each member might represent several governments, as do most of the executive directors of the World Bank. A system of weighted voting reflecting the shares of different countries in total world imports might be necessary. Also, the treaty might require more than a majority of votes for some issues, such as the setting of tax rates.

Fifth, the treaty would come into effect when it had been ratified by countries the value of whose imports equaled a specified percentage of world trade. Provision would be made for adhering governments to withdraw after giving specified advance notice. A conference to review the operation of the treaty might also be provided for in the treaty.

Whether the treaty would also specify in more than very broad terms how the proceeds of an international trade tax would be used is an open question. Participating governments would certainly want to have some control over the eventual disposition of the taxes that they would collect. In theory, there would appear to be no reason to earmark the proceeds of this tax for any specific purpose; in practice, however, it is unlikely that governments would agree to an international tax unless they knew the purposes for which the proceeds would be used. The question of how the ultimate use of these funds might be determined will be explored later in this chapter.

Taxes on Polluters

Imposing taxes on polluters would also best be done by treaty. Because the problems involved in revenue taxes and pollution taxes are so different, and because they must be justified on different grounds, it would be difficult to negotiate an agreement about both kinds of taxes simultaneously. A separate treaty on pollution taxes would therefore probably be necessary. There would be some logic in including all taxes on the same effluent (such as oil) in one treaty, but the novelty of the concept of international taxes argues in favor of dealing initially with only one pollution tax. For purposes of the present discussion, it will be assumed that the first such tax would be on oil spills by tankers in the course of routine operations.

In a general way, the provisions in a treaty imposing a tax on tankers would parallel those of a treaty imposing a trade tax; there would, of course, be substantial differences in content. As was true of the trade tax, it is most unlikely that all problems with respect to a tanker tax could be settled definitively. A continuing body, which will again be referred to as the executive council, would be needed to see to the detailed application of the provisions of the treaty.

In the case of the tanker tax, the tax base would be the deadweight tonnage of each tanker, which would not be difficult to determine. As was explained in chapter 4, the tax rate would be based on the past operating experience of each category of tanker. The rates for individual tankers would be reduced to the extent that their operators could prove that their emissions were below the average for their class. Some means would have to be provided in the treaty both for maintaining data on tanker operations and for checking the claims of improved performance by some tanker operators. These tasks might well be among those assigned to the executive council.

Enforcement of the tanker tax would be primarily in the hands of the port authorities of participating nations. Tankers that did not carry certificates showing that the tax for the current year had been paid would not be permitted to leave port until all back taxes had been paid. Certificates could be issued by the executive council or its designated agents.

An important question to be decided by the drafters of the treaty would be whether to apply the tax to all tankers using the ports of participating nations, or only to tankers flying the flags of such nations. The former approach would have the obvious advantage of exerting greater leverage on one major source of marine pollution. It would also produce more revenue. Perhaps of greatest practical importance, it would avoid creating an incentive for tanker operators to shift their registration to nonparticipating nations. This approach might, of course, be resented by nonparticipating nations as high-handed taxation without representation, but they could remove this injustice at any time by acceding to the treaty.

Since the tanker tax could be enforced at either end of a voyage, and since a relatively few countries account for the bulk of the international trade in oil, only a handful of countries could, if they wished, impose the tax on most of the world's tanker fleet. The political wisdom of doing so would be questionable, since action of this sort by a small minority might worsen prospects for broader international cooperation on other important financial and environmental questions. Failure to obtain the adherence of nations whose citizens own a substantial part of the world tanker fleet could cause especially difficult problems, possibly extending to an organized refusal to accept cargo originating in, or destined for, treaty nations. The treaty might therefore provide that it would come into force only after ratification by a specified minimum number of nations, including nations accounting for a specified percentage of the ship-borne international trade in crude oil and refined products and for the ownership of a specified portion of the world tanker fleet.

The treaty establishing a tax on tankers would also provide for withdrawal after advance notice and for review of the operation of the treaty after a period of years. No special sanctions against treaty violators, other than holding up the departure of tankers without current tax certificates, would appear to be necessary.

As was pointed out in the earlier discussion of a treaty establishing a revenue tax on international trade, the precise terms of a treaty imposing a tax on tankers cannot be predicted. The terms would be determined by negotiation. Such a treaty might, however, include the following major points:

First, governments adhering to the treaty would agree to require all tankers using their ports to carry certificates showing that their operators had paid the tanker tax for the current year. Tankers without such certificates would be held in port until certificates had been obtained from the executive council or a designated agent.

Second, an executive council representing all participating governments would be established with power to set tax rates per deadweight ton for each category of tanker on the basis of guidelines specified in the treaty. The executive council would also be authorized to grant tax reductions to operators of tankers who could demonstrate better-than-average performance with respect to oil emissions in the course of normal operations.

Third, the treaty would come into effect when it had been ratified by twenty-five nations that were involved, either as importers or as exporters, in at least 50 percent of the ship-borne international trade in crude oil and refined products, and whose firms or citizens owned at least 50 percent of the world tanker fleet. As in the case of the treaty establishing a tax on international trade, provisions would be made for withdrawal from the treaty after advance notice and possibly also for review of the treaty's operation after a specified period.

The treaty might also include some provision for the eventual disposition of the proceeds of the tax. This subject will be addressed later in the present chapter in the context of the management of international revenues from a variety of sources.

The legal and administrative arrangements for other possible taxes on polluters would be generally similar to those outlined for the tax on tanker emissions. Some taxes might, however, be levied on a regional basis. (The tanker tax could not be limited in this way because tanker operations are global in scope and individual tankers are often shifted from one run to another.) Taxes on spillage from offshore oil exploration and production might well be limited to particular regions, since the sponsors and beneficiaries of such taxes could be regional conventions established to deal with the problem of marine pollution in specific areas. Such an approach would tend to make investment in the exploitation of offshore oil resources in the region subject to the tax somewhat less attractive than investment in similar resources in other areas. But this distortion of investment decision is the inevitable result of many efforts by individual nations, or groups of nations, to protect their environment. In the absence of effective international coordination of environmental protection measures, national governments must decide in each case whether such economic distortions are more serious than continued damage to the environment.

Borrowings in Capital Markets

In contrast with the other two possibilities discussed above, borrowing money can scarcely be regarded as a new means of financing international programs. Funds raised by the World Bank and other international lending agencies have long been a major source of development assistance. In the context of the present study, the problem to be considered is how more money might be channeled from the world's capital markets into international environmental programs.

In theory, this goal might be realized by borrowing explicitly for environmental purposes. In practice, this would be quite difficult. The only international agency with a broad mandate in the environmental field is the United Nations Environmental Programme (UNEP), and it has neither the borrowing authority nor the financial backing by governments that would enable it to raise funds in the capital markets.

As a practical matter, the question is whether or not more of the resources of the World Bank Group and the regional development banks can be devoted to development projects with important environmental aspects. The relative emphasis accorded environmental problems by the World Bank and the regional development banks must be decided by the governing boards and managements of those institutions. New legal and administrative arrangements might, however, be devised that would facilitate increased attention to environmental concerns, if that is desired. Such a change in the priorities of these financial institutions would not result in an increase in the total funds available for international purposes, but only in a modification in the way in which existing financial resources would be used.

The World Bank has a small environmental unit that reviews all projects for their environmental consequences. Informal relations also exist between the Bank and UNEP. No special procedures have as yet been developed, however, to ensure that environmentally important projects will be developed and considered for financing by the Bank or by its affiliate, the International Development Association (IDA).

A precedent for such procedures may be provided by the existing relationships among the Bank, the United Nations Development Programme (UNDP), and several UN Specialized Agencies.[3] UNDP sponsors and pays for preinvestment surveys and studies for projects that are, in the majority of cases, subsequently financed by the Bank. Much of the preinvestment work sponsored by UNDP is in fact delegated to the Bank, but much is also delegated to other UN Specialized Agencies, such as the Food and Agriculture Organization (FAO). Even in the latter case, the Bank is involved in that it comments informally on the terms of reference for UNDP-sponsored surveys and studies in which it may be interested and on plans for carrying them out. The Bank also has formal cooperative arrangements with the United Nations Educational, Scientific and Cultural Organization (UNESCO); the World Health Organization (WHO); the United Nations Industrial Development Organization (UNIDO); and FAO. The Bank helps these agencies to finance the assistance that they give governments in identifying projects and preparing proposals.

These arrangements have ensured the World Bank a flow of carefully prepared proposals for development projects. The precedents provided by these arrangements suggest that UNEP might work with the Bank in several ways for the purpose of providing the Bank with a larger flow of proposals for environmental projects.

First, UNEP might assume a role similar to that of UNDP and sponsor preinvestment studies and surveys of environmental projects for eventual consideration by the Bank. The UN Specialized Agencies that UNEP

3. The origin and nature of these relationships are described in Edward S. Mason and Robert E. Asher, *The World Bank since Bretton Woods* (Brookings Institution, 1973), pp. 307–15, 566–76, and 749–52.

would call on to carry out this work would presumably include some of the same agencies that now cooperate with UNDP.

Second, UNEP might assist governments to identify environmental projects and prepare proposals for consideration by the Bank.

Third, UNEP might perform preinvestment studies and surveys for UNDP.

The first course of action would probably require larger amounts of money than are now available to UNEP. The possibility that the Bank might pay UNEP to conduct or sponsor preinvestment studies and surveys cannot be ruled out, although such a step would run counter to the precedent established in the Bank's relationships with UNDP. The alternative, under present circumstances, would be for UNEP to solicit additional contributions to the Fund of UNEP. In so doing, UNEP would be able to argue that modest expenditures on preinvestment studies and surveys could be expected to result in the commitment of much larger amounts of money by the World Bank to environmental projects.

The second course of action would not create a financial problem for UNEP. If the Bank saw merit in UNEP's working with governments to identify environmental projects and prepare proposals, it would presumably be willing to pay the bulk of the costs incurred, as it does now for several UN Specialized Agencies. UNEP might, however, fear that the second course of action might in time distort its role within the UN system. Rather than playing the catalytic role to which it now aspires,[4] UNEP might become merely one more representative of a sectoral interest, much like the UN Specialized Agencies.

The third course of action could also be seen by UNEP as endangering its assigned role, since UNEP's relationship with UNDP would be little different from that of one of the UN Specialized Agencies. Accepting money from UNDP for helping to conduct preinvestment studies might be financially attractive to UNEP, but it might also be seen as implying an unwelcome subordination to UNDP.

Any problem of this nature could be avoided if UNEP sought only an advisory role in the preinvestment process and not that of a full participant. In the near future, it would, in fact, appear more likely that UNEP would provide informal advice to the various organizations involved in preinvestment work than that UNEP would enter into any of the three

4. See "Catalytic Role of UNEP," UN Doc. UNEP/GC/82, January 16, 1976.

more formal relationships described above. Adoption of such a role would require no special legal or administrative arrangements. UNEP's assumption of an advisory role in the preinvestment process would be a natural evolution of the informal consultative relations already established with the World Bank and the other organizations concerned.

Each of the other possibilities described above would require a more formal understanding between UNEP and the other organizations concerned. Any of these courses of action could be expected to facilitate a greater commitment of the Bank's resources to environmental projects than less formal means would be likely to bring about. If, as has been suggested, UNEP would not find the second and third courses attractive, the practical question is whether the Bank and UNEP could agree on the first course.[5] There is no way to answer this question in the abstract. If, however, agreement did prove to be possible, the existing understanding between the Bank and UNDP would provide a directly relevant precedent.

It may be asked whether the proposed restructuring of the economic and social work of the United Nations is likely to affect prospects for channeling more of the World Bank's resources into environmental projects. In the absence of a clear indication of the form that restructuring may take, no confident answer to this question is possible. The report of a group of experts commissioned by the General Assembly to study the restructuring problem provides, however, a useful basis for speculation.[6]

A principal recommendation of the group of experts was the creation of a United Nations Development Authority (UNDA) that would assume control of all UN funds for technical assistance and preinvestment activities, including the funds now managed by UNDP and UNEP. Although the separate identity of existing funds would be preserved, placing all funds under a single management would almost certainly affect the emphasis given to environmental considerations in the preinvestment process. The name proposed for the new authority (and the likelihood that it would be created simply by expanding the role of UNDP) suggests that environmental concerns might be subordinated to development goals even more than they are at present. On the other hand, the proposed con-

5. This expansion of UNEP's role might also have to be approved by the Economic and Social Council (ECOSOC) or the General Assembly, and possibly by both. For present purposes, it will be assumed that ECOSOC and the General Assembly would go along with anything worked out by the Bank and UNEP.

6. *A New United Nations Structure for Global Economic Co-operation*, UN Doc. E/AC. 62/9, May 29, 1975, especially pp. 41–42.

solidation would facilitate a broadening of the existing preinvestment process to include studies and surveys of environmental projects. Which of these contrary possibilities would come to pass would depend on the management of the new authority and on the policies set by ECOSOC and by the new Operations Board that would directly supervise the authority.

As for the regional development banks, UNEP might be able, by various informal means, to facilitate the financing of more environmental projects (and development projects with important environmental aspects) by these institutions. On a selective basis, UNEP might informally assist governments in drawing up project proposals for submission to regional banks. Similarly, UNEP might stand ready to help regional banks evaluate proposals that deal significantly with environmental problems.

Management of Expanded Means of Financing International Programs

If substantial new means of financing environmental and other international programs are ever to become available, agreement must be reached not only on how the new funds are to be generated but also on what is to be done with them. The key questions are who controls the disposition of the funds, and who benefits from their use?

The management of borrowed funds would pose no new problems. They would be put to use by the borrowing agencies—the World Bank Group and the regional development banks—under procedures similar to those followed at present. Channeling more resources into environmental projects according to the possible new arrangements that were discussed earlier in this chapter would not represent fundamental changes in the ways in which these agencies manage their financial resources. Managing the other three kinds of funds under discussion here—revenue taxes, taxes on polluters, and revenues from nonliving ocean resources—would, however, pose new problems and would require new arrangements.

Funds from any given source can be thought of as passing through three stages of management: acquisition, allocation, and expenditure by an operating agency. The first of these stages poses no special legal or administrative problems. The international agreement under whose authority the new funds would be generated would specify how they were to be acquired and where they were to be deposited initially. The initial depository of newly generated funds is usually self-evident. Thus, in the case of revenues from nonliving ocean resources, the first recipient would presumably be the international ocean authority, if and when it is created. The proceeds of both revenue and pollution taxes would go to the executive councils that were suggested above.

The allocation function is both more complicated and more likely to be the focus of international controversy. Several difficult decisions must be made with respect to the allocation of each new source of financing. The first question to be decided is whether the allocation of funds to operating agencies should be discretionary or automatic. If the allocation is discretionary, what institution or institutions should make the decisions, and subject to what guidelines? If the allocation is automatic, what principle or formula should control the allocation of funds? A mixed system—partly discretionary and partly automatic—is also conceivable. One possibility of this nature would be an arrangement under which a predetermined share of an international revenue tax was retained by the nations collecting it.

Another major issue is whether the range of choice of the institutions making discretionary allocations should be limited by earmarking some kinds of funds for specific purposes. This question is, of course, particularly important for the present study with its special emphasis on the financing of environmental programs.

Finally, there is the question of what institutions should be given responsibility for the discretionary allocation of various funds, whether earmarked or not. The alternatives, as will be seen, include both existing institutions and new institutions created specially to perform the allocation function.

Discretionary versus Automatic Allocation

Many developing countries would probably prefer that all new sources of financing be allocated directly to national governments in accordance with a mechanical formula that would reflect relative developmental needs. As was noted in chapter 5, there is a fairly good chance that they will get their way with respect to revenues from nonliving ocean resources —if agreement is ever reached on an international regime to control the exploitation of those resources.

The Communist countries would also be likely to support automatic allocation of some or all of the new funds as a means of demonstrating their solidarity with the developing countries. Some of the less developed Communist countries would also see automatic allocation as a means of obtaining convertible currency, which is normally in short supply.

Automatic allocation would be opposed by the developed free-market countries, whose firms and citizens would bear the major burden of any likely international taxes. It would be hard to convince those countries that an international tax had merit unless its proceeds were to be used prudently to advance some agreed upon objectives. This would probably be taken by the developed countries to require discretionary allocation by an institution in which they would have strong influence, if not control. It is conceivable, however, that the developed countries would agree to automatic allocation of some of the new funds as part of an effort to meet some of the demands of the developing countries for a new international economic order.

Despite the strong possibility that revenues from nonliving ocean resources would be allocated automatically, it will be assumed that at least a portion of such revenues, as well as the two other kinds of funds under discussion, would be handled in a discretionary manner. This assumption will facilitate a fuller exploration of the other issues related to the allocation process.

Earmarking Funds for Specific Purposes

The next question that arises is whether any of the funds under discussion should be earmarked for particular purposes. In the context of the present study, this question can be phrased more specifically: Should any of these funds be reserved solely for activities related to the environment? Both environmental programs that benefit all countries (for example, programs for global monitoring or ocean protection) and development programs with a major environmental component (for example, projects to combat the spread of deserts) could be included in the general category of environment-related activities.

If money were to be borrowed for environmental purposes—which is unlikely for reasons mentioned earlier in this chapter—there would be no question about its being earmarked. There may be no other situations, however, in which earmarking can be said to be inevitable. The decision to devote certain revenues to limited areas of expenditure must be made on political grounds. Proponents of earmarking see it as a legitimate means of setting social priorities. Opponents argue that every spending decision should be made in the context of the broadest possible range of alternatives and that this principle cannot be followed if some funds have already been earmarked for certain purposes. According to the traditional argument, expenditures should theoretically be allocated so that the last dollar spent on any given expenditure category would yield benefits equal to those produced by the last dollar spent on each of the other categories. Earmarking introduces a rigidity in spending decisions that would make achieving this ideal objective impossible. This argument against earmarking is probably most valid, however, in single countries that enjoy a high degree of political integration and confidence in the government and appears largely irrelevant in the context of the proposed international taxes.

The appropriateness of using the proceeds of a tax on pollution from oil tankers to pay for programs to overcome the effects of marine pollution will seem self-evident to many people. Similar attitudes would probably prevail with respect to pollution taxes on other merchant ships and on off-shore drilling activity. Some people might argue that revenue from non-living ocean resources should also be earmarked for purposes associated with the protection of the marine environment. As was previously noted, however, development programs would appear to be the most likely beneficiaries of any such revenues that escape automatic allocation.

In principle, there is no reason why some or all of the proceeds of revenue taxes could not be earmarked for environmental purposes or for any other specific purpose, such as financing the safeguards system of the International Atomic Energy Agency or even meeting deficits in the central UN budget. For purposes of the present discussion, however, it will be assumed that all of the proceeds of international revenue taxes, plus any revenues from nonliving ocean resources that are not allocated automatically, will be designated for general developmental or environmental purposes, subject to such restrictions and guidelines as may be specified in the relevant treaties. Thus, the discussion of institutional alternatives that follows will be concerned with only two kinds of funds: general development funds and environmental funds.

Institutional Alternatives

The agencies that initially acquire each of the new sources of revenue under discussion here could conceivably allocate them to end users. Thus, the international seabed authority and the executive councils administering revenue and pollution taxes could make grants and loans directly to a variety of national, international, and local organizations. This approach would no doubt have considerable appeal to the governments of some industrialized countries, if weighted voting gave them a large voice in the direction of those agencies. This approach would, however, further fragment the management of international financial resources. It would be virtually impossible to coordinate the actions of the various agencies—both old and new—so as to achieve something approaching a rational distribution of funds among receiving organizations. Also, it would force the agencies concerned to develop staffs that would duplicate the functions of existing international organizations.

At the opposite extreme, the new funds might be subjected to some kind of centralized budgetary control by the United Nations. Ideally, the central budgetary process should determine both the amounts of funds that are to be generated from new, as well as old, sources of finance and the disposition that is to be made of those funds. In practice, the United Nations could exert only limited influence over the generation of new funds, since that process would be controlled by autonomous agencies that would not necessarily even belong to the UN system. The agencies administering seabed resources and pollution taxes would actually have little control over the magnitude of their revenues. The most that could be hoped for would be that the agency (or agencies) in charge of revenue taxes would give some weight in setting tax rates to advice by the United Nations concerning the levels of revenue that would be desirable in future years.

A major advantage of centralized budgetary control—that is, the ability to adjust revenues to fiscal requirements—would therefore be largely lacking. The only advantage in turning the new funds over to the United Nations for distribution would be the theoretical one of facilitating choice among a large number of alternatives. Whether the United Nations could perform this function in a manner satisfactory to the industrialized countries whose citizens and firms would provide most of the funds to be distributed is doubtful. From the perspective of these nations, the process would be certain to become politicized and would be to their disadvantage.

A more feasible course than allocation by either the revenue-acquiring agencies or the United Nations would be to entrust this function to institutions with special competence in the fields of developmental and environmental problems. As will be seen, a number of institutional alternatives exist in the cases of both general development funds and environmental funds.

GENERAL DEVELOPMENT FUNDS. The choice of institutional arrangements for managing new general development funds would be certain to involve considerable controversy. If the Communist countries joined the new international revenue system, new institutions might well be required. If those countries did not join, it would be somewhat more likely that the new funds could be allocated by existing institutions.

The World Bank—or more likely, its affiliate, the International Development Association (IDA)—could receive part of the proceeds of revenue taxes and pollution taxes and revenues from the exploitation of nonliving ocean resources and lend them in accordance with existing procedures. The increased volume of lending by the Bank would expand requirements for preinvestment studies and surveys by UNDP and for assistance by several UN Specialized Agencies to governments in identifying and preparing project proposals. Part of the new funds received by the Bank might therefore be passed on to UNDP and to the UN Specialized Agencies. An alternative arrangement would be for the new general development funds to come initially to UNDP, which would determine how much should be passed on to the World Bank (and possibly also to the regional development banks), how much should be retained to pay for its own preinvestment work, and how much should go to the UN Specialized Agencies.

Both of these alternatives would be opposed vigorously in some quarters. The Bank and UNDP now have separate sources of funding, and neither of these institutions could be expected to welcome subordination to the other. A more fundamental difficulty, however, would flow from the predictable opposition of different groups of countries to giving either institution the upper hand. The developing countries would object to giving the Bank, with its weighted voting rights, both greater resources and implicit authority over UNDP. The Soviet Union, China, and most other countries with centrally planned economies do not belong to the Bank. Insofar as they were able to influence the outcome, they, too, would oppose expanding the Bank's role.[7]

The reverse arrangement would be certain to be resisted by many of the developed countries with market economies. They would feel that they should control the disposition of funds raised largely from their firms and citizens. These developed countries would also fear that giving UNDP control over more money would in time lead to an expansion of UNDP's role into the field of investment, thereby bringing it into direct competition with the World Bank.

Some compromise between these opposing points of view might be possible if the volume of general development funds to be allocated every year turned out not to be very large. For example, the developed market economy countries might go along with making UNDP the primary allocating institution for new general development funds if both its role and the percentage of the funds that it could retain were sharply circumscribed. The countries on the other side of the issue might agree to an arrangement under which UNDP would pass most of the new funds on to the Bank, since the amount involved appeared to be modest.

If, however, very large new general development funds became available—say, several billion dollars annually—the only practicable alternatives would be either to create a new institution or to reform the World Bank to increase the voting rights of the developing countries. Because of the difficulties that would be certain to arise if two large institutions were operating in the general development field, reforming the World Bank is the more attractive alternative. As difficult as this would be, it might be possible—particularly if the Bank had before it the prospect of the creation of another international aid agency with considerable resources and influence. Changing the distribution of voting rights in IDA alone might be more feasible than reforming both the Bank and IDA. It is even conceivable that, if the Communist countries joined a new international revenue system, they would be willing to take the additional step of joining an IDA that was no longer dominated by the industrialized countries with free-market economies.

7. There is no reason to assume that these countries will remain outside the Bank forever. In fact, it is possible that most of them will decide to join both the Bank and the International Monetary Fund within the next decade.

If agreement to turn over the new development funds to a reformed IDA could not be reached, an entirely new institution would be needed.[8] This new institution, which might be called the Special Revenue Fund (SRF), could be given broad authority to allocate funds to other institutions which would in turn allocate them to the institutions that actually carry out projects and programs. SRF could be established by the UN General Assembly, but a compromise on the critical issue of voting rights might more easily be reached as part of the negotiation of a treaty creating one or more international revenue taxes. This approach would also avoid the anomaly of permitting nations that had declined to participate in the treaty to have a say in the disposition of the money resulting from the treaty. Also, it might be more acceptable to developed free-market countries that have become increasingly skeptical about the decision-making processes of the General Assembly. In order to obtain the essential agreement of the developed free-market countries on the imposition of taxes, the developing countries and the Communist countries might give some ground on the issue of control over SRF. The outcome might be a system of voting weighted somewhat in favor of the developed free-market countries, but to a lesser degree than in the case of the World Bank.

Many other questions would also have to be settled before the SRF could be established. One basic question is whether it should be allowed to make allocations directly to operating institutions (such as national governments) that carry out specific projects and programs, or be confined to dealing with intermediaries (such as the World Bank) that would make the final allocation to operating institutions. The first course would run the risk of duplicating specialized capabilities that are present in the intermediary institutions. This course would also make SRF something like a second World Bank and would make it difficult to distinguish the functions of the two organizations. The second course would deny SRF a certain amount of useful flexibility and might make the allocation process cumbersome and overly bureaucratic. A possible compromise would be to require SRF to deal with intermediaries, except in the cases of direct allocations larger than a specified amount.

---

8. The proposal to create a new UN Development Authority to administer all existing preinvestment funds does not go far enough to meet the institutional problem under discussion. The proposed UN Development Authority would be only a super-UNDP, limited like UNDP to the preinvestment phase of developmental and other forms of assistance.

The selection of intermediary institutions by SRF would be another problem. For example, should SRF be free to make unlimited allocations to the World Bank Group? In terms of efficiency, a positive answer is clearly indicated, but this course might be politically objectionable to the developing countries and would certainly be opposed by countries, such as the Soviet Union, that do not belong to the Bank.

Other issues that would have to be faced in establishing SRF would be the purposes for which it could allocate funds, the terms of its allocations, and whether or not it would be permitted to raise money on the capital markets. The last of these problems is probably the least difficult. Since the SRF would be set up to handle a continuous flow of funds from new sources, it would be able to function without borrowing. It could, of course, expand its allocations by borrowing, but to do so would bring it into competition with the World Bank and the regional development banks. All of these institutions depend on borrowed funds, and the competition of SRF might interfere with their ability to borrow—and thus to relend—on favorable terms.

The question of the purposes to which SRF money should be devoted can be answered in terms of the functions of the recipient organizations. Thus, SRF might be authorized to finance any or all of the following expenses of specified organizations: administration, operations (that is, programs directly conducted by the organizations), and grants or loans to other entities. Most of the organizations specified would belong to the UN system, although the regional development banks might also be included. The purposes for which SRF could allocate funds would, in effect, be delimited by the charters of the recipient organizations. There is no reason why the specified organizations could not include some with environmental responsibilities or why some SRF funds could not be used for environmental purposes.

On the question of the terms of SRF allocations, both grants and loans should be permitted. When funds are provided, directly or indirectly, to finance activities in countries with satisfactory foreign exchange positions, repayment should be required. The terms of repayment, however, need not be hard, since SRF's funds would be relatively free of cost. If necessary, repayment could be scheduled over an extended period, a grace period could be provided, and interest rates could be low. Even very soft loans, however, would not be appropriate in countries that were in foreign exchange difficulties. In such cases, grants would be necessary.

SRF could use its ability to make grants and soft loans by helping the World Bank to finance projects for borrowers who could not afford the Bank's normal terms. Just as the Bank now is able to soften the terms of loans by blending Bank and IDA money, a blending of SRF and Bank resources could produce more favorable terms than would be possible if the Bank acted alone.

Particularly if a new institution were created to handle new general development funds, a framework for considering developmental needs and the means of meeting them could be quite useful. One proposal to this end calls for the periodic preparation of a world development budget, which would set forth the capital requirements of the developing countries, estimate the funds that might be available from all sources to meet those requirements, and identify major problems and shortfalls.[9]

ENVIRONMENTAL FUNDS. Existing institutions do not appear to be well-equipped to allocate more than modest amounts of environmental funds. The Fund of UNEP could, in theory, assume this role at the primary level, but this would require a drastic change in UNEP's philosophy, and possibly some increase in staff. The Fund of UNEP, which is financed by voluntary contributions from member governments, spent only $12.4 million in 1975.[10] The philosophy that guides the allocations of the Fund of UNEP to other organizations is that of providing seed money in support of UNEP's catalytic role. Large-scale allocations, whether to operating or intermediary institutions, would represent a drastic change in the role that is, by design, currently being played by the Fund of UNEP.

A number of possible institutional innovations might be considered as means of allocating new funds that have been earmarked or otherwise set aside for environmental purposes. One possibility would be to establish a new environmental affiliate of the World Bank. Another would be to expand the functions, as well as the resources, of the Fund of UNEP. Still another would be to set up an autonomous environmental fund.

The great advantage of the first of these three possible ways of handling environmental funds would be the Bank's expertise in financing large projects in many parts of the world and its established working relation-

---

9. See Edward R. Fried and Philip H. Trezise, "The United States in the World Economy," in Henry Owen and Charles L. Schultze, eds., *Setting National Priorities: The Next Ten Years* (Brookings Institution, 1976), pp. 217–18.

10. "Proposed Fund Programme Activities," UN Doc. UNEP/GC/62, January 30, 1976, p. 3.

ships with other UN Specialized Agencies. Moreover, the Bank has experience in lending not only for self-financing projects but also for projects that are unable to earn a sufficient rate of return to pay back money borrowed at close-to-conventional rates of interest. Experience with handling these concessional funds would be especially useful if it is assumed that a considerable portion of the new financial resources would be used for programs that are not self-financing.

On the other hand, establishing an environmental affiliate of the Bank would have a serious disadvantage. The basic purpose of the Bank is to promote development by transferring resources from the rich countries to the poor countries. It would therefore not make sense for the Bank to finance environmental programs, such as global monitoring, that are not related to development. Thus, if an environmental affiliate of the Bank were created, a separate institution would still be needed to finance environmental programs of benefit to both developed and developing nations. Moreover, the development programs with a strong environmental aspect that a new affiliate could properly finance could be financed by the Bank and the IDA as now constituted.

The second possible institutional innovation, an expanded Fund of UNEP, could provide greater support for the environmental priorities established by UNEP's Governing Council. Such a fund would also retain the advantage of free access to the specialized environmental skills present in UNEP's staff. The third alternative, an autonomous environmental fund, would have none of the advantages of affiliation with either the World Bank or UNEP. It would also involve creating yet another separate entity in a system that many believe is already too large, complex, and poorly coordinated. This third alternative would clearly be the least desirable of the possibilities considered here. On balance, expanding the functions and resources of the Fund of UNEP would be the best course to follow.

A variant of the second alternative would be to leave the present Fund of UNEP with its present role and establish alongside it an Environment Foundation that would be given new functions and larger financial resources. This Environment Foundation would be subordinate to the same Governing Council as UNEP and might be managed either by the same executive director or by a separate officer. The following observations about an expanded Fund of UNEP apply equally to a new Environment Foundation linked to UNEP.

Some problems would clearly be encountered in turning over large new resources to the Fund of UNEP. The issue of voting rights would be sure to arise. However, a compromise between the developing and the developed countries could probably be reached more easily than in the case of a new World Bank affiliate, because the precedent for future control of the Bank, the International Development Association, and the International Finance Corporation would be less direct or compelling. Decisions would also be needed on the function of the expanded Fund of UNEP and on its relation with other entities, including most notably the World Bank.

The expanded Fund of UNEP could invest directly or indirectly in concrete environmental programs and projects, including the financing of technical assistance. It could also continue to provide seed money in support of UNEP's catalytic activities. And it could enable UNEP to assume a preinvestment role similar to that of UNDP.

The expanded Fund of UNEP could cooperate with the World Bank in jointly financing developmental projects with important environmental aspects. Because the money at the disposal of the fund would be relatively cost-free, it could allocate some of its resources as grants and the rest on soft terms like those extended by IDA. As in the case of Bank-SRF cooperation discussed above, a blending of Bank money and money from the expanded Fund of UNEP would make possible the financing of some projects on easier terms than would be possible if the Bank acted alone.

The environmental fund should not be authorized to supplement its resources by borrowing in capital markets. The chances that it could borrow on favorable terms would be poor. Moreover, the environmental fund would not have to borrow in order to continue to function, since it would enjoy a continuous flow of funds from earmarked pollution taxes and possibly from other sources.

Many of the allocations made by the expanded Fund of UNEP would go directly to operating institutions, such as national and local governments and specialized international agencies. However, in a field as complicated as the environmental field, and in a world characterized more by diversity than uniformity of physical conditions and human institutions, the use of intermediaries to assist in the allocation of some environmental funds is all but essential. Ideally, there should be a mosaic of global, regional, and national institutions that could receive funds for purposes stated in fairly general terms and could reallocate them to operating institutions charged with the execution of specific projects. The commissions which are being organized to serve as secretariats for the emerging regional conventions formed to deal with the environmental problems of specific parts of the ocean or enclosed seas could become important parts of this mosaic. One example is the secretariat established by UNEP to oversee the implementation of the Convention for the Protection of the Mediterranean Sea Against Pollution, which was signed by fourteen states in 1976. (The treaty is expected to go into force in 1977 after ratification by a sufficient number of states.) The activities of the preliminary secretariat, which is funded by UNEP and by contributions from various nations and regional bodies, include the establishment of a regional oil-combating center in Malta to deal with major oil spills, the development of a regional approach to planning for management of the resources of the Mediterranean Basin, and the provision of a framework to monitor certain pollutants and organisms.[11]

Other examples of institutions which might be suitable as intermediaries in the allocation of funds for environmental programs are the United Nations Habitat and Human Settlement Foundation and the Global Environmental Monitoring System (GEMS). One way of organizing the field activities of GEMS might be along the lines of most programs run by the World Meteorological Organization (WMO). The WMO has a relatively small budget compared with other UN agencies, yet it has some of the most successful programs in the entire UN system. Basically, the WMO serves as a coordinator of various meteorological programs and services, and of research efforts that are operated and financed by national governments. GEMS might serve as coordinator of various global monitoring efforts, which would be conducted by participating national governments who would draw on scientific expertise in their governments, universities, and research centers. The main difference between the global monitoring service and the world weather programs would be in the financing. Since national governments are clearly more willing to pay for meteorological services than they are for global environmental monitoring, the funding for the latter might appropriately come from a new source of international revenue.

11. "Final Act of the Conference of Plenipotentiaries of the Coastal States of the Mediterranean Region for the Protection of the Mediterranean Sea—Barcelona, 2–16 February 1976," UN Doc. UNEP/GC/61/Add.3, March 24, 1976.

Conclusions

The generation of revenue taxes and taxes on polluters would require formal international treaties. Since the terms of such treaties could not easily cover all problems and contingencies, continuing bodies would have to be created to oversee execution of the treaties and to make a variety of decisions within guidelines specified in the treaties. Obtaining revenues from nonliving ocean resources would probably also require a formal international agreement, although less formal arrangements are possible on an interim basis. Only the fourth source of financing considered, borrowing from capital markets for environmental purposes, would require no new formal agreement. Such borrowing could best be handled by the World Bank and the regional development banks operating within the terms of their existing charters. The channeling of greater World Bank resources into environmental projects could be facilitated by having UNEP assume a preinvestment role in the environmental field similar to that now played by UNDP in the field of development assistance.

Most of the funds considered would probably be allocated on a discretionary basis, although automatic allocation of the proceeds from any of the revenue sources is possible. In principle, all of the funds could be used for any agreed upon international purpose. Earmarking any of them for environmental programs or any other special purpose would be a political decision and not the inevitable consequence of something inherent in the funds or their sources. Nevertheless, it is virtually certain that the governments agreeing to the generation of new international revenues would insist on knowing how those revenues would be used, either by earmarking them for specific purposes or by establishing specific restrictions and guidelines.

For present purposes, it is assumed that two categories of funds would be involved: general development funds and environmental funds. Choices among institutional alternatives must be faced for both kinds of funds. General developmental funds could, in principle, be administered and put to use by existing international institutions, primarily the World Bank and UNDP. Disagreements could be anticipated, however, between the developed and the developing nations over the roles and relative influence of these two organizations. Particularly if very large general purpose funds became available, a new institution might have to be created to manage them. However, a reform of the World Bank (or the International Development Association) that gave greater voting rights to developing countries would be a possible—and preferable—alternative.

A substantial flow of new funds that are either earmarked or otherwise designated for environmental purposes could best be handled by expanding the functions of the existing Fund of UNEP, or by creating an Environmental Foundation closely linked with UNEP. With increased resources, the fund or foundation could make substantial investments in environmental programs and projects. Seed money in support of UNEP's catalytic role could continue to be provided by the expanded Fund of UNEP or, if the Environmental Foundation were established, by the present Fund of UNEP. The fund or foundation could also provide UNEP with financing for preinvestment studies and surveys, if UNEP were to undertake such work in the future.

CHAPTER SEVEN

Problems
and Possible Solutions

IN FUTURE YEARS, the international community will almost certainly need increasing amounts of money to deal with major international problems, such as assisting in the development of the poorer nations of the world, expanding and improving the system of nuclear safeguards, maintaining peacekeeping forces, and meeting threats to the environment. Present means of mobilizing funds for international purposes—principally assessments on governments, voluntary contributions by governments, and borrowing from capital markets—cannot be expected to meet growing needs.

Review of Financial Options

This study has examined a wide variety of possible new sources of finance. For one reason or another, most of them have been set aside. The small number of remaining possibilities fall into two groups: those that could be used to finance any agreed upon international programs, including environmental programs; and those that might appropriately be earmarked solely for environmental purposes.

General Funds

Three sources of general revenue deserve serious consideration: shadow taxes on governments, economic rents from the exploitation of nonliving resources of the ocean beyond national jurisdictions, and taxes

195

on international trade and on the international transfer of profits from international investments.

Shadow taxes would do no more than provide another way of calculating assessments on governments. If, however, they imparted an increased flexibility, as well as a degree of automaticity, to the present assessment system, they might enable the United Nations and the UN Specialized Agencies to adjust revenues more easily to rising requirements. The most attractive shadow tax would probably by one levied on the gross domestic products of member governments. Substituting such a shadow tax for the present schedule of assessments could be done without any new formal international agreements. A strong impetus for financial reform in the United Nations and the UN Specialized Agencies would, however, be required.

The manganese nodules found on many parts of the deep ocean floor appear to be the only resource lying beyond the present or prospective jurisdiction of coastal states that could generate substantial amounts of revenue for international purposes in the foreseeable future. Perhaps as much as $200 million a year could be appropriated by 1985 from the economic rents generated by exploitation of nodule deposits. Whether nodule mining will yield any revenue for international purposes probably depends, however, on whether agreement can be reached on an international regime to manage the exploitation of nonliving ocean resources. Even if such a regime is established, it is possible that any economic rents that it might appropriate would be distributed directly to developing countries on the basis of a mechanical formula, rather than being used to pay for agreed upon international programs.

The third source of general revenues—international taxes on all or part of international trade and on certain financial transactions—has several major advantages: large revenue-raising potential, great flexibility, and freedom from dependence upon annual appropriations by governments. The direct imposition of taxes on private firms and individuals on behalf of the international community would, however, be a revolutionary step. A formal treaty would be required, plus administrative arrangements for which there are no close precedents.

Environmental Funds

Any of the three sources of general revenue might be used to support international environmental programs. In addition, several other possible means of finance might be used exclusively for environmental purposes. The more promising of these appear to be: the solicitation of private contributions and the sale of technical services by the United Nations Environment Programme, the channeling of more of the resources of the World Bank Group and the regional development banks into environmental projects (and development projects with important environmental aspects), and the imposition of taxes on polluters of the ocean.

Of these possible sources of environmental funds, private contributions and the sale of technical services could be generated without any unusual new legal and administrative arrangements or any great departure from past precedents. Their revenue-raising potentials, however, are uncertain and probably are quite limited.

An increase in loans for environmental purposes by the World Bank Group and the regional development banks could be facilitated by involving UNEP in the preinvestment process, thereby providing those financial institutions with a flow of well-prepared environmental projects. How large an increase in environmental financing could be achieved in this way, however, would depend on the resources available to those institutions and on how they and their clients resolve the perceived competition between developmental and environmental goals.

Imposing taxes on polluters of the marine environment would only incidentally be a revenue-raising measure. The principal purpose of such taxes would be to induce polluters to reduce their emissions as a means of gaining reductions in their tax liabilities. Nevertheless, these taxes could yield significant revenues, since most polluters would find it cheaper to pay some tax than to reduce their emissions to zero. These revenues could be used for any agreed upon international purpose, but the international community may see a special propriety in devoting them to environmental purposes.

Like general revenue taxes, taxes on polluters would represent a revolutionary step and could be imposed only by means of a formal treaty. One possible category of taxes might be levied on activities that chronically emit oil or refined petroleum products into the ocean—namely, tanker operations, other merchant shipping, and offshore drilling operations. A serious, but not necessarily insuperable, obstacle to the imposition of taxes on oil spillage is the absence of reliable information on the damage, expressed in monetary terms, inflicted on the marine environment by various levels of emissions of the pollutants to be taxed.

Problems Requiring Solution

Some of the possible financial measures noted above raise practical problems that would have to be solved before they could be put into effect. Some measures would involve actual or potential conflicts between international and national interests. Some, taken separately, would result in a distribution of burdens among nations that would be viewed by many as inequitable. Most of the measures would be regarded differently by various nations, depending upon circumstances such as their levels of development and the nature of their economic systems. Obtaining the participation of a sufficient number of nations could prove to be a problem. Problems of enforcement and collectibility would be certain to arise with respect to several of the possible new sources of finance. Finally, if substantial new funds for either general or environmental purposes are to be generated, new institutional arrangements would probably be required to collect such funds and to handle their allocation.

Conflict with National Interests

The fundamental basis for friction between various national interests and some of the possible international revenue systems under discussion lies in the fact that nations will fear some loss of sovereignty to international institutions. Obviously, this is not a step which many governments are eager to take. Although the powers of the international institutions could be carefully defined and circumscribed in an international treaty establishing a revenue system, the potential for conflict would remain. The most obvious point of stress is that the international revenue system would be competing with national systems for revenues from the same sources. Some potential for conflict between national and international policies might also exist.

National governments already levy duties on imports, tax income from international investments, and impose a variety of taxes on oil and other forms of energy and on minerals—whether imported or produced domestically. As for revenue from mineral production from the deep ocean floor, if an international seabed authority with powers to collect and distribute revenues from mineral exploration and output is not created, then presumably national governments would tax mining companies operating in the ocean in the same way that they tax companies engaged in mining activities on land. If a seabed authority with revenue powers is created, then some of the economic rent which otherwise would have gone entirely to national treasuries would be siphoned off by the seabed authority. No national government now taxes pollutants discharged directly into the oceans from tankers and other ships. Thus, international taxes on such discharges would not directly infringe upon present revenue sources. Various taxes are, however, imposed on private shipping companies and on the oil industry. The international taxes on oil discharges would therefore indirectly compete with existing national revenue sources.

If an increase in loans for environmental purposes from existing institutions such as the World Bank and the regional banks was sought, the lending institutions either would have to curtail their lending for other purposes or would have to expand their ability to make loans by raising more money in capital markets. If the latter course was followed, the international bank would be competing with the national government or private firms in the country that were also trying to borrow in the capital markets. Thus, whenever the World Bank decides it wants to market bonds in a particular capital market, the matter is carefully negotiated with the host government before the Bank attempts to borrow in that country.

The general revenue taxes probably pose the most serious potential conflict with national interests since they coincide with existing national taxes on trade and financial transactions. The problems that this circumstance might create can probably be minimized, however, if the international tax rates are kept very low. It should be noted, moreover, that in the developed countries revenues from tariffs are not generally a principal source of income to national treasuries. In the analysis in chapter 3, the tax on general trade used for illustrative purposes is levied at an ad valorem rate of 0.1 percent. Compared to various levels of import duties that are imposed by most national governments, this tax rate is quite low. Again, the tax rate used as an example to explain the international tax on oil is 0.1 percent ad valorem. When compared with the taxes which many national governments impose on crude oil and petroleum products, this illustrative tax also appears quite low. Low rates of international taxation, such as these, should not cause any significant reduction in national revenues. In fact, an international trade tax would not directly divert revenue from the customs duties imposed by national governments. It would only depress the yield of such duties indirectly by raising the price of imported goods and causing a slight reduction in their consumption, thereby decreasing somewhat the flow of goods on which duties are collected.

On the whole, possible conflicts with national policies appear to be less serious than potential infringements on national revenue sources. Thus, the conflict between international taxes on polluters and national regulations imposing compulsory design standards on tankers is more philosophical than real. A shipowner conforming to good national design standards could claim a reduction in his international pollution tax for any consequent reduction in oil emissions.

Similarly, an international trade tax and a tax on income from international investments would, in principle, run counter to the policies of those governments that are committed to the reduction of barriers to commerce among nations and to the free flow of capital. But, if the rate of these taxes was very low, their practical effects on progress toward freer trade and their interference with flows among world capital markets would probably be relatively minor.

A more difficult problem is posed in the case of exploitation of minerals on the ocean floor. The international interest in deriving revenue from such minerals runs counter to the interest of a few countries that depend heavily for foreign exchange on the export of these minerals. A solution to this problem requires either compensating the countries affected or restricting ocean mining to the extent necessary to avoid an unacceptable fall in prices.

Burden Sharing

How the burden of public expenditures should be distributed is one of the most fundamental and persistent issues in both national and international politics. At the national level, the question is principally one of how heavily different groups of individual taxpayers—defined in terms of criteria such as level of income, occupation, and so forth—should be taxed. This question could also arise in connection with the financing of international activities. At the international level, however, the issue is much more likely to be how the burden of a particular means of finance should be shared among nations, rather than among firms and individuals.

Perceptions of what distribution of burdens is fair differ. Some spokesmen for developing countries would probably resist the imposition of any additional burden on their countries, arguing that what is needed is a straightforward transfer of resources from the rich nations to the poor nations of the world. At a minimum, many developing countries could be expected to insist that the tapping of new sources of finance not excuse the industrialized countries from meeting the internationally agreed upon target of devoting 0.7 percent of their gross national products to official development assistance. Some developing countries would refuse to accept any new burdens whatsoever, so long as the industrialized countries failed to meet this target. Many governments of industrialized countries might go along with some degree of preferential treatment of the developing countries, but they would probably insist that no participating country be totally exempted from any new scheme to raise money for international purposes.

For present purposes, it will be assumed that all disagreements over burden sharing could be solved through negotiations that would strike a compromise among the points of view of differently situated nations. An important component of such a compromise would probably be an understanding of how the proceeds of new sources of finance were to be allocated. Such an understanding could be either substantive or procedural, but most likely it would be both. That is, agreement would be reached on how both broad priorities and specific allocations would be made. In the latter connection, the distribution of voting rights would be crucial.

The importance of the issue of burden sharing varies greatly among the various possible new sources of international funds. The issue would not arise with respect to private contributions, except to the extent that governments that provide tax benefits to individuals and firms making gifts to international organizations would claim credit for that fact in general debates over burden sharing. Much the same would be true of the sale of technical services, although it is possible that some developing nations might argue that charges for such services should be varied with ability to pay. This would amount to a claim that the "burden" of paying for these particular benefits should be allocated in a particular way.

Efforts to channel more of the resources of the World Bank Group and the regional development banks into environmental programs would raise problems about the distribution of burdens only if these institutions decided to increase their lending capacities by soliciting additional contributions from member governments. No questions of burden sharing, as that term is used here, have come up in the debate over the exploitation of nonliving ocean resources beyond national jurisdictions.

International taxes on polluters are an intermediate case. There can be no doubt that such taxes would have different impacts on different nations, and this fact could become a source of controversy. On the other hand, the primary purpose of these taxes would be to change the behavior of polluters and only incidentally to raise revenue for international purposes. The question of whether the burden of such taxes was distributed fairly would probably be overshadowed by the desire to protect the environment that would provide the motive for imposing them.

In the cases of international revenue taxes and shadow taxes, however, there can be little doubt that the issue of burden sharing would be of fundamental importance. Of these two means of finance, revenue taxes have by far the greater potential for raising large amounts of money and therefore for imposing large burdens. Shadow taxes have only relatively limited utility as a substitute for the assessment schedules now used by the United Nations and the UN Specialized Agencies, or as a complement to revenue taxes. The following discussion will therefore focus on the problem of burden sharing as it arises in connection with one of the revenue taxes singled out for special attention in this study, an ad valorem tax on all internationally traded commodities. The problem of burden sharing raised by this tax will serve to illustrate the somewhat similar problems that would be created by other possible international revenue taxes.

As was brought out in chapter 3, a given nation's share of total world imports can be taken as a rough index of the share that it would bear of a tax on internationally traded commodities.[1] Thus, a large nation, most of whose trade is internal, would be taxed a much smaller fraction of its gross

1. This approach is, at best, approximate since it ignores the fact that some nations run trade deficits and surpluses for prolonged periods and would pay more or less than their normal shares if—as is assumed here—the tax were levied on imports. This approach also does not take account of the effects of differences in the elasticities of demand and supply for various commodities and differences in the commodity compositions of the trade of various nations.

national product (GNP) than would a small nation whose economy is heavily dependent on foreign trade. Consequently, there would be no correlation between the burden of the tax and even as crude a measure of ability to pay as GNP. The developing countries would in fact argue that making the burden proportionate to GNP would not be enough and that the rich countries should pay a larger share of GNP than the poor countries.

In principle, the international trade tax could be brought into line with any agreed upon standard of international equity in several ways: tax rates could be varied from country to country, or different rates could be applied to different categories of goods; part or all of the imports of some countries could be exempted from the tax; part or all of the taxes collected on the imports of some countries could be rebated to the governments of those countries, or those governments could retain part of the tax proceeds that they collect, with the proportion retained varying inversely with the size of the country; the trade tax could be coupled with another revenue-raising measure whose burden would be distributed in such a way as to compensate for the deficiencies in the distribution of the burden of the trade tax; or the proceeds of the trade tax could be used for purposes that would bring about a distribution of net burdens (taxes paid minus benefits received) that would be regarded as equitable. Combinations of these approaches are also conceivable.

Sole reliance upon differential tax rates as the adjustment mechanism would not be desirable. If the objective were only to distribute the tax burden in proportion to GNP, the imports of countries whose international trade is only a small fraction of their GNP would have to be taxed at rates so high as to distort existing trade patterns and possibly disrupt existing international agreements on trade and tariffs. Exemptions—which would amount to applying a zero tax rate to part of total trade—would be subject to similar objections from the point of view of international trade policy. Moreover, exemptions alone probably could not achieve an acceptable distribution of the tax burden without a very large, and therefore undesirable, contraction of the tax base.

Rebates or retentions of a portion of the tax would not have the distorting effect on trade patterns that would be caused by differential rates or exemptions. From the point of view of the international community, however, rebates or retentions would be subtractions from the funds being

204 New Means of Financing International Needs

raised for its general benefit. This loss could be made up by raising the tax rate. In chapter 3 a formula for calculating the proportion of revenues to be retained by each country was developed. This formula would produce the same annual yield at a tax rate of 2 percent ad valorem as a tax rate of 1 percent with no retentions.

Coupling the international trade tax with another revenue-raising measure in order to bring about a combined burden distribution that would be regarded as equitable is attractive in principle, but difficult in practice. A domestic sales tax or a value-added tax would move the burden distribution in the right direction, if the objective were to impose burdens roughly proportionate to GNP. These taxes would not, however, completely eliminate the advantage enjoyed by large countries under the international trade tax, unless higher rates were applied to them in collecting a sales tax or a value-added tax. This is so because (assuming similar economic structures) levying a sales tax or a value-added tax on all countries at the same rate would impose equivalent burdens as proportions of GNP. But what is required is a greater burden—and therefore higher rates— on the countries taxed relatively lightly by the international trade tax. Determining what rate should be applied to each country would be quite difficult and would be certain to arouse endless controversy. A more fundamental obstacle to the use of a sales tax or a value-added tax for international purposes is the likelihood that many governments would view this use of traditional internal revenue sources as inappropriate and, in some subtle way, an infringement on national sovereignty.

A more acceptable, and technically less difficult, way of evening out the perceived inequities in the international trade tax would be to levy special assessments on nations that bear shares of the burden of the tax that are too small. These balancing assessments would have to be calculated, explicitly or implicitly, on the basis of a schedule of total obligations from which deductions would be made for amounts collected by means of the international trade tax. It might therefore be asked why the schedule of assessments could not be used without going to the trouble of collecting the trade tax. A partial answer is that the tax would bypass the annual appropriation process and reduce somewhat the political cost of diverting substantial sums of money to international purposes. At the same time, it must be recognized that, by focusing attention on total national obligations, a schedule of assessments would tend to impose a ceiling on the amount that could be raised by means of the international trade tax.

As was noted above, the distribution of the burden of the international trade tax can be adjusted at the expenditure, as well as at the collection, end of the fiscal process. In fact, any means of raising money for international purposes is certain to be judged on the basis of who benefits from use of the money, as well as on the basis of where the money came from. The only question in this regard is whether understandings can be reached in advance that would cause nations that believe their share of the tax burden is too large to conclude that this inequity will be eliminated when the tax proceeds are spent. Advance commitments to spend specified amounts in specified countries would not be desirable, since there would be little chance that such an expenditure pattern would conform to any rational system of international priorities. Perhaps the most that could be done would be to reach agreement on the general purposes for which the tax proceeds would be used and on how allocations to specific programs and projects would be made.

The conclusion that emerges from the above review of possible means of adjusting the burden of the international trade tax is that all approaches involve problems and no single approach can be relied on to achieve an acceptable result by itself. It is probably best to regard each approach as a possible subject for negotiation and the totality of approaches as a complex area for international bargaining. Thus, if a climate favorable to the imposition of an international trade tax were to arise, the treaty providing for the tax could prove to be a complicated document. Provision might be made for differential rates, exemptions, rebates, or retentions. The detailed administration of these provisions would probably be delegated to a continuing body that would act within guidelines set forth in the treaty. A system of balancing assessments might also be included. Almost certainly, agreement would be required on how the proceeds of the tax were to be used.

The variations in the different adjustment mechanisms and in the ways that they might be combined are almost infinite. It may be useful, however, to give one hypothetical example as a means of illustrating what is possible. The governments desiring to create an international trade tax might: (1) set a low tax rate to ease the fears of the industrialized countries, (2) levy compensating assessments on large countries that trade relatively small percentages of their GNPs, (3) exempt essential imports of countries with annual per capita GNPs below $500, (4) rebate all taxes collected from countries with annual per capita GNPs below $200, and (5) agree that at least a stated percentage of revenues be used for developmental or environmental purposes in countries with per capita GNPs below $500.

The above analysis of burden sharing in the case of the international trade tax can be applied with modifications to the other possible revenue taxes discussed in this study. The available adjustment mechanisms, and the problems involved in each, would be quite similar. In some cases, however, determining where the burden of the tax would fall would be more difficult than in the case of the international trade tax. The reason is that it would not be possible to assume that the total amount of tax would be passed on to consumers. For some commodities, a significant portion might be absorbed by producers.

Participation

Several possible sources of funds for international purposes—trade taxes, taxes on polluters, and probably also revenues from exploitation of nonliving ocean resources—could be tapped only by means of formal international treaties. Such treaties would have to specify the number of countries whose ratification would be needed to bring the treaties into force. As will be seen, this requirement would not be the same for all of the revenue sources in question.

The general trade tax would probably need the largest number of adherents, if a revenue structure based on this source were to be effective and fair. This is because non-treaty members could trade with each other and escape the tax entirely. Thus, for example, if the United States and the European Community ratified the treaty, while Japan stayed out, Japan would enjoy a competitive advantage in industrial exports to other non-treaty participants. It might not even be sufficient to have participation by all of the major trading countries, if a number of middle-level exporters (such as Taiwan, South Korea, South Africa, and Brazil) were nonmembers.

This problem would probably not be serious if the tax rate were kept extremely low. A rate of, say, 0.1 percent ad valorem would not affect prices very much, and treaty members would not be placed at any significant disadvantage with respect to non-treaty members. At substantially higher tax rates, however, the only escape from the need for widespread participation would be through refraining from taxing exports of treaty members to non-treaty countries. This approach would, of course, reduce the revenue-sharing potential of the general trade tax, and it would be less desirable than obtaining the participation of as many countries as possible.

A tax on internationally traded crude oil and refined petroleum products would require far fewer participating nations than would a general trade tax. Only thirteen countries account for 76 percent of world oil imports, and only eleven countries originate 86 percent of exports. Participation of twenty-four countries would therefore permit taxation, at either the export or the import end, of the great bulk of the international trade in oil.[2]

Comprehensive coverage would be quite desirable. On the assumption that the oil tax would be largely, if not entirely, shifted forward to consumers, oil-importing countries that stayed out of the treaty would gain the advantage of a cheaper source of energy than would be available to treaty countries, unless their oil imports were taxed at the point of export. Similarly, oil-exporting countries with excess productive capacity might hope to expand their sales by offering oil at a price below that of treaty participants, unless their oil were to be taxed at the point of importation.

A tax on all energy trade (except nuclear fuel) would require participation by a few more countries than a tax on oil alone. The principal conventional energy sources besides crude oil that are presently involved in world trade to a significant degree are coal and natural gas. The principal flows of coal are from Eastern Europe to Western Europe and from the United States and Australia to Japan. The major flows of natural gas at present are from the Soviet Union to Eastern Europe, from North Africa to Western Europe, and from Southeast Asia to Japan. The principal importers of coal and gas are, in most cases, major oil importers. Thus, if a treaty were expanded from oil trade to all energy trade, these major importers would already be participants. The principal additional countries whose participation might be desirable would be Poland, the Soviet Union, and Australia.

A tax on oil spills from tankers would require acceptance by roughly the same countries as a tax on crude oil trade. The pollution tax on oil discharges would probably not be collected for each voyage. In the absence of adequate on-board monitoring devices which could measure the

2. *World Energy Supplies, 1950–1974,* UN Doc. ST/ESA/STAT/SER.J/19, 1976, pp. 193–227.

amount of oil discharged by a given tanker during a particular voyage, the tax would be calculated on the basis of estimated average oil spillage during the course of a year. The amount of spillage, and therefore the amount of the tax, would vary with vessel size, with the tanker's design, and with the type of pollution abatement technology with which the tanker was equipped. The simplest procedure for collection might be an annual tax. When the tax was paid, the tanker owner would be provided with certification papers or a sticker, which would be shown to port authorities in participating countries as proof of payment.

Participation by the countries that are the principal importers of crude oil would be sufficient, along with adherence by the small number of countries that are the major exporters of crude oil. However, it would be prudent also to have treaty participation by the relatively small number of countries in which ownership of the world's tanker fleet is concentrated. About 75 percent of the world tanker fleet is owned by governments or individuals and corporations of some nine countries.[3] Even though the tanker owners might be able to pass along the tax burden to the consumer, it is difficult to imagine this tax being put into effect by the international community if the countries where tanker ownership is concentrated refused to adhere to the treaty.

A tax on oil spills from ships other than tankers would require more widespread formal acceptance than the tax on tankers. Ships owned by nationals or governments of non-treaty countries could be used in trade with other non-treaty countries with impunity. However, efficient routing and utilization of cargo vessels normally require great flexibility. A vessel has to be ready to stop at whatever port may be necessary from a commercial point of view, and the port could as easily be located in a treaty country as in a country that remained outside the treaty. Thus, it might be sufficient to have ratification by only ten countries, which together accounted for more than half of the world's trade (excluding oil).[4]

A special problem affecting all of the means of finance under discussion here is the participation of the Soviet Union, China, and the other countries with centrally managed economies. Most of these countries have not joined the major financial institutions—the World Bank and the Inter-

3. U.S. Department of Commerce, Maritime Administration, *A Statistical Analysis of the World's Merchant Fleets* (1975), p. 4.

4. United Nations, Department of Economic and Social Affairs, *Yearbook of International Trade Statistics* (1974), vol. 1, table A, pp. 16ff.

national Monetary Fund—that form part of the UN system. They might therefore also remain outside any new system established to raise money to support international programs. On the other hand, it is possible that their strong interest in some programs, such as efforts to create a global environmental monitoring system or more effective nuclear safeguards, might induce some of them to join. Participation of these countries would affect the institutional arrangements required to manage the system and very possibly would affect the purposes for which some of the funds are spent. Participation by the Communist countries is clearly desirable on political grounds. Their refusal to participate might cause some other countries to take a similar position, thereby making it difficult or impossible to institute some of the new revenue-raising measures. Thus, every reasonable effort should be made to facilitate participation by these countries. As noted in chapter 6, it may be possible for the centrally planned economies to join a restructured International Development Association, which might manage part of the revenues from the new system.

From a purely technical point of view, however, participation by the Communist countries would not be essential. The trade of these countries with the rest of the world, although growing, is a very small percentage of total international trade. Their nonparticipation would therefore not seriously detract from the technical feasibility of a general trade tax or a tax on specific commodities moving in international trade. Refusal of the Communist countries to participate in pollution taxes on tankers or other merchant ships would also pose no special problems. Much of the trade of these countries moves overland, rather than by sea, so failure of their port authorities to enforce these taxes would detract very little from the overall effectiveness of the taxes.

Enforcement and Collectibility

Even if the international community were able to agree on the establishment of one or more of the revenue systems discussed here, enforcement of payment of the revenues would be much more difficult than enforcement of a national revenue system. The international agency managing the revenue system would not have the powers to impose penalties that a national government possesses, and enforcement of any of the revenue systems would depend on the cooperation of treaty members.

Nevertheless, the general revenue and pollution taxes analyzed in this study have an advantage over purely voluntary contributions by or assessments on national governments in that these taxes can be collected within the territory of more than one country. Thus, the knowledge by a government that, if it refused to collect a tax on imports, the commodities involved could be taxed at the exporting end (possibly at a higher rate) ought to provide at least some leverage with respect to payment of the tax. A tax on the international transmission of profits from international investments could also be collected at either end of each transaction. Similarly, a pollution tax on petroleum emissions from tankers and other cargo ships would be enforceable if the authorities in only one of the ports at which it called would not allow it to leave without a certificate indicating that the annual tax had been paid.

As for collection of revenues from deep ocean mining by an international seabed authority, the method of enforcement would depend on the type of revenue accruing to the seabed authority. No problem should arise if the authority itself engaged in mining operations. If, however, the authority derived revenue from a tax on the profits of private operators or by auctioning off exploitation rights, collection might require the cooperation of the governments of the countries in which the private firms were based. Such cooperation would almost certainly be forthcoming, since those countries would presumably be parties to the treaty establishing the seabed authority.

A variety of disputes are certain to arise concerning the various means of financing international programs, and these disputes could interfere with the collection of revenues. For example, a participating country might claim a larger rebate than the body administering an international tax would be willing to approve, and as a consequence the country might suspend its cooperation in collecting the tax. Or a tanker operator might contend that his ships should be taxed more lightly than the average because they were responsible for lower levels of emissions of oil into the ocean and withhold part of the tax levied by the administering authority.

Some means of adjudicating these and other disputes would have to be provided. Disputes between an international tax authority and private firms or individuals might be brought before national courts in the country of residence or incorporation of the private party concerned. Disputes between an international tax authority and national governments might be subjected to binding arbitration by a board created by the treaty under the authority of which the tax was levied.

Nonconvertible currencies pose still another kind of problem for an international revenue system. This problem has arisen in the past principally in connection with payments by Communist countries. Most of the contributions and payments of assessments by these countries to the United Nations and the various UN agencies have been in their own currencies which are not convertible.

Assuming an interest on the part of Communist countries in joining the revenue system, an important question is whether a means can be devised for payment of the revenue and pollution taxes in convertible currencies. This is one place where the system of collecting the tax at more than one point can be useful. Thus, the port authorities of importing countries could collect trade taxes on exports from Communist countries in convertible currencies, just as they now collect port fees from Communist ships in hard currencies. With respect to exports to Communist countries, arrangements could be made for the tax to be collected at the exporting end, again in convertible currencies.

Institutional Arrangements

If adoption of some of the possible new financial measures discussed in this study produced large amounts of money for international purposes, new institutional arrangements might be needed to collect the money, manage it, and put it to good use. The treaties providing for the levying of international revenue and pollution taxes would probably have to establish continuing bodies to represent the states involved in administering the taxes. If agreement is ever reached on a regime to control and exploit the resources on the ocean floor beyond national jurisdictions, a new seabed authority will probably be created to administer the agreement along with an operating agency to carry out, or contract for, the mining of manganese nodules and any other resource that may become commercially exploitable in the future.

Some funds might, by international agreement, be earmarked for specific purposes (such as environmental programs) and be channeled by the collecting agency directly to an institution entrusted with the handling of such funds. Other funds, which may be thought of as general purpose funds, might be turned over to the existing international development institutions.

These institutions—principally the World Bank Group and UNDP—

would be technically capable of handling any likely new flow of general purpose funds. If, however, the amount of money involved were very large—say, on the general order of $1 billion a year or more—opposition could be anticipated to giving either the World Bank or UNDP the leading role in allocating the new funds. The developing countries, supported by the Communist nations, would probably resist turning over large new resources to the World Bank in which weighted voting gives control to the major industrialized countries with free-market economies. The industrialized countries, on the other hand, would probably argue that, since they would bear the largest part of the burden of providing the new funds, they should have a greater voice in deciding how the funds should be used than they possess in UNDP. The only way out of this possible impasse might be through creating a new institution that would give the industrialized countries more influence than they have in UNDP, but less than they enjoy in the World Bank and its affiliates. An alternative solution would be to reform the voting system of the World Bank—or more likely IDA—to give more influence to the developing countries.

Existing institutions are not well equipped to handle large new funds earmarked for environmental purposes. The present Fund of UNEP handles relatively small amounts of money obtained through voluntary contributions by member governments. The Fund of UNEP would have to undergo a substantial transformation if it were to become the means of channeling large funds in support of major environmental programs. In particular, the Fund of UNEP would have to acquire somewhat greater financial and managerial skills than its present operations require. An expanded Fund of UNEP (or alternatively, an Environmental Foundation established alongside the existing Fund of UNEP) could both invest in specific environmental programs (directly or through intermediaries, such as the Global Environmental Monitoring System and regional conventions to protect the marine environment) and provide the financial support that UNEP would need if—as appears desirable—it were to assume a preinvestment role similar to that of UNDP. If UNEP were to work with some of the UN Specialized Agencies in the preparation of well-chosen and well-planned environmental projects, the use of a larger part of the resources of the World Bank Group and the regional development banks in such projects could be greatly facilitated.

New institutions established to handle either general purpose funds or environmental funds could work with existing institutions, such as the

World Bank. The funds entrusted to such new institutions would be nearly cost-free. By blending, for example, revenues from a tax on international trade, or a tax on polluters of the ocean, with the money that the World Bank borrows at commercial rates of interest on the capital markets, borrowers in developing countries could be extended loans on more favorable terms than the Bank could provide using only its own resources.

Potential Role of New Means of Finance

The problems that would be encountered in establishing new means of financing international needs are, as the above analysis has demonstrated, complicated and difficult. They are by no means insuperable, however. In every case solutions can be found.

The difficulties that must be surmounted in creating a new international financial system must be weighed against the benefits that such a system would bring. By agreeing on revenue-raising measures, such as the levying of international trade taxes or the establishment of an international regime to regulate the exploitation of nonliving ocean resources, the international community can greatly increase its ability to raise funds to meet developmental, environmental, and other needs. In this way, moreover, the mobilization of financial resources for international purposes can be made more automatic and less vulnerable to the shifting fiscal priorities of individual national governments.

Taxes designed to internalize the social costs of international polluters and to induce them to abate their pollution of the commons can be an important part of a new international revenue system. Although such taxes would only incidentally produce revenue—and probably only in modest amounts—they would mobilize substantial revenues in support of an international objective by giving polluters an economic incentive to make large expenditures on pollution-abating technology.

Despite these evident benefits, it is by no means certain that the international community will adopt any of the major new means of financing international needs discussed in this study. What is required, and today is lacking, is recognition that rising needs cannot be met by currently available means. With such recognition, it might be possible to create support for a new, more workable, international revenue system. Whether that support is to be created—and if so, how—is a problem for the political leaders of the world. The conclusion of the present study is only that the means of mobilizing large financial resources for international purposes exist and can be made to work if the political will is present.

Technical Appendix
on Selected International Taxes

THIS APPENDIX presents more detailed analyses of the means of adjusting the burden of a general tax on international trade and of the incidence of the various taxes discussed in chapters 3 and 4.

Adjusting the Burden of a General Tax on International Trade

The distribution of the burden of a straight ad valorem tax on international trade would not be politically satisfactory because of the low burdens in relation to gross national product on the United States and the Soviet Union and the high burdens on numerous small countries. It is therefore desirable to try to find some means of adjusting the tax burden to achieve a more satisfactory distribution between large and small nations.

A number of statistical relationships were tested between the ratio of imports, c.i.f. (cost, insurance, and freight), to GNP and the independent variables, population and per capita GNP.[1] A good fit was obtained by the equation:

$$(1) \qquad r = 0.522 - 0.0901 \ln P - 0.0033\, Y',$$
$$ (12.0) \qquad (6.0) \qquad\quad (0.036)$$

$$\bar{R}^2 = 0.226; \text{ standard error } = 0.236; N = 119$$

where r is the ratio of imports (c.i.f.) to GNP for 1974; $\ln P$ is the natural

---

1. The authors acknowledge the valuable assistance of David Leahigh of Georgetown University in this testing work.

logarithm of population in millions; and Y' is the per capita GNP in mid-1974 U.S. dollars.[2] The numbers in parentheses are t values. A slightly better fit was obtained by:

(2) $r = 0.521 - 0.0878 \ln P + 0.0236 \ln Y'$,
                 (13.5)   (6.0)   (1.5)

$$\bar{R}^2 = 0.2404; \text{standard error} = 0.235$$

where $\ln Y'$ is the natural logarithm of per capita GNP. Clearly, the influence of per capita income level on the trade ratio is insignificant since the sign changes when per capita income is expressed in logarithms. If per capita GNP is dropped from the first of these equations, an equation with only one independent variable, population, can be written:

(3) $r = 0.51 - 0.089 \ln P$.

$$\bar{R}^2 = 0.233; \text{standard error} = 0.236$$

This equation can be taken as defining the normal relationship between a country's size and the ratio between its imports and its GNP. For a country of average size (30 million population), imports tend to be 21 percent of GNP; for a small country (1 million population), the ratio tends to be 43 percent; for a large country (200 million population), the ratio tends to be 10 percent.

Equation 3 can also be written:

(4) $I/Y = 0.51 - 0.089 \ln P$,

or

$$I = Y(0.51 - 0.089 \ln P),$$

where I is imports and Y is total GNP. The expected tax yield (T) for countries with normal imports for their size becomes

(5) $T = tY(0.51 - 0.089 \ln P)$,

where t is the tax rate expressed as a ratio on imports. And the ratio between the tax yield and GNP (or the tax burden) is

(6) $T/Y = t(0.51 - 0.089 \ln P)$,

2. Measures of significance are: $\bar{R}^2$, the adjusted multiple correlation coefficient; the standard error of estimate; and N, the number of observations (countries) in the regression.

or, in the case of a 1 percent tax,

$$T/Y = (0.51 - 0.089 \ln P).$$

This equation reflects the fact that large countries tend to import less relative to GNP than small countries and therefore would be taxed less heavily.

Equation 6 can be used to construct a tax-retention formula that offsets the extra trade dependence of small countries and makes the tax burden high or low depending on the relation of actual imports to normal imports for a country of that size. The formula is

$$(7) \qquad\qquad f = \frac{0.435 - 0.089 \ln P}{0.51 - 0.089 \ln P},$$

where f is the fraction of taxes collected by a particular country that it would be permitted to retain. The numerator of this tax-retention formula has been written in such a way as to reduce the net burden of a 1 percent trade tax to 0.075 percent of GNP for all normal trading countries (that is, countries whose ratio of imports to GNP is exactly explained by equation 3). For example, in the case of a country with a population of 1 million, $\ln P$ would equal zero and the tax burden without retention (equation 5) would be 0.43 percent of GNP. The tax-retention formula would reduce the burden as follows:

$$(8) \qquad\qquad 0.51 - \frac{(0.435 \times 0.51)}{0.51} = 0.075.$$

For countries with populations of more than 1 million, $\ln P$ is greater than zero and the tax retention is correspondingly reduced in order to achieve the desired net burden of 0.075 percent of GNP for normal trading countries. If a country's actual ratio of imports to GNP is higher or lower than the expected value for its size, the adjusted burden of a 1 percent tax would be higher or lower than 0.075 percent of GNP in the same proportion. This adjustment formula does not work for countries with populations of 150 million or more, because at the 150 million level the numerator (and therefore also the retention fraction) becomes zero.

The net burden of a 2 percent tax on normal trading countries under the tax-retention formula would be 0.15 of GNP, which is roughly the average burden for all countries of an unadjusted 1 percent tax. See table

3-3 for a comparison of the burden distributions of an unadjusted 1 percent tax and a 2 percent tax with variable tax retentions.

The value 0.435 in equation 7 serves the function of identifying the target rate of tax in terms of GNP for any country whose ratio of imports (I) to GNP is exactly explained by the regression equation 4. In this case the ratio of tax to GNP with the retention formula and a 1 percent tax, is

$$(9) \quad T/Y = 0.01(0.51 - 0.089 \ln P)\left[1 - \left(\frac{0.435 - 0.089 \ln P}{0.51 - 0.089 \ln P}\right)\right],$$

which reduces to

$$T/Y = 0.01[(0.51 - 0.089 \ln P) - (0.435 - 0.089 \ln P)],$$

$$T/Y = 0.01(0.51 - 0.435),$$

$$T/Y = 0.01(0.075).$$

Of course this breaks down whenever the population is so large that the expected ratio of imports to GNP is less than 0.075, which happens at a population of about 150 million.

Incidence of a Tax on Internationally Traded Oil

The incidence of a tax on internationally traded oil will be considered, first in the long-run situation and, then, in the short-run situation.

Long run

We first assume a tight cartel control over outputs of OPEC members, with an ad valorem tax of, say, 10 percent of the sales price. It is well known that for a monopolist optimum price and output are those for which marginal revenue equals marginal cost. As can be seen from figures A-1 and A-2, the effect of an ad valorem tax depends on the shape of these curves.

In figure A-1, the demand curve, AR, has a constant elasticity slightly more than 1.0, and the related marginal revenue curve is MR. An ad valorem excise tax reduces marginal revenue by the percentage tax rate (the resultant new net marginal revenue curve is MRT). The intersection of MRT and MC, the marginal cost curve, determines a lower output, C, and a higher price, NP.

Figure A-1. *Incidence of a Tax on Internationally Traded Oil in the Long Run: Constant Elasticity*

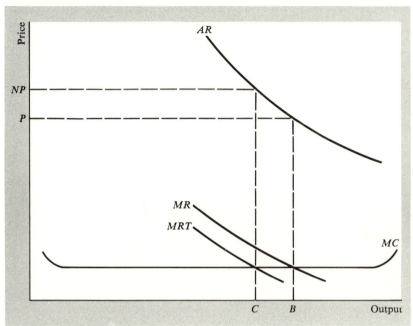

Figure A-2 differs by showing a demand curve that becomes more elastic as the price rises. Here the tax causes less fall in output and consequently less increase in price. As drawn, figure A-1 indicates full shifting of the tax to consumers, and figure A-2 indicates that the price rises by less than half of the tax.

For the Middle East oil producers who are the key decision makers in the cartel, the marginal cost curve is probably flat over a considerable range of output at a level of about $1 a barrel.[3] A market price of about $10 a barrel (in 1970 dollars) for oil f.o.b. (free on board) in the Persian Gulf could be consistent with the optimum long-run price of a cartel with

3. This includes the commonly cited lifting cost of Persian Gulf oil of about $0.15 plus an allowance for user cost of about $0.85. User cost is equivalent to a royalty, the discounted value of some future output that is precluded by current production. This was estimated for Persian Gulf oil at $0.47 in 1970 prices; see William D. Nordhaus, "The Allocation of Energy Resources," *Brookings Papers on Economic Activity, 1973:3*, p. 554. We have raised the Nordhaus figure for current price levels, particularly the prospective prices of oil substitutes.

Figure A-2. *Incidence of a Tax on Internationally Traded Oil in the Long Run: Greater Elasticity with Higher Price*

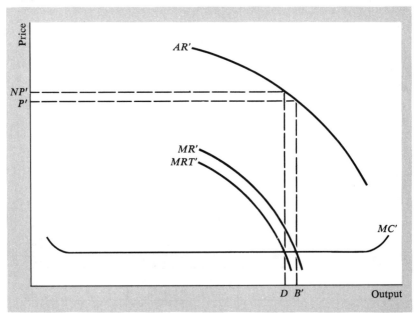

the marginal cost equal to $1 a barrel if the elasticity of demand at the equilibrium price and output is 1.1.[4]

A demand curve with a uniform elasticity of −1.1 and constant marginal cost is consistent with figure A-1, that is, the tax is passed on in full to the customers. With the tax, output falls until the marginal revenue after tax equals marginal cost. At this point, the formula cited in footnote 4 indicates that the price net of tax will be the same as it was before. The producers suffer a decline in income because the volume of sales falls.

4. A well-known formula that relates price, marginal cost, and elasticity is:

$$P = MC \left[e/(e - 1) \right],$$

where P is the market price, MC is the marginal cost, and e is the point elasticity of demand. See Charles E. Ferguson and Charles Maurice, *Economic Analysis*, rev. ed. (Irwin, 1974), p. 275. With elasticity demand at 1.1, price will be about 10 times marginal cost. If this elasticity is 1.0 or less, marginal revenue becomes zero or negative and the tight cartel assumption breaks down. Oil producers should then reduce production and raise price further until marginal revenue equals marginal cost.

We think the real state of affairs is that the demand for crude petroleum becomes more elastic as the price rises. Customers will use less oil; more oil will be produced within the consumer countries; and, in the long run, more energy substitutes will become economically feasible—for example, oil from shale, electricity from coal, liquefied or gasified coal, solar energy, nuclear energy, and so forth. This seems quite likely at prices more or less in the plausible range.[5]

It does not seem feasible to estimate a long-run elasticity more precisely than this. The prospective costs in, say, 1985 of energy from shale, solar energy, and so forth, are merely educated guesses and, when we say long run, there is some vagueness about whether the long run is 1985 or 1990 or beyond. All we draw from this discussion is that in the long run even with a tight OPEC cartel there would be enough substitutes for imported oil that the oil-exporting countries would have to absorb a large portion of the tax.

This result—that tax shifting depends on the long-run elasticity of demand for OPEC oil—is not changed if we assume that OPEC is merely a loose cartel, in which a few key countries carry the burden of keeping prices high by restraining output, while the smaller producers try to take advantage of the situation by producing to capacity. In this situation an oil price increase to cover the tax would not incur any competitive output response from the smaller OPEC producers because they would face the same tax increases. Tax shifting still depends, as it did before, on the elasticity of demand.

There is a more subtle long-run problem connected with the cartel, however. Any tax that is passed on will require lower output; this, in turn, will necessitate allocating the production cutbacks among producers, and will be a disruptive force in the cartel. If enough countries decided that cutting output was becoming too costly and shifted to a high output policy, it would become impossible for the cartel to pass on the tax in higher prices.

On the whole, we conclude that in the long run it is quite likely that much of an oil tax would be borne by the producers.

5. See Massachusetts Institute of Technology, Energy Laboratory Policy Study Group, *Energy Self Sufficiency* (American Enterprise Institute, 1974), p. 52; Federal Energy Administration, *Project Independence Report, November 1974* (1974); K. C. Vyas and W. W. Bodle, "Coal and Oil Shale Conversion Looks Better," *Oil and Gas Journal* (March 24, 1975), pp. 45–54.

Short run

What is conspicuous about the short-run oil price situation is that in
the short run the demand for oil is very inelastic. The profit-maximizing
strategy for a cartel is to increase prices until the marginal revenue equals
marginal cost (and to reduce it later if need be). It seems clear that OPEC
has not exploited the full monopoly potential of the short-run price. Why
OPEC has not demanded a still higher price for crude oil is a matter for
speculation. Whether the tax would affect the short-run price depends on
how it relates to the particular constraint that explains the short-run price.

One circumstance that may explain the price constraint is a general un-
easiness about the development of oil substitutes and other oil production
within the consumer countries (North Sea oil, oil from the outer continental shelf of the U.S. east coast, and so forth). Another possible explanation is OPEC's fear that higher prices would constrict the size of the
oil export market and increase strains within OPEC over the division of
the market. These considerations appear to influence OPEC's members in
varying degrees, and the organization's price policies are determined by
a process of private bargaining at its periodic meetings. Under the circumstances, a tax levied at a low rate would probably not have much effect on
OPEC's price policies. In any event, it would be virtually impossible to
determine whether, or to what extent, the price set by OPEC was any
higher because of the tax than it would have been if there were no tax.

Summarizing this analysis of the tax incidence, we conclude that, both
in the long run and in the short run, the bulk of the tax would probably
fall on the producers of export oil. In both cases, however, it is possible
that some of the burden would fall on consumer countries.

Incidence of a Tax on Internationally Traded Mineral Raw Materials

The analysis of the incidence of a tax on internationally traded raw
materials must cover a variety of market situations. If possible, the analysis should take into account whether a broad or a narrow view of the tax
base is being used. This analysis has some similarity to the prior discussion
of an oil tax, except that here it is necessary to allow for greater competition among sellers. As in the case of oil, due account must be taken of

parent–subsidiary relationships between sellers in exporting countries and purchasers in importing countries.

If there is substantial competition in the production of a particular raw material, for example, iron ore, the important implication as regards tax incidence is that mining companies would in the long run earn normal profits. The long-run burden of the tax would in this case be divided between the owners of the ore-bearing land and the consumers of iron and steel products. Only if profits are above normal (that is, above the level required to attract and retain needed capital) could the mining companies absorb part of the tax. If, as is assumed, the tax is imposed on all imports of a given raw material, a large number of competitive suppliers would face the tax, their demand curves would be relatively inelastic, and most of the tax would fall on consumers.

One special case that has to be looked into is competition between foreign exporters and domestic producers in the consuming country. How much of the tax is shifted to consumers globally depends upon the overall elasticity of demand for the taxed commodity. How much of the tax is shifted to consumers in a given country depends upon the elasticity of demand in that segment of the world market and upon the responsiveness of domestic suppliers to changes in price (that is, the elasticity of supply in that country).

The case in which imports supply a substantial part of a country's consumption of a mineral raw material is shown in figure A-3. Domestic producers will supply the part of the market H_1, defined by the part of their supply curve, HS, that lies below the world supply price, FS. Imports are total supply, T_1, less home supply, H_1. When the world price goes up because of the tax (but not necessarily by the full amount of the tax), domestic producers are enabled to increase their share of the market to H_2. Foreign suppliers not only lose this part of the market, but also absorb the shrinkage in the total market defined by the difference between T_1 and T_2.

In the case of substantial imports, represented by figure A-3, the competitive implications are quite small. Figure A-4 was drawn so as to show more impact on the import business; this requires a low level of imports. For this to be an important case, the combination of two circumstances is required: the imports must be relatively small in the market of the importing country and, at the same time, these "marginal" imports must be a substantial part of the exporters' business. For example, a small mineral operation in Canada which exports most of its product to the United

Figure A-3. *Incidence of a Tax on Internationally Traded Mineral Raw Materials in Case of Substantial Imports*

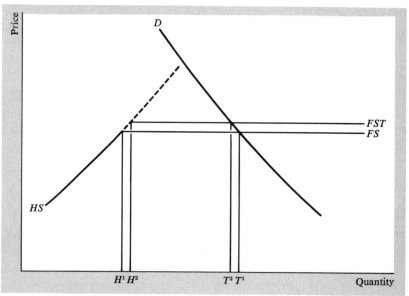

States, where it competes with domestic producers, would find that it has to absorb the tax.

The freight costs of raw materials are usually high relative to the value of the product. This means that quite different markets can exist around the world, and it is possible that the international tax would work to the disadvantage of some small exporters. The actual frequency of this phenomenon could be determined only through a careful, case-by-case analysis. The best guess is that it would be relatively rare, and it is safe to conclude that the long-run impact would be on consumers.

In the short run, the important determinant of incidence is the shape of the supply curve. Two alternatives are depicted in figures A-5 and A-6. In figure A-5, despite the elastic demand curve, the price would fall partly on the producer because of the very steep supply curve. In this case, the producer can neither cut output nor expand it. In the area of hard minerals this seems to be a very unlikely situation. A producer could be expected to have alternatives to use more or less labor in mining. If costs can be cut by reducing output, the situation is as depicted in figure A-6, where the

Figure A-4. *Incidence of a Tax on Internationally Traded Mineral Raw Materials in Case of Low Level of Imports*

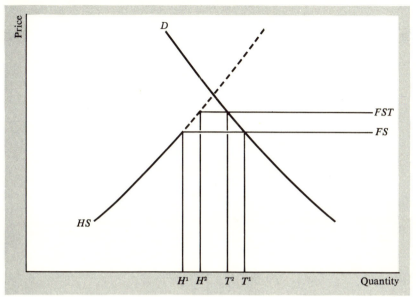

elasticity of the demand curve dominates the price reaction and the tax is shifted through a rise in the price.

If a mineral is controlled by a monopoly, there is still little reason to change the expectation that the burden will generally fall on consumers. A monopolist could be expected to operate below full capacity so the supply curve would be relatively flat.

It is worth noting that by relating the tax to the percentage of mineral content in the commodity imported, a potential problem of discouraging refining in less developed countries is avoided. If the tax were imposed on the refining markup, the burden would fall on producers in the exporting countries in a manner similar to that depicted in figure A-4. Small refining operations in exporting countries, which were just getting into the processing business, would be in competition with large established refiners in importing countries. It would be difficult for such small refiners to pass on a tax on the refining markup, because refiners in the importing countries could reduce their taxes by importing crude materials and doing their own refining. By basing the tax on the metallic content, rather than on the total

Figure A-5. *Effects of Steep Supply Curve on Incidence of a Tax on Internationally Traded Mineral Raw Materials*

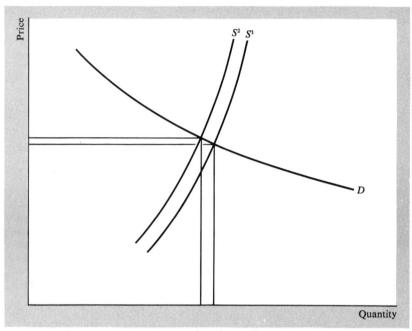

value, any penalty on refining within the exporting countries would be avoided.

Incidence of a Tax on International Investment Income

Analyzing the incidence of a tax on international investment income is a unique question since these incomes are almost universally subject to tax in either host or home countries and it becomes possible to modify the incidence by practices with regard to tax credits (that is, the government that gives a tax credit for the new tax bears the burden). For purposes of the present discussion, it will be assumed that no credit is allowed against any other income tax. In this case, the international investment income tax will be a partial income tax which, in general, can partly be shifted in the short run away from the investor.[6]

6. Otto von Mering, *The Shifting and Incidence of Taxation* (Philadelphia: Blakiston, 1942), p. 209.

Figure A-6. *Effects of Flat Supply Curve on Incidence of a Tax on Internationally Traded Mineral Raw Materials*

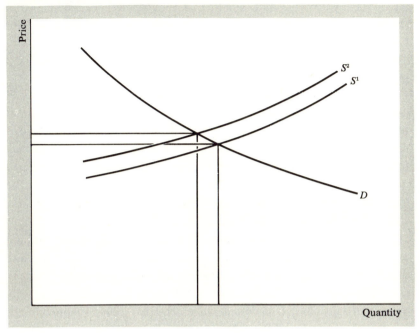

To clarify the issue, a two-market model with only equity funds is assumed. In a financial center (*FC*) country there is a large supply and a large demand (*d*) for investment funds. In the other market (*LDC*) there is less demand for funds, but still less supply. Initially, there should be an equilibrium rate (*r*) in *FC,* and (consistent with a new flow of funds from *FC* to *LDC*) a rate of $r + d$ in *LDC* ($d > 0$). A tax rate is imposed on ($r + d$) when proceeds are transferred internationally.

Initially, there should be no change in the stock of capital in either *FC* or *LDC*. If it is assumed that business firms set prices and outputs in the short run to maximize profit, it would follow that there would be no change in the before-tax profit rate, and the tax would fall on the investors.

In an oligopolistic industry, firms may not seek to maximize profit; instead, they may follow a strategy such as achieving a target rate of return, or limiting profits to a level that would not attract competition. Under such a strategy, a profits tax even in the short run could be shifted forward as higher product prices, since competitors would be faced with a similar tax. With this forward shifting, the incidence would be diffused, some falling on the host country and some falling on customers for the exports of the host country. There is no way to determine the exact extent of such price strategies. We prefer the profit-maximizing model and its implication of no short-run shifting.[7] No flat prediction of the incidence of a profits tax is possible.

In the long run, the tax could be described as moving the supply of capital curve to the left; the amount of international investment funds forthcoming at a 10 percent return with a 10 percent tax should approximately equal the amount that would have been provided at a 9 percent return tax free. How this will affect the rate of return on international capital and its gross flow depends on the supply and demand elasticities. (See figure A-7.) We do not expect to find any precise measurements for these elasticities, but some speculation might be fruitful.

In theory, the case of uniform elasticity of one in the supply and demand curves should result in half of the international tax being shifted into higher rates and the flow of such investment falling by one-half of the tax rate (figure A-7, A). If both curves are very elastic, but equal elasticity prevails, the tax is still half shifted, but now the flow of international funds falls by more than half the tax rate (figure A-7, B). With equally inelastic curves, half shifting with little drop in the flow of funds occurs. If the supply curve or the demand curve is notably inelastic, we can be confident that the flow of funds will not change much, but the tax will be borne by investors in the inelastic supply case (figure A-7, C) or will be shifted in the inelastic demand case (figure A-7, D).

Qualitatively, elastic supply means that investors are finely tuned to small differences in the rate of return between foreign and domestic investment, and they quickly shift to domestic investment when the tax differential appears, unless compensated. Herbert G. Grubel has published estimates of rates of return (on equity, after tax) for U.S. domestic and foreign investment for the period 1960–69, classified by fourteen countries. The rates by country vary from 25 percent to 9 percent. The average

---

7. The point of issue is similar to the question of short-run shifting of a corporate income tax. We are impressed by Gordon's evidence of little shifting, in Robert Gordon, "The Incidence of the Corporation Income Tax in U.S. Manufacturing," *American Economic Review,* vol. 57 (September 1967), pp. 731–58.

Figure A-7. *Shifting of a Tax on Investment Income*[a]

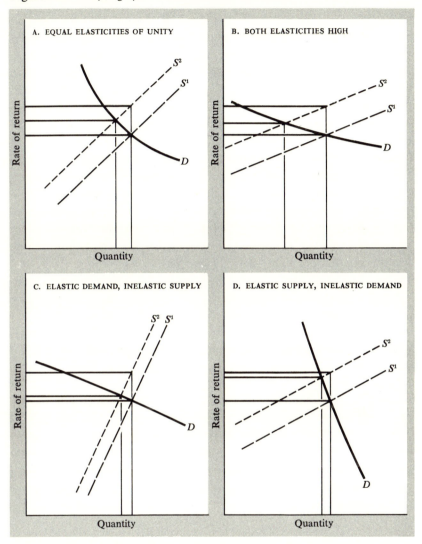

a. In each graph the top horizontal line indicates the price of capital, the rate of return that would be required to shift the tax completely away from the investor. The lower horizontal line indicates the before-tax rate of return. The middle horizontal line indicates more or less shifting as it is closer to the top line or the bottom line.

D is the demand for capital; S^1 is the supply of capital before the tax; and S^2 is the supply after the tax.

rate of return on foreign investment was 13.4 percent, compared to an average rate of return on domestic investment of 11.5 percent.[8]

The very wide spread of rates in these data suggests that investment decisions abroad are influenced by numerous strategic factors, such as protecting market positions, avoiding tariff walls, and so forth. Therefore, there is not a precise equalization of profit rates at the margin. The data, of course, represent only average profits and are not inconsistent with much more uniformity of marginal rates of return. The spread of rates, however, looks quite high and suggests no fine tuning to small rate differences.

The demand curve should reflect two factors, the substitution of labor for capital (as costs of capital change) and the substitution of domestic capital for foreign capital. There is an extensive, but controversial, literature about the substitution between capital and labor (based on experience in developed countries). This literature is divided between some writers who estimate an elasticity of unity and others who estimate a very inelastic relationship.[9] The relevant curve here should be more elastic than the one usually debated in growth economics. The higher prices on international capital should cause capital users to shift to domestic capital sources, and nationals of the host country could be expected to reduce their foreign investment and invest domestically instead.[10] Very tentatively, these speculations lead to a guess of moderately elastic demand and moderately inelastic supply—that is, in the direction of figure A-7, C— with little shifting but not much reduction in the flow of funds.

So far as portfolio investment goes, the short-run incidence is entirely on the lender-investor since the contract is fixed. In the long run, the supply curve would probably be relatively flatter than in the case of direct foreign investment, since portfolio investment is more exclusively influenced by the rate of return. The volume of international lending could therefore be expected to fall more substantially than the volume of direct foreign investment.

8. Herbert G. Grubel, "Taxation and the Rates of Return from Some U.S. Asset Holdings Abroad, 1960–69," *Journal of Political Economy,* vol. 82 (May/June 1974), pp. 468–88.

9. Robert E. Lucas, Jr., "Labor-Capital Substitution in U.S. Manufacturing," in Arnold C. Harberger and Martin J. Bailey, eds., *The Taxation of Income from Capital* (Brookings Institution, 1969), pp. 223–67.

10. Some writers put much weight on this kind of effect when they are considering the impact on a host country of an increased inflow of foreign capital, namely, that domestic investment is discouraged. See Richard J. Barnet and Ronald E. Müller, *Global Reach* (Simon and Schuster, 1974), pp. 148–84.

We now turn to the unique feature of a tax on investment income: that the tax may be taken into account in the levying of national income taxes. Many of the Western countries already allow a credit for foreign taxes. Extending a foreign tax credit for the international tax would result in shifting the burden to the treasury of the country that is the source of the capital. However, the data for U.S. corporations in 1964 suggest that, for the most part, an additional tax credit would be unused.[11] Some countries, for example, the Netherlands, impose no tax on foreign income. On the whole, the operation of the tax credit would only slightly shift the impact of the tax on direct foreign investment from companies to the treasury of the country that was the source of the capital. With the credit, the impact of the tax on interest from private bonds sold internationally would be almost entirely on the treasury of the source country.

Incidence of the Tax on Chronic Oil Emissions by Tankers

The initial incidence of the tanker tax would be similar to that of the specific tax per barrel of oil that is analyzed in chapter 4. The demand for tanker services is quite unresponsive to price, since it is dependent largely upon the demand for refined petroleum products.[12] Tanker operators would therefore have no reason not to reflect the tanker tax fully in their freight rates.[13] How much of the resulting increase in the delivered cost of oil would be absorbed by producers and how much would be passed on to consumers would, in theory, depend upon the elasticity of demand for

11. Companies accounting for $115 million of foreign taxes were not cut back by a foreign tax credit limitation, while companies with $2,714 million of foreign taxes were cut back in allowed credits by one of the limitations. (If a new international tax were added, more companies would be under the limitation.) Internal Revenue Service, *Statistics of Income: Foreign Income and Taxes,* Supplement for 1964–65 (1966), pp. 134–40.

12. Since tankers are also used, to some extent, to transport grain and other bulk commodities, the level of trade in those commodities would also influence the price of tanker services.

13. Tanker rates for crude oil and refined products are highly variable over time. At any particular time, however, these rates are at an equilibrium determined by the demand for tanker services and the effective supply of such services, that is, the capacity of the tankers in existence that have not been mothballed or converted to the grain trade. The tanker tax would obviously not affect the demand for tanker services. Nor would it affect the supply, if tanker rates rose by the amount of the tax, since operators would be given no incentive to add to or subtract from the number of tankers engaged in the transport of oil.

refined products. Since time is needed to develop substitutes for oil, or to adopt oil-conserving measures, the demand for oil is quite inelastic in the short run. Most of the burden of the tax would therefore tend to fall on consumers.

In the longer run, as old tankers were replaced by new tankers with antipollution features, most of the tax would disappear, but it would be replaced by the roughly equivalent cost of amortizing the cost of the anti-pollution features. Less forward shifting would probably take place in the longer run for two reasons. First, the cost of transporting oil would fall as a result of reduced spillage, so there would be less extra expense to shift or absorb. Second, and probably more important, with the passage of time, the increased elasticity of demand would make shifting more difficult.

Circumstances could arise in which all of the increased costs attributable to the tanker tax would be absorbed by the oil producers. Imposition of the tax can be thought of as laying down the requirement that the oil industry "produce" (that is, not spill) a certain amount of oil at about $10 a barrel. For all practical purposes, this amounts to the same thing as imposing a fixed tax on the industry. (If the industry were left to its own devices, it could produce any additional oil that it wanted at about $1 a barrel.) If OPEC achieves the ability to function as a monopoly and sets the price of oil at the level that would maximize the net revenues of its members as a group, all of the tanker tax would be absorbed by the oil producers. This is so because a fixed tax does not change the production level at which marginal costs equal marginal revenue.

It may be of some interest to compare the economic burden of the tanker tax with that of a regulation designed to achieve the same end result, that is, the adoption of a less polluting technology by the entire tanker fleet. Under both the tax and the regulation, old tankers without the improved technology would be permitted to operate, but the tax would require their operators to pay for that privilege. In that sense, the regulation would give the operators of old tankers a windfall.

The regulation would, of course, raise freight costs only as operators bought new tankers with the new, more expensive technology. The tax would do so immediately. Over the longer run, however, the effects of the two approaches would be quite similar. The only significant difference would result from the fact that under the tax approach even tankers with the new technology would pay some tax (for spillage not related to ballasting), possibly resulting in a slightly higher delivered cost for crude oil than would be produced by the regulatory approach.

Possible Effects of Oil Spills on Marine Life

THERE HAS BEEN little scientific study of the biological and chemical effects of oil in the open ocean. Numerous studies of the effects of crude oil and many fractions of refined products on various species of marine biota have been undertaken in laboratories and in coastal areas after a major oil spill caused by either a tanker or an offshore drilling accident. In general, most of the laboratory studies and many field studies indicate that oil is toxic to, or has negative sublethal effects on, numerous forms of marine life.[1] However, a number of the field studies show that, after an acute oil spill, the affected area appears to recover fully (that is, things seem to return to normal) after a period of time which can range from a few months to as much as ten years.[2]

In many of the major tanker accidents that have been studied, there was extensive mortality of birds, fish, and other marine biota. Death was usually caused by direct contact with large quantities of oil (by smothering). There is little evidence, however, of reduced fish productivity caused by chronic low-level inputs of oil into fishery areas.

1. For a comprehensive list of published research on oil pollution and marine life, see the reference list in National Academy of Sciences, *Petroleum in the Marine Environment* (Washington, D.C.: NAS, 1975), pp. 100–03; and the bibliography in Donald F. Boesch, Carl H. Hershner, and Jerome H. Milgram, *Oil Spills and the Marine Environment* (Ballinger, 1974), pp. 47–55. For a compendium of relevant scientific papers, see *Proceedings of Joint Conferences on Prevention and Control of Oil Spills*, sponsored by the American Petroleum Institute, the Environmental Protection Agency, and the U.S. Coast Guard (Washington, D.C.: API, 1973).

2. Boesch, Hershner, and Milgram, *Oil Spills and the Marine Environment*, p. 30.

Studies have been undertaken of fisheries along the Louisiana coast, where oil production and fishing are both important offshore activities.[3] Although the studies generally show that there has been no reduction in fishery output over the years, it is not certain that there has been no effect on fisheries because the studies do not take into account technological advances in fishery production. Also, while total output has not declined, one study points out that fish have had to be harvested from increasingly large areas in order to maintain yields (that is, the productivity of a given unit of area apparently has declined).[4] Whether this decline is attributable to oil pollution, to overfishing, or to other causes is not known. In general, overfishing is thought to be the principal reason for a declining rate of increase in world fish harvests. It is difficult to know, however, whether this is the only reason, or whether petroleum or other chemical compounds from sewage runoffs, industrial wastes, fertilizer, and so forth, are also part of the explanation.

Occasional examples of apparent local impacts on fisheries do not constitute sufficiently strong evidence that oil pollution is causing considerable damage to ocean fisheries generally. Oil pollution in one type of area in the marine environment, however, causes considerable concern among marine biologists. This area is the coastal wetlands, which are nursery, feeding, and dwelling areas for various species of birds, commercial fish, and other marine biota. In temperate climates these wetlands, which are frequently situated in the vicinity of oil-polluting activities, are often salt marshes with tall vegetation. A number of studies have been made of the effects of oil spills on marshes, particularly on the plants, and a few have focused on marsh-dwelling animals.[5] By and large, these studies showed that marsh plants and animals suffered considerable damage when they were affected by chronic spillage, but the studies showed less certain impacts in the case of a single oil spill. Although these studies strongly suggest that nursery and breeding areas may be severely damaged by chronic oil pollution, these effects have not as yet been related to any known reduction in commercial fish production.

In addition to the concern about possible toxic effects of oil on fisheries and on coastal nursery and breeding areas, there is concern about the

3. See ibid., pp. 14–15, for a description of several studies.
4. NAS, *Petroleum in the Marine Environment*, p. 89.
5. Boesch, Hershner, and Milgram, *Oil Spills and the Marine Environment*, pp. 21–23.

potential damage to marine biota that feed on oil-infested sediments on the ocean floor. Oil has a natural affinity for sediment particles, and oil emitted into the marine environment that does not evaporate or weather finds its way to bottom sediments. One study, which draws on studies of coastal areas in its treatment of benthic organisms feeding on bottom sediments, notes:

> How much and what kinds of oil prevent a species from utilizing a substrate . . . are largely unknown, but in view of available data, the presence of low-to-medium boiling point aromatic hydrocarbons at concentrations as low as 10 to 100 parts per billion may chemically perturb many species. The effects of higher boiling, insoluble materials depend on how much an organism relies on his particular substrate and how much it is altered by oil. Species depending on a substrate only for passive support may be little affected by habitat changes caused by oil. But those living in the substrate or otherwise actively depending on the substrate are surely more vulnerable.[6]

In referring to the impact of oil pollution on seabed organisms, another study notes:

> The effects of oil pollution on subtidal seabed organisms have been seriously neglected. Yet oil is often deposited in high concentrations on the bottom, where it may persist and chronically pollute an environment. . . . The chronic effects of such contamination remain unstudied, and it is unknown if petroleum hydrocarbons can be transmitted to fishes feeding on oil-contaminated seabed organisms.[7]

In addition to the potential toxic effects discussed above, there is concern about possible sublethal but harmful effects of chronic oil spillage. Very little scientific research has been done in this area. Based on results in the small number of relevant studies, marine scientists are suspicious about the possible long-run dangers to marine biota both in nearshore areas and in the open ocean. Broadly speaking, the list of concerns includes: (1) possible harmful effects on the metabolism (through changes in photosynthesis and respiration) of some marine biota;[8] (2) interfer-

6. Council on Environmental Quality, *OCS Oil and Gas—An Environmental Assessment*, vol. 1 (April 1974), p. 106.

7. Boesch, Hershner, and Milgram, *Oil Spills and the Marine Environment*, p. 21.

8. See E. S. Gilfillan, "Effects of Seawater Extracts of Crude Oil on Carbon Budgets in Two Species of Mussels," in API, *Proceedings of Joint Conferences on Prevention and Control of Oil Spills*, pp. 691–95; P. Krauss and others, "The Toxicity of Crude Oil and Its Components to Freshwater Algae," in API, *Proceedings of Joint Conferences on Prevention and Control of Oil Spills*, pp. 703–14; and P. L. Parker, "Experimental Design for an Environmental Program: Hydrocarbon Analysis in

ence with chemical communication between marine animals (many marine animals communicate via smell); and (3) possible negative effects on reproduction and spawning of some animals.[9]

an Oil Producing Area," in R. E. Smith, ed., *Proceedings of Conference/Workshop on Marine Environmental Implications of Offshore Drilling Eastern Gulf of Mexico* (State University of Florida, Institute of Oceanography, 1974), pp. 279–89.

9. See S. M. Jacobson and D. B. Boylan, "Seawater Soluble Fraction of Kerosene: Effect on Chemotaxis in a Marine Snail, *Nassarius Obsoletus*," *Nature*, vol. 241 (January 19, 1973), pp. 213–15. This study showed harmful effects on the findings of food by predators. See also S. D. Rice, "Toxicity and Avoidance Tests with Prudhoe Bay Oil and Pink Salmon Fry," in API, *Proceedings of Joint Conferences on Prevention and Control of Oil Spills*, pp. 667–70. This study shows that oil in seawater prevented salmon from entering their home spawning area.

APPENDIX C

Estimated Chronic Oil Spillage in 1985

TABLE C-1 shows rough forecasts of principal oil imports (crude oil and products) for 1985. Table C-2, which is based on table C-1, shows major oil shipping movements. Note that refined products as a proportion of total oil shipments are higher in table C-2 (about 27 percent) than such products are as a percent of total oil imports. This is because table C-2 includes some transshipments. For example, in table C-2 both voyages of the journey are included in the case of crude oil that is shipped on very large crude carriers (VLCCs) from the Middle East to refineries in the Caribbean and then shipped on small product tankers (called handy tankers) to New York. Also included are estimates of the amount of refined products shipped in regional trade in Western Europe.

The forecast of the total volume of oil imports in 1985 (about 1.6 billion metric tons) is based on an assumed price for crude oil of $12 a barrel (or $88.24 a ton) in 1975 dollars f.o.b. (free on board) the Persian Gulf. If the world price for crude oil declined in real terms by 1985, oil consumption might be considerably higher than the demand level implied in table C-1.

Table C-3 shows the number of tankers required in each of three representative size categories to carry the projected oil shipments to the principal importing regions and the amount of oil spillage from all operating tankers for 1985. The three tanker categories are: VLCCs, with an assumed average size of 250,000 deadweight tons; intermediate tankers, with an assumed average size of 74,000 deadweight tons; and "handy"

This appendix was prepared with the assistance of Aeran Lee.

238

Table C-1. Projected Major Interregional Trade in Crude Oil and Refined Products, by Region of Origin and Destination, 1985

Millions of metric tons per year

Importing region	Total	Exporting region					
		Middle East and North Africa	Subsaharan Africa	Indonesia	Caribbean and Latin America	Other
World	1,614	1,198	135	75	144	60
Crude oil	1,342	1,055	132	67	70	18
Products	272	144	3	7	75	42
United States	299	134	40	0	120	5
Crude oil	204	120	40	0	45	0
Products	95	15	0	0	75	5
Japan	453	332	25	75	0	20
Crude oil	408	300	22	67	0	18
Products	45	32	3	7	0	2
Western Europe	613	483	70	0	25	35
Crude oil	543	448	70	0	25	0
Products	70	35	0	0	0	35
Developing countries[a]	249	249	0	0	0	0
Crude oil	187	187	0	0	0	0
Products	62	62	0	0	0	0

Sources: Estimates for total imports to Western Europe and Japan are derived from Organisation for Economic Co-operation and Development, *Energy Prospects to 1985*, vol. II (Paris: OECD, 1974), pp. 25, 28 ($9 projection). For the United States it was assumed that imports would be held at about 299 million metric tons. Estimates for the developing countries are based on the analysis by Edward R. Fried in Joseph A. Yager and Eleanor B. Steinberg, *Energy and U.S. Foreign Policy* (Ballinger, 1974), p. 257. The countries from which the various importing regions would receive oil are the authors' estimates. Estimates of imports of refined products were based on a combination of factors, including announcements of refinery construction in various producing states and a continuation of imports of products from Caribbean refineries to the United States. The Soviet Union and Eastern Europe are expected to be roughly self-sufficient in oil in 1985 and are not included in this table. Canada, Australia, and New Zealand are expected to participate in world oil trade only to a limited degree and also are not included.

This table shows final imports only and does not show flows of crude oil to refineries in a second country for reexport to third countries. For example, exports of Middle East crude oils to refineries in the Caribbean which are then shipped to the United States appear only in the column showing exports of refined products from Caribbean and Latin America to the United States. All figures are based on an assumed world price of crude oil of $88.24 a metric ton ($12 a barrel) in 1975 dollars f.o.b. the Persian Gulf. Figures are rounded.

a. Excludes not only OPEC countries but also other developing countries which are net oil exporters.

Table C-2. *Major Shipments by Tanker of Crude Oil and Refined Products, 1985*
Millions of metric tons per year

Importing region	Total	Exporting region				
		Middle East and North Africa	Subsaharan Africa	Indonesia	Caribbean and Latin America	Other
World	1,778	1,106	279	75	144	174
Crude oil	1,391	961	276	67	70	18
Products	387	144	4	8	75	156
United States	349	184	40	0	120	5
Crude oil	254	169[a]	40	0	45	0
Products	95	15	0	0	75	5[b]
Japan	453	324	35	75	0	20
Crude oil	408	291	31	67	0	18[c]
Products	45	32	4	8	0	2[c]
Western Europe	737	349	204	0	25	149
Crude oil	543	314	204	0	25	0
Products	184	35	0	0	0	149[d]
Developing countries[e]	249	249	0	0	0	0
Crude oil	187	187	0	0	0	0
Products	62	62	0	0	0	0

Sources: Imports for developed countries are derived, in part, from OECD, *Energy Prospects to 1985*, vol. 1, pp. 47, 50, and 53 ($9 case); and, in part, from authors' estimates. Estimates for the developing countries are based on the analysis by Edward R. Fried in Yager and Steinberg, *Energy and U.S. Foreign Policy*, p. 257.

This table attempts to show major oil shipments by sea of both crude oil and products, in order to provide a basis for calculating tanker requirements and oil discharges from tankers for 1985. Comprehensive statistics are not available for all shipments of oil because of the complexities related to transshipments. However, major flows of this type, such as shipments of Middle East crude oil to Caribbean refineries which are then reexported to the United States, and intraregional trade in refined products in Western Europe are included. Estimates of transshipments of oil are incomplete and many shipments are undoubtedly not included. All figures are based on an assumed world price of crude oil of $88.24 a metric ton ($12 a barrel) in 1975 dollars f.o.b. the Persian Gulf. It was assumed that major oil exporters (except for Venezuela) would export about 12 percent of their total exports in 1985 in the form of refined products. Venezuela was expected to continue to export about one-half of its total oil exports as products. The Soviet Union was assumed to be self-sufficient in oil; Soviet exports to Eastern Europe and Western Europe were expected to move by pipeline (or rail) and are not shown. Figures may not add up to exact totals because of rounding.

a. Includes 49.8 million tons of crude oil from Middle East to Caribbean refineries for reshipment to United States. This 49.8 million tons is also included in the column showing exports of refined products from Caribbean and Latin America to the United States.

b. From Western Europe.

c. From United States (Alaska).

d. Includes 114.5 tons of refined products moving by tanker among West European countries and 34.9 million tons of products from U.S.

e. Assumes that 75 percent of imports are crude oil and 25 percent are refined products. For present purposes, all imports were projected to come from the Middle East and to be supplied to three major representative developing countries: India, the Philippines, and Brazil. Imports are shown only for developing countries that are not oil exporters.

Table C-3. *Tanker Requirements for World Oil Shipments and Projected Oil Spillage from Routine Tanker Operations, 1985*

Oil spillage in thousands of metric tons

Importing region	Very large crude carriers (VLCCs)		Intermediate tankers		Handy tankers		Total	
	Number of vessels	Oil spillage	Number of vessels	Oil spillage	Number of vessels	Oil spillage	Number of vessels	Oil spillage
Japan	318	663	22	21	217	103	557	786
Western Europe	241	962	105	280	348	401	694	1,643
United States	151	391			200	207	351	598
Developing countries	34	195	114	195	248	140	396	530
Total	744	2,210	241	496	1,013	850	1,998	3,556

Sources: Tanker requirements were derived from 1985 forecasts of oil shipments moving to each of the major importing areas (see table C-2). Representative ports in exporting and importing regions were used to calculate distances in order to estimate the number of vessel round trips a year. See text for discussion of assumptions about the size of vessels to be used in 1985. Metric tons of oil were converted to deadweight tonnage and divided by the number of vessel round trips a year.

Spillage was calculated on the basis of total 1985 oil shipments in each of the three vessel-size categories for each major importing region. Spillage varies with vessel size, distance, and whether or not a tanker is assumed to utilize the "load on top" (LOT) system for reducing oil discharges. Separate estimates of spillage from ballasting were made for tankers assumed to be practicing LOT and for tankers (including product tankers) which will not be able to utilize LOT. The spillage rate for shipments using LOT with 80 percent efficiency was 0.07 percent. The spillage rate for vessels not utilizing LOT was 0.35 percent. Spillage estimates were also calculated for emissions from dry-docking operations, from terminal operations, and from bunkering and disposal of wastes. All calculations were based on estimates and formulas provided in National Academy of Sciences, *Petroleum in the Marine Environment* (Washington, D.C.: NAS, 1975), pp. 8–9. (The only adjustment applied to the estimates there was that LOT was assumed to operate at an efficiency rate of 80 percent instead of 90 percent.)

It should be noted that about 20 percent of total spillage calculated for 1985 comes from product tankers, which cannot utilize LOT. Spillage from this source is normally omitted in estimates of oil spills from routine tanker operations. It was assumed that, for half of the shipments of refined products in 1985, shore reception facilities will be used for disposal of oily ballast and that the spillage from ballasting for these trips will be zero. For the other half of the product shipments, it was assumed that oily ballast water would be dumped at sea and a 0.35 percent spillage rate was used.

Figures are rounded.

tankers, with an assumed average size of 23,000 deadweight tons.[1] The total oil spillage from routine tanker operations (usually referred to as chronic spillage) is projected at 3.5 million tons for 1985. Most of the spillage will come from VLCCs, which are projected to carry nearly 70 percent of total oil shipments in 1985.

Largely because of the vast price increases in 1973–74 and subsequently, world consumption of oil is expected to grow more slowly than had been forecast previously. Consequently, a considerable excess of tanker capacity—particularly in the VLCC category—is expected to prevail from the mid-1970s well into the next decade. In spite of this projected excess tanker capacity, it is assumed here that all tankers in operation will work on a full-time basis, and that the rest will be mothballed, scrapped, or possibly converted to other uses. Thus, only those tankers in use will be subject to the tax.

In calculating the number of tankers needed in each category to carry the projected oil shipments in 1985, it was assumed that VLCCs will be used whenever possible because of the significant saving in freight costs (attributable to economies of scale) afforded by the large tankers. Therefore, it was assumed that VLCCs will be used for all crude oil shipments from the Middle East and Africa to Japan, and for 90 percent of the Persian Gulf crude oil shipped to Western Europe, with 10 percent moving through the Suez Canal on intermediate tankers. (VLCCs cannot now pass through the canal.) The United States was assumed to have built sufficient superport capacity by 1985 to handle all oil imports, so that all crude oil imports would be carried on VLCCs. For the developing countries, it was assumed that 50 percent of crude oil imports would be carried on VLCCs and the remainder on intermediate tankers. The Soviet Union was assumed to be more or less self-sufficient in oil requirements, with exports moving by pipeline or by rail, so that the Soviet Union would not be involved in the shipping of oil to any significant degree.

---

1. There is a considerable range in the deadweight tonnage of vessels included in each category—for example, the VLCC class normally comprises tankers in the 200,000 dwt–450,000 dwt (or larger) range. For all calculations in this appendix, all tankers in each category are assumed to be the average size indicated.

Bellagio Conference on New Means of Financing International Needs, March 26–29, 1977

EIGHTEEN scholars, government officials, and officials of international organizations from fourteen nations on five continents (see the list at the end of this appendix) met in Bellagio, Italy, from March 26 to 29, 1977, to discuss a fundamental problem confronting the international community: the growing gap between the financial resources needed to deal with international needs and the funds that are being raised through the present system of essentially voluntary contributions by national governments. The conference was convened by the Brookings Institution to consider new means of financing international needs. The Rockefeller Foundation provided conference facilities and accommodations for participants in its Bellagio Study and Conference Center. The Ford Foundation and the United Nations Environment Programme helped to meet conference expenses.

A draft study on new means of financing international needs by members of the Brookings staff, which was jointly sponsored by the Rockefeller Foundation and the United Nations Environment Programme, was made available to participants as background for their deliberations. The authors of this study took part in the conference and briefed other participants on the results of their work. The conference was not asked, however, to take a position on the study, either in whole or in part.

In order to encourage a free exchange of views, the proceedings of the conference were off the record. Moreover, it was understood that participants spoke only for themselves and not for their governments or the organizations with which they were affiliated. No formal consensus was sought on the matters discussed. The purpose of the conference was not to make recommendations, but to initiate a wider consideration of a problem that must increasingly concern the entire international community.

General Principles

Early in the conference, several participants pointed out that the conference was not an isolated event. The problem of financing international needs is not new but has long concerned the international community. In fact, in the early days of the United Nations a coordinating committee under Secretary General Trygve Lie considered the feasibility of international taxes. Moreover, the conference must be viewed in the context of other contemporary developments, including the Conference on International Economic Cooperation, the Law of the Sea Conference, and—most notably—the continuing effort to create a New International Economic Order.

The need to base new revenue measures on a clear definition of international needs was emphasized by a number of participants. Two broad kinds of needs were seen: meeting the financial requirements of various agreed upon international programs and transferring resources to the developing nations to assist them in improving the living standards of their people. Of these two kinds of needs, the second was seen as the larger and the more important. The past practice of defining developmental needs in terms of specified rates of growth in gross national product was regarded by some participants as inadequate. An alternative approach would be to identify specific, high priority requirements (for example, basic human needs) and seek the continuing transfer of resources needed to satisfy them.

Some participants strongly urged that the adoption of new sources of finance be reviewed as supplementary to more fundamental structural reforms. Specifically, a shift in the international terms of trade could bring about a more equitable distribution of the world's income and reduce the magnitude of the direct resource transfers required to meet the needs of the developing nations. Some means must also be found of dealing with the large debt burden borne by many developing countries.

Broad support was expressed for the proposition that as many countries as possible, including those with centrally managed economies, should participate in any new international revenue system.

New Sources of Finance

The new sources of finance considered by the conference fall under three headings: international revenue taxes, charges on polluters of the international commons, and a variety of other possible measures that cannot easily be classified. Each of these categories will be taken up briefly in turn.

International Revenue Taxes

Among the various possible revenue taxes, most attention was devoted to ad valorem taxes on international trade. The possible utility of a trade tax on selected commodities was not excluded, but the only two examples of such a tax that were discussed in any detail—a tax on internationally traded oil and a tax on internationally traded mineral materials—received little support. Some participants believed that the tax on oil was unfair to the oil-exporting countries and that the tax on minerals would be an undesirable burden on some of the important exports of developing countries. A general tax on international trade was viewed somewhat more favorably because of its great revenue-raising potential, but reservations were expressed about such a tax from a number of points of view. Several participants feared that a general trade tax would both interfere with the efficient international division of labor and impose a special burden on countries that depend heavily on international trade. Some in this group thought that it would be both more desirable and more feasible to seek an increase in governmental contributions.

Other participants were concerned about the fact that the burden of an unadjusted general trade tax would not be distributed in accordance with ability to pay. They pointed out that adjustments could be made to make the tax less regressive and that its net burden would depend on how the revenue that it produced was spent. Doubts remained, however, concerning the possibility of arriving at an equitable distribution of the burden of a general trade tax.

Particular concern was expressed over the possibility that middle-income developing countries would have to absorb most of a tax on their exports of manufactured goods, because such goods must compete with similar goods produced in the industrialized countries in which they are marketed. Possibilities for compensating this group of developing countries by devoting some of the new tax revenues to their needs were seen as poor, given their own preference for self-reliance and the fact that they do not qualify for concessional financing under the established policies of international financial organizations.

There was general agreement that a tax on trade (or indeed any other new source of revenue) should not excuse the industrialized countries from meeting the internationally agreed upon target of devoting 0.7 percent of their gross national products to official development assistance. One view expressed was that, rather than being an excuse for continued delinquency, the trade tax could be used as a means of partially meeting the agreed upon target. Another view was that revenues collected by the trade tax should be regarded as additional to resource transfers made pursuant to the 0.7 percent target. Still another view was that all tax revenues collected from developing countries should be rebated to those countries, until the industrialized countries were in full compliance with the agreed upon target. Otherwise, the tax would be unacceptable to the developing countries.

The possibility of taxing the international transfer of profits on private international investments was also discussed. The imposition of such a tax was not completely ruled out, but several participants expressed concern over the difficulty that would be encountered in enforcing it. Attention was also called to the fact that the Communist countries do not receive profits from private investments abroad, and hence could not participate to any great extent in raising this source of revenue.

Other possible revenue taxes were discussed more briefly. One participant proposed a tax on arms transfers or defense budgets. Another suggested taxes on commodities of little or no social value, such as tobacco and alcoholic beverages. Still another proposal was a tax on international travel.

International Taxes on Polluters of the Commons

The general principle that polluters should pay for the damage that they cause the international commons had wide acceptance among participants. (One participant believed, however, that imposing charges on polluters in effect gave them a license to pollute.) There was also general agreement that oil discharges into the marine environment are a form of pollution of the commons that deserves urgent attention. The conference concentrated on the possibility of using taxes on chronic oil emissions by tankers, by other merchant ships, and by offshore drilling operations to bring about a reduction in this kind of pollution of the marine environment. Greatest attention was devoted to a tax on tankers that would be designed to induce operators to buy new tankers with segregated ballast tanks when existing tankers are retired.

One participant feared that the tanker tax would impose an unfair and unnecessary burden on countries that already enforce strict antipollution regulations on tankers flying their flags. A number of participants, however, expressed the view that the tanker tax was both feasible and desirable. Several thought that this tax was more likely to win early international approval than any other financial measure considered by the conference.

Some participants pointed out that this fact could pose a problem. Would it be wise, they asked, to press first for adoption of an international tax that is primarily designed to change the behavior of polluters and only incidentally to raise modest amounts of revenue? Would such an effort prejudice later efforts to obtain agreement to levy a revenue tax, such as a general tax on international trade?

No conclusive answer to this problem was reached, but most participants agreed that the tanker tax should be dealt with on its merits and that it was more likely to provide a precedent for the imposition of revenue taxes than to divert attention from their serious consideration in international forums.

Other Possible Sources of Finance

In addition to revenue taxes and charges on polluters of the international commons, the conference discussed a number of other possible ways of raising money to finance international needs.

The conference noted the impasse at the Law of the Sea Conference over the nature and powers of an international regime to control the exploitation of nonliving ocean resources beyond national jurisdiction. Participants who spoke on the subject agreed on the importance of establishing such a regime as a means of ensuring that any economic rents produced by exploitation of the resources of the deep ocean would be available for agreed upon international purposes.

Several participants urged the use of the International Monetary Fund's Special Drawing Rights (SDRs) to help meet the needs of the developing nations. The strong opposition of some industrialized nations to the SDR "link" was, however, recognized, as was the fact that SDRs are at present issued only to meet requirements for international liquidity.

One participant suggested that substantial funds could be obtained for international purposes by establishing a reserve requirement of, say, 10 percent for the Eurocurrency deposits held by banks in a number of Western European countries. This requirement could be imposed by agreement among the central banks most directly concerned, or it could conceivably be adopted by the International Monetary Fund. Apart from its advantage as a means of financing international needs, this arrangement might appeal to financial authorities as a way of gaining some control over a part of the international monetary system that is now virtually unregulated.

The conference discussed a number of possible charges for the use of the international commons. Some participants expressed the view that such charges were appropriate only if a scarce resource (such as telecommunication channels) was involved, or if the commons were degraded by a particular use (as is the case with ships that pollute the marine environment). Others argued that the international community could properly charge for any use of the commons, such as transport and communication.

The possibility was raised that the waters and the seabed surrounding Antarctica might provide revenue for international purposes. The waters are known to contain enormous quantities of krill, which are a useful source of protein, and there may be substantial deposits of oil in areas offshore Antarctica. It is not possible, however, to evaluate these possibilities on the basis of presently available evidence.

Legal and Institutional Arrangements

The conference discussed various legal and institutional arrangements that might be adopted to generate and manage new means of financing international needs. Participants agreed that formal international treaties would be needed if most new sources were to be tapped. The relative merits of using existing institutions or creating new ones to manage new funds were considered. Several participants believed that the distribution of voting power among member governments would have to be reviewed if existing institutions, such as the World Bank Group, were to be involved in the management of new funds. One suggestion was that it might be possible to change the weighted voting system of the International Development Association (IDA) to give the developing countries a greater role in financial management and, further, that additional Communist countries might join a reorganized IDA.

Another suggestion was that the proposed World Development Budget under discussion in various forums could provide a useful framework for determining how the funds raised from new sources of finance should be allocated.

The general view of participants speaking on the subject was that no firm decisions on legal and institutional questions were required at this point, but that the problems involved were clearly not insuperable.

Conclusion

In concluding their deliberations, participants joined in expressing the hope that the conference will help to promote a wider discussion in other forums of the problem of mobilizing the financial resources needed to meet pressing international needs. There was wide support for the view that some kind of new international revenue system was needed, in order to mobilize larger resources and provide greater automaticity in the financing of international needs. Some of the new means of finance discussed at the conference appeared to be promising. It was hoped that the possibility of adopting these means will be given high priority on the international agenda.

Conference Participants

Gerard M. Brannon *Chairman, Department of Economics, Georgetown University*

Rodrigo Botero Montoya *Former Finance Minister of Colombia*

Adriano Buzzati-Traverso *Senior Scientific Adviser, United Nations Environment Programme*

William C. Clark *Vice President, World Bank*

Robert K. A. Gardiner *Commissioner for Economic Planning, Ghana*

Paul-Marc Henry *President, OECD Development Center*

Ali Mohammed Jaidah *Secretary General, Organization of Petroleum Exporting Countries*

Manfred Lachs *Member, International Court of Justice*

Jan Meijer *Netherlands Foreign Ministry*

Philip Ndegwa *Director, Program Division III, United Nations Environment Programme*

Hisao Onoe *Director, Institute of Economic Research, Kyoto University*

Manuel Perez Guerrero *Minister of State for Economic Affairs, Venezuela*

Ralph W. Richardson, Jr. *Director, Natural and Environmental Sciences, Rockefeller Foundation*

Eleanor B. Steinberg *Brookings Institution*

Maurice F. Strong *Chairman, Petro-Canada (Conference Chairman)*

Tamotsu Takase *Chairman, International Studies Program, Kyoto Sangyo University*

Mostafa K. Tolba *Executive Director, United Nations Environment Programme*

Joseph A. Yager *Brookings Institution*

Index

251

effect of nodule mining on price of, 149, 152; estimated production from nodules, 148

Cornell, Nina W., 146–47, 151–53

Costs of environmental programs, 4–6. *See also* Social costs

Council on Environmental Quality, 100n

CRISTAL. *See* Contract Regarding an Interim Supplement to Tanker Liability for Oil Pollution

Cuba: earnings from nickel exports, 162; international oil tax burden on, 67, 71

Damage function, 104, 105

Defense, proposed tax on national budget for, 42

Dennis, J. V., 129n

Desert lands, international program for, 5

Developing countries: burden of international taxes on, 67, 71, 76, 201; compensation for losses from nodule mining, 161–64; demand for share of world's resources, 2–3; duties imposed on primary commodities of, 81; environmental problems of, 3–4; net capital flow to, 2; oil-importing, 2, 12, 13; UN efforts to increase financial resources of, 3; World Bank and, 212

Diamond, Peter A., 92n

Eatwell, John, 22n

ECOSOC. *See* United Nations Economic and Social Council

Effluent tax: alternatives to, 21, 105–06; based on damage and abatement functions, 104, 105; determining level of, 104; effluent standards versus, 104; origin of, 103; purpose of, 102

Eklund, Sigvard, 6n

Environmental programs: allocation of funds for, 189–92; cost of, 4–6; earmarking funds for, 182–83; effect on capital requirements of developing countries, 3–4; expenditures for, 15–16; financial requirements for, 2; insurance for, 41–42; international revenue taxes for, 189–92, 193, 196–97. *See also* Financing international environmental programs

Exports, international tax on, 49, 62

FAO. *See* Food and Agricultural Organization

Finance, international taxes on, 29–30

Financing international environmental programs: allocation of funds for, 180–82; by charges for technical services, 39–40; by gold sales, 44–45; by insurance against environmental damage, 41–42; international revenue system for, 195–97, 213; by loans, 38–39, 197; from ocean resources, 33–38, 158–60, 196; by pollution taxes, 30–33, 197; by private contributions, 40–41; by shadow taxes, 20–24, 196; by Special Drawing Rights, 42–44; by taxing national defense budgets, 42; by taxing trade and financial transactions, 29–30, 45–46; by use charges, 26–29

Fish: effect of oil pollution on, 100–01, 132–33; production costs of, 134; proposed international tax on, 34–35

Fisher, Anthony C., 131n

Flag-of-convenience, 116, 119

Food and Agricultural Organization (FAO): financial operations of, 10; financial requirements of, 1; preinvestment work for development assistance, 177

Francis, Jonathan H., 52n

Fried, Edward R., 2n, 65n, 189n

Gardner, Richard N., 12n

Gaskell, T. T., 142n

GEMS. *See* Global Environmental Monitoring System

Geneva Convention on the Continental Shelf, 137–38

Geological Survey, U.S., 143

Geosynchronous orbit, 27

Gibrat, Robert, 31n

Global Environmental Monitoring System (GEMS), 192, 212; proposed program for, 5–6

Gold sales, 44–45

Gross domestic product (GDP), 19–20

Gross national product (GNP): imports and, 54, 62; international tax burden as percent of, 67, 71, 76, 81, 203–06; tax on components of, 42; UN assessments on basis of per capita, 10

Growth rate: capital flow to sustain, 13; targeted for developing nations, 2

Gulland, J. A., 36n

Hammond, Allen L., 144n

Hershner, Carl H., 110n

Holdgate, M. W., 36n